PUBS AND BREWERIES
Of The BLACK COUNTRY

PUBS AND BREWERIES OF THE BLACK COUNTRY

STEVE JAMES

BREWIN BOOKS

BREWIN BOOKS
19 Enfield Ind. Estate,
Redditch,
Worcestershire,
B97 6BY
www.brewinbooks.com

First published in Great Britain by Voxlumina 2022
This revised edition published by Brewin Books 2024

© Steve James 2022 & 2024

The author has asserted his rights in accordance
with the Copyright, Designs and Patents Act 1988
to be identified as the author of this work.

All rights reserved. No part of this publication may be reproduced, stored in a retrieval system, or transmitted in any form or by any means, electronic, mechanical, photocopying, recording or otherwise, without the prior permission in writing of the publisher and the copyright owners, or as expressly permitted by law, or under terms agreed with the appropriate reprographics rights organisation. Enquiries concerning reproduction outside the terms stated here should be sent to the publishers at the UK address printed on this page.

The publisher makes no representation, express or implied, with regard to the accuracy of the information contained in this book and cannot accept any legal responsibility for any errors or omissions that may be made.

A CIP catalogue record for this book is
available from the British Library.

ISBN: 978-1-85858-769-1

Printed and bound in Great Britain
by Hobbs The Printers Ltd.

CONTENTS

Foreword vii
Introduction ix

PUBS
AMBLECOTE 3
BILSTON 5
BLACKHEATH 7
BLOXWICH 9
BRIERLEY HILL 11
COSELEY 15
CRADLEY & COLLEY GATE 17
CRADLEY HEATH 19
DARLASTON 21
DUDLEY
 • home-brew pubs 23
 • famous names and local trades 25
GORNAL
 • Upper & Lower 29
GREAT BRIDGE 33
HALESOWEN 35
HILL TOP & HARVILLS HAWTHORN 41
KATES HILL & TIVIDALE 43
KINGSWINFORD & WALL HEATH 45
LANGLEY 47
LYE 49
NETHERTON 55
OLDBURY 59
OLD HILL 61
OLDSWINFORD 63
PELSALL 65
PENSNETT 67
QUARRY BANK 69
SEDGLEY & WOODSETTON 73
SMETHWICK 77
SPON LANE 79
STOURBRIDGE
 • a century ago 81
 • music scene 83
SWAN VILLAGE & GREETS GREEN 85
TETTENHALL & PENN 87
TIPTON 89
WALSALL
 • famous names and local trades 91
 • old pubs 95

WEDNESBURY 97
WEDNESFIELD 99
WEST BROMWICH
- famous names and local trades 101
- Golden Mile 105
WILLENHALL 109
WOLLASTON 111
WOLVERHAMPTON
- famous names and local trades 113
- oldest pubs 119
WORDSLEY 121

BREWERIES
BROWNHILLS
- William Roberts 125
DUDLEY
- Breweries 127
- Batham's 129
- Holden's 133
- Simpkiss 135
LANGLEY
- Crosswells Brewery 137
- Holt, Plant & Deakin 139
MICRO-BREWERIES 141
NETHERTON
- Breweries 143
SMETHWICK
- Cheshire's Brewery 147
STOURBRIDGE
- Breweries 149
WALSALL
- Breweries 151
WEST BROMWICH
- Breweries 153
- Darby's Brewery 155
WOLVERHAMPTON
- Breweries 157

Acknowledgements 161
Notes on Pub Information 165

FOREWORD

It gives me great pleasure to introduce this informative and absorbing book, which is a labour of love devoted to the history of the many fascinating pubs and breweries of the Black Country.

Public houses are the centre of local communities, forming a microcosm of human nature and the setting for all human drama. They also provide a welcoming social environment and venue for local groups and societies. Pubs see it all: love and laughter, happiness and distress, pity, anger, grief, solitude, gaiety and all the rest. They are supported by those who produce the principal products that are consumed there – breweries provide the beer!

The Black Country has a wealth of pubs and breweries serving the local population of its many towns and communities. This book aims to cover the many hundreds of pubs in the Black Country that have served their local communities over the years, telling some interesting stories about the pubs, their landlords and customers. It also covers most of the breweries in the area, ranging from small home-brew pubs to the many commercial breweries that have existed over the years.

It is certain that, over the years, inns and pubs have changed personnel and their clientele. Landlords move on to other pubs or other places. Customers get older and new ones come and go. The character of the local pub inevitably changes with the moods and trends of the day. But even though we have lost hundreds of pubs in the Black Country alone, many soldier on steadfastly, providing an essential service to the local community. Pubs close, reopen or are converted to other uses, whilst new pubs and bars, such as micro-pubs, add to the variety of licensed venues. Similarly, breweries come and go, leaving not only the larger commercial breweries, but also a new breed of micro-breweries.

The information in this definitive book is the result of a great deal of painstaking research into the history and development of the pubs and breweries in the Black Country. It not only offers a compendium of most of the recorded pubs and breweries in the area, but also tells the story of their evolution, including personal tales of the landlords and their customers, and events that have taken place.

I was born in Wordsley, still live in the Black Country, and my first novel *The Black Country* was published by Salt Publishing in 2015. It was written as my thesis piece at Manchester Writing School at Manchester Metropolitan University. And I also love real ale! I am familiar with the author's work, since he regularly contributes to *The Blackcountryman*, the magazine of the Black Country Society. He also writes regularly for the *Black Country Bugle* newspaper about Black Country pubs and breweries as well as for other local magazines. I know that he is passionate about the history of pubs, breweries and beer, and I'm sure you will be fascinated by the stories he tells. You'll also probably learn more about the pubs and breweries of the Black Country than you ever knew!

Kerry Hadley-Pryce MA
Editor – *The Blackcountryman*
Author of *The Black Country* (2015) and *Gamble* (2018)
Visiting Lecturer at the University of Wolverhampton
March 2022

INTRODUCTION

"Beer is proof that God loves us and wants us to be happy" – Benjamin Franklin

The Black Country has a wealth of pubs and breweries serving the local population of its many towns and settlements. This book is based on a series of articles published in the *Black Country Bugle* newspaper and *Blackcountryman* magazine during 2020-2022.

Steve James is passionate about beer, pubs and breweries. He is a lifelong member of CAMRA (Campaign for Real Ale) and a member of the Black Country Society, Brewery History Society, Pub History Society and Friends of Highgate Brewery. He is also a member of the British Guild of Beer Writers, where he has been nominated in the past for awards. He has written many articles on the history of pubs and breweries in the Black Country as well as wider afield for the *Black Country Bugle*, *The Blackcountryman*, local CAMRA magazines and other publications. He also produces bespoke histories for individual pubs and contributes to the historical research of pubs and breweries.

This book aims to cover the main towns and settlements of the Black Country, detailing the many hundreds of pubs that have served the local communities over the years, telling some interesting stories about the pubs, their landlords and customers. It also covers most of the breweries in the area, ranging from small home-brew pubs to the many commercial breweries that have existed over the years.

The research involved has been extensive and time consuming, but the bedrock of information comes from two main sources. Firstly, from Tony Hitchmough's database contained in *Hitchmough's Black Country Pubs*, and secondly, from the books and articles written by the late John Richards. These friends were the inspiration for this book and it is effectively dedicated to them. Other research comes from published books and articles, along with contributions from friends and colleagues. A full list of acknowledgements is included at the end of this book.

It is almost inevitable that such a wide-ranging book may not be completely comprehensive and up-to-date. The author has done his best to ensure that all relevant pubs are included and has checked the details of those that remain open. He has also visited all the towns and settlements individually – but not necessarily all the pubs! However, the information will change over time, so readers are asked to check with individual pubs for opening times on their websites and social media.

In the meantime, let's start with some background to the Black Country and the history of the public house.

The Black Country

The Black Country is an area of the West Midlands to the west of Birmingham, based around the South Staffordshire coalfield. Its precise boundary is hotly disputed, but historically, it covered the southern part of Staffordshire and the northern part of Worcestershire. In modern-day terms, this extends over most of Dudley, Sandwell, Walsall and Wolverhampton metropolitan boroughs. Some say that Dudley is the undisputed capital of the Black Country.

The area began to change from a rural backwater with the arrival of the Industrial Revolution. By the late 19th century, it had become one of the most heavily industrialised areas in the country. Iron and steelworks, foundries, brickworks and glassworks began to be established, using the local mineral resources of coal, limestone and fireclay. The area also made railway locomotives, carriages and wagons, bicycles, motorbikes and cars, axle boxes and hollow shafts, shipware, anchors and chains, fenders and fire-irons, keys, locks, buckles, nails, nuts and bolts, leather-wear, saddles, bridles and horseshoes, gun barrels and pistols, scales and spring balances, cutlery and utensils, saucepans and hollow-ware, ornamental ironware, enamel-ware and glass-ware, coffee mills, textiles, clocks, spades and steel toys, steam gauges, gas tubes and water pipes. There were also several maltings supplying the local breweries who provided beer to the many local pubs serving the thirsty workers. Much of the large-scale heavy industry that once dominated the Black Country has now gone, but there are still plenty of smaller-scale manufacturing firms remaining.

There is much discussion about why the area is called the Black Country. Some say it was because of the heavy industry in the area, creating pollution and black smoke. Even Queen Victoria ordered the blinds to be drawn when she travelled through the area by train. Others believe it was more related to the black gold of the collieries.

The Black Country is also home to a distinctive dialect, which is spoken slightly differently in various parts of the area. Many Black Country folk are intensely proud of their heritage, culture and dialect, which is reflected in the presence of the Black Country Living Museum in Dudley, where there's even a preserved pub!

All this heavy industry was thirsty work, and so literally hundreds of pubs sprang up to serve the thirsty miners and factory workers, supplied by many local breweries. In the early days, most pubs brewed their own beer, before being bought up by the commercial breweries. The Black Country once had many hundreds of pubs, ranging from the street-corner and terrace local, commercial hotels and inns, to more modern flagship pubs, purpose-built by local architects for the main brewery companies.

Today, perhaps fewer than 10% of the total number of licensed premises remain, but many of these include traditional, historic pubs, with plenty of character and "characters". Some of the smaller pubs often serve only a limited range of beers from a specific brewery, whereas others offer a much wider range of beers from local breweries and those further afield, including the newer micro-breweries.

Without doubt, the choice of beers and other drinks in local pubs is much wider than it used to be, and in many cases, the pub offers a much more enjoyable overall experience than in earlier days. So, it's probably time now for a brief history of the pub...

History of the Public House
The public house has become part of British culture, and one of the focal points of the community. The British public house can be traced back to the Roman tavern or tabernae, and later the Anglo-Saxon alehouse. This became so popular that in 965, King Edgar decreed that each village should have no more than one alehouse. He also standardised weights and measures so that all alehouses sold ale in the same quantities. In 1266, the Assizes of Brews and Ale were introduced to control the prices of these staple commodities in line with the current prices of corn and malt. By 1300, boroughs could impose fines for brewing beer too weakly, giving short measure or selling too cheaply. As long ago as 1393, King Richard II compelled all landlords to erect a sign outside their premises, which allowed people to identify the alehouse by the picture on the sign, since many folks could not read or write at that time. From the 14th century, Ale Connors (ale tasters) were appointed to inspect and taste the ale.

By 1460, boroughs were regulating common brewers and later specified licensing hours and fixed prices for selling ale. They also imposed fines for drinking after hours or gambling on the premises. Pub licensing began with the Alehouse Act of 1552, when magistrates were given the power to license alehouses. In the 18th century, gin replaced ale as the most popular drink, after the Dutch brought it here in the late 1680s. It was cheaper, more alcoholic, and readily available.

Drunkenness became commonplace, and on several occasions the government introduced legislation in an attempt to reduce the problem. It was in this atmosphere that the modern public house was born.

At that time, beer was considered to be a harmless, nutritious alternative to gin, and people were actively encouraged to drink it. It was often healthier than drinking the local town water supply, which was sometimes contaminated. This led to the passing of the 1830 Beerhouse Act, introduced by the Duke of Wellington, which brought in new and radical changes in the law to combat the evils of gin drinking. It allowed any householder and tax payer to obtain a licence to brew and sell beer on their premises in exchange for a 2 guinea licence fee. Licensees were not allowed to sell spirits or fortified wines, and anyone doing so would be closed down and heavily fined. In the first three months after the Act came into force, over 24,000 new licences were issued, leading to a rapid rise in the number of pubs and the new class of licensed premises, the beerhouse.

Beerhouses were often family homes, where beer was usually sold in the front room and dispensed from a jug, or served directly from the barrel. The room was simply furnished with bare floorboards, wooden benches and trestle tables. Some of the early beerhouses carried names, just like pubs, but some were disorderly and unhygienic. To address this situation, a new Act was introduced in 1834 specifying three kinds of publican's licence. A full publican's licence could be granted annually by local magistrates, and beerhouses were divided into on and off sales. Beerhouses flourished until the introduction of the Wine & Beerhouse Act of 1869, which prevented the opening of new beerhouses and tightened local magistrates' control of the industry, including granting licences for beer, wines and spirits and selling alcohol off the premises. In the early 1900s, some local magistrates were becoming concerned about the sheer numbers of beerhouses and public houses in their towns and began to limit or even revoke licences, encouraged by the Temperance movement. By the early years of the 20th century most beerhouses had disappeared.

Many of the early pubs were coaching inns, so called because horse-drawn coaches or omnibuses would stop there to change their horses, and pick-up and drop-off passengers and mail. From the early 1800s, they became focal points in the town, where travellers were provided with food, refreshments and often accommodation, with stables for the horses. Coaching inns relied on the regular coaching traffic, which in turn relied on the state of the roads. In the 18th century, road improvements and maintenance were undertaken by the Turnpike Trusts, who collected tolls from road users at turnpike toll houses. The owners of coaching inns also did what they could to assist in improving roads, such as landlord Fletcher of the George Hotel in Walsall who obtained an Act of Parliament to build the road between Walsall and Stafford. But horse-drawn coaches and omnibuses quickly disappeared after the coming of the railways and trams, which were faster and more reliable.

Some of the larger pubs and hotels became the social and commercial centres of the town, and were used for holding meetings of the local boards and trustees, for inquests and other formal occasions. They also provided venues for local societies, such as Friendly Societies, Freemasons and other organisations. On market days, pubs would not only slake the thirst of traders, but much business would also be carried out during their extended opening hours, which is why there were many pubs clustered around the marketplace. They were also the venue for heated political meetings and workers' groups, like chainmakers and colliery workers.

The 18th and 19th centuries were a period of tremendous social and economic change in England. The Industrial Revolution and growth of industry led to a rapid increase in the urban population, with more pubs and alehouses opening to cater for the thirsty workers. The development of road transport helped many coaching inns to flourish, while pubs opened alongside canals to cater for boatmen and canal traffic. Workers at the local iron and steelworks would often send out lads to fetch beer from the local pubs to quench their thirst, since it was safer than drinking tap water. Some pubs allowed workers to have a tab and run up large bills, which often resulted in arguments and sometimes fights. Workers would often pass their pints around their friends, and if refused, would often offend. Entertainment became more popular in pubs, with billiards in vogue in the 18th century, supplementing old favourites such as dice, dominoes, darts and cards. Cockfighting, bull-baiting and dog fights were also very popular at this time, on which substantial bets were won or lost, and often made the landlord plenty of money.

In the 18th and early 19th centuries, most publicans brewed their own beer in the brewhouse behind the pub, and sometimes supplied it to other pubs and beerhouses. In the second half of the 19th century, common brewers began to replace home-brewers, and it became quite common for a brewer to own or supply a number of pubs, which led to tenants having to sell his beer. Some breweries behind pubs developed into commercial breweries, and some moved sites to establish free-standing breweries. The owners of these new commercial breweries became important local figures in their own right, donating money to local causes, providing land for community facilities and other philanthropic causes. Family brewers became respected members of the local community, with some becoming local councillors and MPs. The larger breweries had their own social life, with football teams and brass bands. William Roberts of the Station Brewery, Brownhills, even provided and paid for the town's first fire engine!

The traditional English pub evolved into several separate rooms, each with its own purpose. The bar, with a counter, was copied from gin houses, in order to serve customers quickly and keep an eye on them. The taproom, or public bar, was developed for the working classes. It had simple wooden bench seats, cheap drink and bare floorboards or tiles that were often covered in sawdust to absorb spillages and spit. The saloon bar or lounge appeared in the latter part of the 18th century, as a comfortable, carpeted and well-furnished room with an admission fee or higher priced drinks. It catered for more affluent people, often with entertainment and drinks served at the table.

Another room, the snug, sometimes called the smoke room, was a small, private room where people could drink without being seen. The windows were made of frosted glass and the room had a separate entrance, so that people could enter and leave without being noticed. There was usually access to a separate section of the bar, where a higher price would be paid for drinks. The snug was often used by ladies, at a time when the pub was perceived to be for men only, and also by courting couples, who liked their privacy. There was often an off-licence, where beer, wines and spirits could be bought for home consumption. It was either a small room or counter, or just an open window, where customers (including children) could take back bottles to be filled with beer. The bottles would be sealed with paper to prevent children drinking the contents on the way back home!

During the 19th century, more legislation governed licensing, gaming and brewing, including defining closing times for the first time. As the century progressed, innkeepers and brewers faced increasing pressure from the Temperance movement and the local magistrates to reduce the number of pubs and beerhouses. At the annual Brewster Sessions, Licensing Justices took the opportunity to close down many pubs, resulting in owners and brewery companies being forced to improve standards and facilities in their pubs. This sometimes involved building new pubs, often on the site of old ones, destroying many ancient inns and alehouses. Most of these new pubs conformed to a similar architectural style, with ornamental and terracotta brickwork and ornamental glass, making these new pubs stand out in their surroundings.

The early 20th century saw another flurry of legislation to restrict sales to children, tighten licensing regulations and improve standards of comfort and hygiene in pubs. When local authorities began to embark on programmes of slum clearance, many historic inns and alehouses were swept away. In some cases, owners were able to transfer the licences from these old, cramped pubs to new ones, either in town or in the new suburban housing areas. The 1930s and 1950s saw more pub building campaigns, with architects favouring a fairly solid brick style, with provision for car parking, and the development of the road-house style pub.

Public houses have always been associated with music, from a simple sing-song, to musicians who performed in the saloon bars. A piano was an essential part of the local pub, encouraging talented customers and musicians to entertain the locals with a variety of popular and traditional tunes. In Oldbury, Jack Judge played the piano at the Malt Shovel and is believed to have written his famous *It's a Long Way to Tipperary* there. Some of the larger pubs had their own concert room, where live entertainment, variety shows and plays were performed. Games have been played in pubs for a long time, including billiards, snooker, card games, dominoes and skittles, with darts being played from at least the 17th century.

Many pubs had their own football team, often playing in the local Sunday league, whilst others had their own bowling green and bowls team. Some even had their own gym for boxing and sponsored local boxers. A popular Black Country pastime was pigeon racing, with followers joining one of the many clubs based at a local pub who had their own pigeon loft. Another popular activity was cycling, which led to the formation of countless cycling clubs throughout the country, often based at local pubs. In the early days, before it was banned in 1849, many pubs hosted cock and bull fighting, some even having their own cock pit, as well as prize-fighting between local folk heroes, such as the Tipton Slasher. Pubs have served some form of food or snacks for a long time. Originally, it would have been simple bar snacks, such as crisps, peanuts, pork scratchings or pickled eggs, or a simple cold plate like a ploughman's lunch. This gradually evolved into the high-quality home-cooked meals that many pubs now offer, particularly after the advent of the microwave oven.

Many landlords had other occupations as well as running the pub. Some pubs were not profitable enough to support the licensee and his large family, so they ran a second business, often based in part of the pub. Sometimes they were maltsters or brewers, whilst others were butchers, keeping pigs in the back yard, slaughtering them and hanging joints of meat upstairs to be cured. Pork and bacon would be sold in a separate room off the bar. Some licensees were also involved in local trades, such as making guns and locks, files, glassware and chains, often in their own workshops behind the pub. Others might own local shops or farms, or work in local collieries or factories. A few licensees became affluent by investing their money in land and property, selling off building plots or becoming local auctioneers. Many pubs were kept by the same local families over many generations, and became known by that family's name, such as Pick's or Jasper's. Others had local names, due to some feature of the pub, like the Coffin Handles because of its brass door fittings, or recalling the brewery supplying the beer, like the Top Wrexham.

Some pubs have been rebuilt on the site of much older inns and alehouses, and may retain features of the older building, such as the cellar or outbuildings. In some cases, they were rebuilt because they were too small or structurally unsafe. Others were replaced by much larger road-houses in the 1930s, in the quest to provide larger, family-orientated pubs. In 1930, Birmingham brewer, Mitchells & Butlers, published a commemorative book on their 50th anniversary, extolling the virtues of their estate of modern pubs. These were sometimes referred to as Fewer and Better pubs, often designed by in-house or local architects who began to specialise in distinctive styles, including art-deco and mock-Tudor. Many have since become buildings formally listed for their historic or architectural importance.

Local brewery companies wanted to "improve" the overall experience of the pub, widening its clientele to include families and providing a more spacious, comfortable venue, often offering hot meals. In more recent times, focal buildings such as courts, libraries, banks, cinemas and theatres, have been converted into pubs, many of which are well worth visiting. But there has also been a trend to introduce theme pubs, such as Irish pubs, sports pubs, gastro-pubs and the like. And whatever you may think about Tim Martin's Wetherspoon's chain of pubs, they offer a good range of economically-priced beers, other drinks and meals. Apparently, they have their roots in George Orwell's 1946 essay about his "perfect" pub – the Moon Under Water, which several of his pubs are actually called, and reflect the qualities of the "improved" pub, almost a century on. Even echoes of the old beerhouse can be seen in the relatively new phenomenon of the micro-pub, with its single room, friendly atmosphere and beer served directly from the cask.

Pubs have always been more than just places selling drinks. They are at the heart of the local community, catering for all ages, families and individuals, rich and poor. They are social and commercial centres, where societies and organisations hold their meetings and functions. Many pubs tended to be used mainly by the working class community, including factory workers, and with the loss of these industries, some pubs have inevitably disappeared. Some people now prefer to drink at home, taking advantage of cheaper beer, wines and spirits from supermarkets, whilst some younger people prefer to drink in clubs and nightclubs. The ban on smoking and tougher drink-driving regulations have all had an adverse impact on the hospitality industry, and the more recent experiences of the Covid pandemic have only served to reinforce people's preference and habits to drink at home.

Pubs may be vanishing at an alarming rate, but many are still evolving to cater for people's changing requirements and tastes. There are still many old hotels, which continue to serve the local community, as well as providing overnight accommodation. Many pubs now offer proper meals, with some pub companies spending large sums of money refurbishing and converting pubs into restaurants, catering for the young, elderly and families alike. However, many traditional pubs remain, often largely unaltered from when they were originally built. Some are now historic buildings in their own right, protected by law. We may have lost many of the smaller-scale breweries, but several new micro-breweries have been established in the Black Country, brewing both traditional and modern craft beers. And there are still a few pub companies and independent owners who spend equally large sums of money refurbishing traditional pubs to serve the real ale drinker. So hopefully, they will all still be a central part of our community life for many years to come. Long may they prosper! Surely, it must be beer o'clock, so let the journey begin...

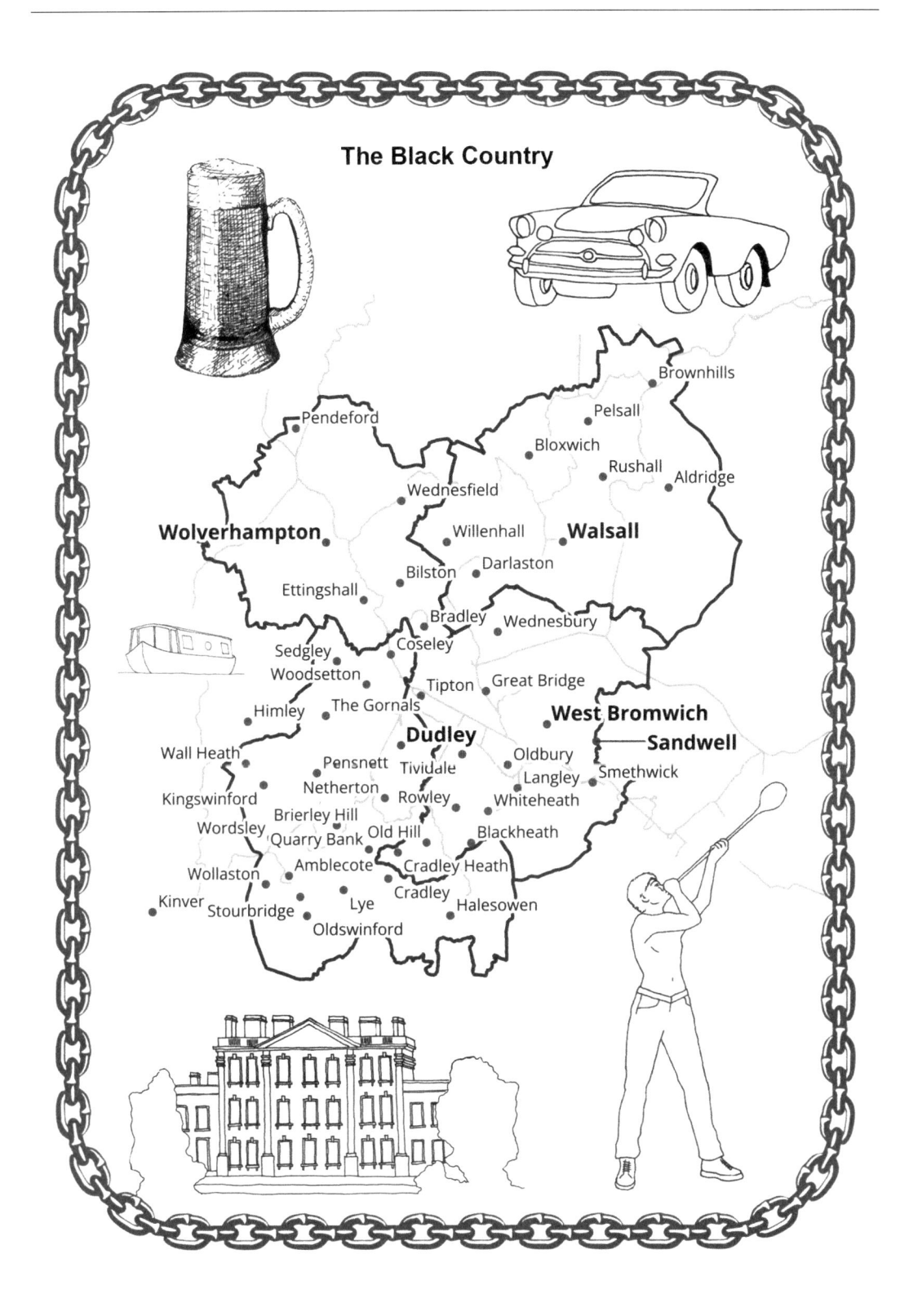

The Black Country

- Brownhills
- Pendeford
- Pelsall
- Bloxwich
- Rushall
- Aldridge
- Wednesfield
- **Wolverhampton**
- Willenhall
- **Walsall**
- Darlaston
- Ettingshall
- Bilston
- Bradley
- Wednesbury
- Sedgley
- Coseley
- Woodsetton
- Tipton
- Great Bridge
- Himley
- The Gornals
- **West Bromwich**
- **Dudley**
- **Sandwell**
- Wall Heath
- Pensnett
- Tividale
- Oldbury
- Kingswinford
- Netherton
- Langley
- Smethwick
- Brierley Hill
- Rowley
- Whiteheath
- Wordsley
- Quarry Bank
- Old Hill
- Blackheath
- Wollaston
- Amblecote
- Cradley Heath
- Kinver
- Lye
- Cradley
- Stourbridge
- Halesowen
- Oldswinford

xv

PUBS

AMBLECOTE

Amblecote is a historic township just north of Stourbridge. Originally in Staffordshire, it became the country's smallest urban district in 1898; the council actually met in the Fish Inn at Coalbournbrook. Amblecote was incorporated into Stourbridge in 1966 and eventually into the larger Dudley metropolitan borough in 1974. After many years as an agricultural village, the Industrial Revolution saw Amblecote become a place of mines and factories, producing coal, clay, sand, bricks, iron, shipware and glassware.

From the early 17th century, the glassmaking industry was established here, with Huguenot glassmakers from the Lorraine region of France. By Victorian times, it was one of the world's leading glass manufacturing districts, with renowned glassmakers such as Webb Corbett, Stuart, Tudor Crystal & Royal Brierley. Interestingly, some of the early pub landlords and families worked in the glassmaking industry. With all this industry and activity, it's not surprising that there were once over 40 pubs serving the district, although little more than a handful survive today.

Most of the pubs in Amblecote were concentrated in three locations. Firstly, around Holloway End, near the River Stour bridge and canal, just beyond the Stourbridge boundary. The **Old Wharf Inn** is now the only surviving pub hereabouts, dating from 1841 and overlooking Stourbridge Canal Wharf and the historic Bonded Warehouse. Previously known as the Barrel Inn and Moorings Tavern and once a home-brew pub, it has recently been reopened by Nickolls & Perks, long-established Stourbridge wine and spirits merchants. Two doors away was the **Foster's Arms,** a former Wordsley Brewery pub dating from 1850, but closed in 1939.

Nearby, the **Navigation** was demolished in 1854 to make way for a railway extension to Bradley's iron foundry. Opposite the railway yard, the **Bridge** was another former Wordsley Brewery pub dating from 1861, but closed in 1906. Near the junction with Vicarage Road was the **Royal Oak,** originally dating from 1829 and known as the Green Dragon. It was rebuilt in 1958, closed in 2013 and is now a veterinary surgery. Opposite the athletic ground was the **Rising Sun,** a former South Staffordshire Brewery/Edward Rutland (Stourbridge) pub, once used as changing rooms for Stourbridge FC (now known as the Glassboys). It was closed in 1926 and demolished in the 1940s. Nearby, the **Holly Bush** dated from 1850, but was known as the Jaguar when it closed in 1981.

The traditional centre of Amblecote was at The Fish crossroads at Coalbournbrook, named after the historic pub at the junction of Stourbridge Road and Wollaston Road, opposite the terminus of the Kinver Light Railway and its tram depot. The **Fish** was probably the oldest surviving pub in the area, originally dating from the early 1800s, but converted into a Chinese restaurant in 1996. It retained some memories of its former use as the council meeting room, including a refurbished civic clock. Nearby was the **Little Pig,** a former home-brew pub and coaching inn dating from 1844. It was rebuilt by T.W. Edwards & Son in 1930, and closed in 2013 and became an estate agents.

Perhaps one of the saddest losses was the **Glassmaker's Arms** on the corner of Collis Street. The original pub dated from 1862 and was a fine building, acquired by Bent's Brewery (Stone) in 1904. It was rebuilt as an uninspiring two-storey building and demolished in 1979. Nearby, on Tobacco Box Hill, the **Queen's Head** dated from 1861, and was a short-lived Diamond Brewery (Dudley) pub, closed in 1907.

Another focal point of Amblecote was the junction with High Street and Brettell Lane. Here, the **Maverick** survives as a real ale tavern and former CAMRA Pub-of-the-Year. Formerly the White Horse and renamed in 1992 to reflect its Wild West theme, it dates from 1829 and was previously a Holt Brewery (Birmingham) pub before passing to Mitchells & Butlers in 1918.

Nearby was the **Old Dial,** dating from 1841 and now a restaurant. On the western side of High Street was the **Board Inn,** dating from 1834, once leased by John Rolinson's Five Ways Brewery (Netherton), but closed by 1913.

Brettell Lane dates from the 1770s and once had 11 pubs, of which only three remain. Strictly speaking, the northern side of the road is beyond the boundary of Amblecote, but the **Red Lion,** dating from 1829, survives as another fine real ale tavern. At the other end of the street, the **Swan** was known as the Swan with Two Necks when it opened in 1841, and has recently been refurbished and reopened. It once housed James Round's small brewery, before being bought by Joule's Brewery (Stone) in 1926. On the corner of Collis Street is the **Starving Rascal** (see below).

In its heyday, other pubs along Brettell Lane included the **Acorn** (1861-1980), **Cross Keys** (1850-1906), **Dog & Partridge** (1869-1936), **Park Tavern** (1861-1920), **Pheasant** (1871-1904), **Roebuck** (1870-1909) and **Unicorn** (1845-1973), some of which survive as shops or houses. The **Builder's Arms** dated from 1850, when it was called the Swan and owned by Job Coley. In 1896, it was acquired by the Sedgley family who changed its name. Joseph Sedgley put it up for auction in January 1936, complete with a small brewhouse, but it closed soon afterwards and became a shop.

Running parallel with Brettell Lane is King William Street, once home to the **Greyhound,** a former home-brew and Eley's Brewery (Stafford) pub dating from 1862, that closed in 1983 and is now a house. Nearby were the **Hope & Anchor,** first known as the Stocking Inn and closed 1971, the **Leamington Brewery Stores,** and **Woodman,** a home-brew pub dating from 1861 and closed in 1906. In Collis Street, the **Robin Hood** dates from 1868 and is a former William Oliver (Talbot Brewery, Cradley) pub, which was sold at auction in 1929 for £1,500. Acquired as a free house by Jean and Max Rawson in 1990, it's another CAMRA award-winning real ale pub.

Amongst the clayfields, collieries and brickworks on the eastern side of Amblecote were a handful of pubs. This area was completely transformed between 1970-1998 with over 8,000 new homes (Withymoor Village). At the end of a lane off Vicarage Road, the **Birch Tree**(1850) served local labourers and was formerly owned by the local Simpkiss Brewery, complete with its haunted cellar! On the nearby Penfields Estate, the modern **Ten Arches** was named after the nearby Stambermill railway viaduct. The **Pear Tree** (Stamford Road) had a bowling green and pleasure gardens, but was closed in 1940, whilst the **Cottage of Content** (Amblecote Bank) lasted only until 1903. The **Spread Eagle** in Vicarage Road was closed in 1912 and the **Waterfall** in Amblecote Lane was demolished in 1919.

A starving beggar at the Dudley Arms

The **Starving Rascal** (formerly Dudley Arms) dates from around 1850. It was renamed in 1974, recalling its alleged ghost of a poor old beggar who arrived at the pub on a Victorian winter's day, begging for food, drink and warmth. The unsympathetic landlord turned him away, and the beggar lay down for the night in the cold pub doorway, but was found dead in the morning. He is said to still haunt the pub, with glasses swinging above the bar and wet footprints appearing on the floor. Once, the TV flew off the shelf, but thankfully hit no-one. It's another local CAMRA award-winning pub, known locally as the Starver, which has recently been refurbished by Black Country Ales.

BILSTON

Bilston was proud of its independent identity as a separate urban district from 1894 and Municipal Borough from 1933, before being amalgamated with Wolverhampton in 1966. Indeed, it was so unhappy about the quality of drinking water supplied by its neighbour that, in 1865, it built its own pumping station at The Bratch, Wombourne. The Industrial Revolution transformed Bilston from a prosperous market town into an industrial centre, with its population increasing from 3,000 in 1780 to over 26,000 a century later. It became a major centre for iron and steel manufacture, as well as coal mining, enamelling, buckle and lock-making.

The first blast furnace was set up at Bradley in 1767, shortly before Springvale Works opened in 1780. More furnaces were built in the 19th and 20th centuries, including Elisabeth in 1954, which produced 275,000 tons of steel a year. All this heavy industry was thirsty work, so pubs were the source of refreshment, not only to quench the thirst after work, but also sending lads out for jugs of beer to drink at the workplace. At the turn of the century, there were no fewer than 113 pubs in the town centre, with more than 300 pubs including the wider Bradley and Ladymoor areas. Of those, barely 20 remain today, with fewer than a dozen remaining in the town centre.

By far the oldest pub in the town is the **Greyhound & Punchbowl.** Originally built as Stowheath Manor in 1438 by John de Mollesley, it became a public house in 1820. In 1936, Wolverhampton brewers W. Butler & Co. employed architect James Swan to renovate this fine timber-framed building, retaining much of the original woodwork, along with the 17th century plaster ceiling and Jacobean fireplaces. Although it's been refurbished several times, some of the original panelling and seating survives, along with its Punchbowl Ghost and the sounds of a baby crying! It's one of the most historic (and haunted) buildings in the area, nationally recognised and listed (Grade II*).

High Street and Church Street form the main thoroughfare of the town, on the original stagecoach route to Wolverhampton. By 1900, there were more than 50 pubs here – virtually a pub on every street corner! Just six remain today, including the **Swan, Greyhound & Punchbowl, Trumpet, Market Tavern** and **Horse & Jockey,** along with a new Wetherspoon's pub, **Sir Henry Newbolt.** This pub is named after Bilston's famous poet who penned the phrase Play up! Play up! and Play the Game! in his 1892 poem *Vitai Lampada*. The **Swan** was a popular boxing venue, but was rebuilt in 1898 and known locally as the Tar Pole. The **Trumpet** dates from 1833 and was first known as the Butcher's Arms, recalling its previous use as a butcher's shop (see below). The **Market Tavern** and **Horse & Jockey** remain, but all the other pubs are long gone, although some buildings survive in other uses.

Around the marketplace was another group of pubs. Nearest the market was the **Market Tavern,** dating from 1851, but the **Barrel, Boars Head, Cricketers Arms, Hop Pole, Leopard, Lion, Shakespeare** and **Vine** are long gone. On the opposite side of the new Black Country Route is the **White Rabbit,** a modern pub recalling the symbolic exorcist who protected local miners. Opposite the Post Office in Hall Street was the **Pipe Hall Hotel,** originally built in 1810 for the local Pipe family and now a listed building (Grade II). In 1869, it became a private girls' school and eventually became a hotel. It had a varied existence as licensed premises, including Carousel, Top Cats and Roar nightclub, before finally closing in 2012, but is now planned for refurbishment. Opposite, the **Great Western** dated from 1864, but was demolished in 1975.

Around the Town Hall, built in 1872, only the **Olde White Rose** survives, where a ghost once haunted the bricked-up cellar. Originally a coaching inn first licensed in 1818, it was rebuilt in 1958. However, there is a new beer café **(Café Metro)** in Church Street, a few doors away, near the site of the Kings Arms, another stop for the mail coaches, but closed by 1890. Next door, the **Town Hall Stores** (1873) was closed in 1965 and is now a shop. Across the road, the **Spread Eagle** dated from 1818, was altered in 1957, but closed in 2011, whilst a few doors away, the **Star** (1858) became a shop. On the corner of Bridge Street was the **Swan Bank Tavern,** known locally as the Blazing Stump; it dates from 1820, but closed in 2008. Of course, we mustn't forget the **Robin 2 Club** around the corner in Mount Pleasant, with its two bars (Woody's & Noddy's).

Oxford Street is another main route through the town, which once had over 20 pubs, on almost every street corner. One of the largest was the **Ship & Rainbow,** once a home-brew pub, but it was demolished in 1970. On the corner of Bradley Street, the **Blue Boar** was memorable for the cellar cut into a coal face, but was demolished in 1965. The **Waterloo** had a small music hall and bowling alley, but was renamed the Oxford in 1907 and closed by 1911. There were other pubs in the back streets, particularly along Temple Street, including the **White Lion,** long kept by the Shelley family. In 1968, this was replaced on the opposite side of the road by the **White Rose,** which was haunted by former landlady, Lizzie, but replaced by housing in 2011.

With all these pubs and people, it's surprising that Bilston never had any large breweries. **William Butler** established his first brewery in 1856 nearby in Priestfield, but in 1873, he built the new Springfield Brewery in Wolverhampton, which finally closed in 1991. Along with **Banks's & Hanson's** (Wolverhampton & Dudley Breweries), they supplied most of the pubs in the town. Other breweries supplying the pubs included **Frank Myatt** (Wolverhampton), **Eley's** (Stafford), **Bent's** (Stone), **Rolinson's** and **Plant's** (Netherton), **Pritchard's** (Darlaston), **Holden's** (Dudley) and **Atkinson's** and **Ansell's** (Birmingham).

In 1897, Richard Harper established the **Hall Park Brewery** in Wellington Road, near the New Bulls Head, supplying around 40 pubs, but this was taken over by Eley's Brewery in 1924 and ceased brewing in 1928. In 1910, Major George Cox established the **Crown Brewery** in Broad Street to supply a dozen local pubs, with the logo: *For Purity of Palate and Nourishment, the Ales of Broad Street Brewery are Unexcelled.* Joseph Marsh operated the **Bilston Brewery** in Oxford Street from 1896-1911, whilst **Peck & Kerrison** brewed at the Pipe Hall Hotel from 1874-1916. In addition, more than 20 pubs are recorded as home-brew pubs, along with 50 individual common brewers. Today, just one brewery operates in Bilston, the **Newbridge** micro-brewery at Tudor House, Moseley Road, which opened in 2013.

So, although Bilston is a shadow of its former self in terms of heavy industry and pubs, we can still enjoy a decent pint of beer in one of the few pubs still remaining!

A tale of the Trumpet

The Trumpet in High Street was first licensed in 1833, when Sarah Vaughan employed Joseph Fellows to keep the pub and brew the beer until 1851. At that time, it was called the Butcher's Arms, since it was originally a butcher's shop with its own slaughterhouse, but was renamed the Royal Exchange in 1877. At one time, it was owned by Bruford & Co., brewers from Wolverhampton, and was eventually acquired by Holden's (Dudley) in 1970. When Les and Ethel Megson took over the pub in 1965, its reputation was so low that it couldn't boast a single customer! But Les was a jazz fan and used to play his favourite jazz records in the pub. When jazzman and comedian, Tommy Burton, heard them, it became a focus for jazz enthusiasts and was renamed the Trumpet in 2006.

BLACKHEATH

Blackheath has sometimes been called a "frontier" town, lying on the historic boundary between Staffordshire and Worcestershire. Prior to the 1830s, Bleak Heath was a place of little significance, but during the Industrial Revolution, it became a "boom town", with the expansion of coal and ironstone mining, brickmaking and other industries, including chain and rivet making. By the time the railway arrived in 1867 and St Paul's Church was built, the population had grown to over 5,400, far outgrowing Rowley Regis. Local people made fortunes by turning old farmhouses into pubs to quench the thirst of local workers. Over the years, several maltings and around 30 pubs served the town, and today a surprisingly large number of the pubs remain open.

The centre of Blackheath was focused around the **Royal Oak,** an old coaching inn dating back to 1775, later owned by the Darby family. Originally a home-brew pub, it soon became a Dare's (Birmingham) house, but was demolished in 1936 when the roundabout in the town centre was constructed.

The **Handel Hotel** occupied a prime position on the corner of Birmingham Road/Oldbury Road, next to the tram terminus and Hippodrome concert hall. First licensed in 1854, it was the main social and commercial hub of the town. Landlord William Laister not only brewed his own beer here, but provided 300 gallons of soup during the nailers strike in 1869. It was also the headquarters of Blackheath Town FC and Blackheath & District Canary Society. John James kept the pub for over 30 years until 1969, when it was demolished to make way for a new Kwik-Save store, now occupied by Wilkinsons. On the opposite corner, the **Shoulder of Mutton** (1854) was originally a Showell's (Langley) pub and became a Holt, Plant & Deakin pub in 1988. It was popular with local miners and is allegedly haunted by three ghosts, including a crying baby and howling dog. Nearby is the distinctive Burton's building, where young Rex Williams practised snooker in the snooker club upstairs.

In High Street, the **Vine** (1865) was originally a home-brew pub used by local miners, nailers and rivet makers, before being rebuilt in 1935. **Manchester House** (1871) was kept by popular landlord Thomas Tom Darby from 1903-1935, before being rebuilt in 1937. It was kept by John Stokes until 1951, but became a building society office in 2003. Local farmer, coalmaster and brickmaker, Joseph Hackett, first licensed the **George & Dragon** in 1834. It was kept by former policeman, Sergeant Frederick Salt in 1896, who gained fame for decimating the Smethwick Slogging Gang, a gang of local muggers. It's remembered for its Saturday night ox roasts during 1920-1939, with travelling entertainers, including a dancing bear. It became the Knight's Quest in 2004.

The **Malt Shovel** (1871) was another Showell's pub, which also became a Holt, Plant & Deakin pub in 1989 and was briefly renamed the Railmakers in 1997. It reverted to its original name in 2006, and is allegedly haunted by a ghost who turns the beer off at inconvenient times! Nearby, the **Royal Exchange** (1861) was demolished in 1984.

In Ross, the **Hawthorns** (1850) was a Cheshire's (Smethwick) Brewery pub, rebuilt in 1926 and kept by Ernest Burden from 1927-1953. In Yew Tree Lane, the **Yew Tree** (1855) was kept by Jess and Eliza Smith from 1936-1962, but was demolished in 1964 and is now a car park. Further along Powke Lane, the **Old Bush Revived** is one of the oldest pubs in the area (see inset).

In Halesowen Street, the **California** was built around 1850 by Benjamin Gould who had found his fortune in gold mining in the USA in the 1830s. It was popular with local miners and used for cockfights and bull terrier contests, but was converted into a shop in 2008. Nearby is a new micro-pub, the **Cyder & Cobb,** which opened in May 2021. A few doors away is the **Beech Tree** (1861), kept by former milkman, Ken "Platty" Platt from 1986-2004. It's recently been renovated and renamed the Little Beech, recalling its local name distinguishing it from the former larger pub with the same name nearby.

The **Britannia** was originally a home-brew pub dating from 1868, where Thomas Chapman brewed, but was rebuilt for Mitchells & Butlers in 1939. Landlord Tony James (1984) was a former wrestler known as Jumping Jimmy James, but after being called the Traveller's Rest for a few years, the pub was refurbished and reopened as a popular Wetherspoon's pub in 2007. At the top of Gorsty Hill, the other **Beech Tree** (Big Beech) dated from 1870, was another Showell's pub. In 1887, landlord Harry Letts displayed the Largest Pig in the World here, and it was allegedly haunted by a ghost in the cellar who turned off the gas and threw glasses around! It was rebuilt later and became a Holt, Plant & Deakin pub in 1984, before becoming apartments in 2015.

At the end of Long Lane (now in Halesowen), the **Ashley Hotel** (1867) was home to Rowley Brewery, where Alfred Cox, George Major and Frank Garrard brewed until 1892. It was rebuilt after a fire in 1894, and in 2013 was refurbished and renamed Windmill's End. Next door, Edward Sturman and his family ran the **Traveller's Rest** (1861), kept over 50 pigs and brewed his own beer until 1935. The pub was allegedly haunted by a ghost, but was demolished in 1997.

In Oldbury Road, the **Railway** (1874) was demolished in 1984 to make way for the ring road. The **Bull's Head** (1881) was popular with commercial travellers, but closed in 1924. Charles Cox built the **New Inn** in 1845 to serve the coal pits and brickworks in Whiteheath. It was once owned by Sadler's Windsor Castle Brewery (Oldbury), and was popular for its dog and cockfighting and bare-knuckle fist fights, but was rebuilt in the late 1920s. Nearby, the **Builder's Arms** (1867) was closed in 1926.

Further along Birchfield Lane, in Whiteheath, the **Bulls Head** (1854) was known locally as "Lowe's Pump" after 17-stone landlord "Billy" Lowe, and was later rebuilt. Almost opposite, the **Whiteheath Tavern** (1845) was originally the New Inn and known locally as Jedknapps, where landlord William Comley ran a steam launch and rowing boats at nearby Titford Pool.

In Rowley Village, John Tom Davenport kept the **Sir Robert Peel** (1855) from 1940-1963, and in the late 1970s, it had female mud-wrestling contests. More recently, the pub raised thousands of pounds for local charities. Further up the hill, the **Britannia** (1868) had several long-serving landlords, including William Dunn and John Pardoe. In 2017, Dean Cartwright moved his Pig Iron micro-brewery from Brierley Hill and renamed it the Britannia Pub & Brewery.

Reviving the Old Bush

The **Old Bush Revived** in Powke Lane was built by Farmer Higgs and first licensed before 1846. Early landlord, Nobby Clarke was a well-known bare-knuckle fighter and close friend of William Perry (Tipton Slasher). The pub was popular for its whippet races, hare and rabbit coursing, and when trade declined, he hired three painted ladies as barmaids and hostesses, who local women dubbed as shameless hussies. Kept by Thomas and Decimus Jess Gaunt from 1851-1923, the Largest Pig in the World was displayed here in 1896. Decimus was a local character, who married twice and had 13 children. In the early 1900s, he served beer to 3,000-4,000 spectators at the annual sports days at Coombs Wood Tube Works football ground. His eldest son, Percival, founded his undertakers business at the pub, making his first coffin in the loft!

BLOXWICH

Bloxwich was a medieval settlement (Bloches Wic), which soon became a market town. It grew rapidly in the 18th century around coal mining, iron smelting and manufacturing industries, including awl blades, keys, locks and buckles, chains, bridles and saddles. The town once boasted more pubs of architectural and historic interest than anywhere in the Walsall area, but most of today's pubs date from the late 19th and early 20th centuries. Over the years, there were more than 90 pubs serving the thirsty workers in the wider Bloxwich area, of which around 20 survive today.

The earliest documentary reference to a Bloxwich inn dates from 1586, when Thomas Ball of The Sign of the Talbot was sued in the Quarter Sessions Court. By the 17th century, Bloxwich had at least six alehouses, including the **Bell** in Stafford Road. This original fine Tudor building was unfortunately demolished and rebuilt in 1900. For most of the 19th century, it was run by the Beech family, including local locksmith, Charles Beech, who wanted to live to 100, but died aged 99. The pub was so popular with miners and metalworkers that it would close at 11.00pm and be open before 6.00am, ready to slake the thirst of the nightshift. Another pub popular with miners and boatmen was the **Barley Mow** in Goscote Lane, backing onto the Wyrley & Essington Canal. Originally a 17th century house, it was converted into a pub by 1827, but unfortunately, it was damaged by fire and demolished in 2012.

Two other pubs dating from Tudor times were the **Bull's Head** in Park Road and the **Wheatsheaf** in Pinfold. The **Bull's Head** was a popular meeting place for workmen and hosted the town's largest Friendly Society in the 18th century. Its name recalls the coat of arms of John Skeffington, a 16th century local landowner. There's an amusing tale about Samuel Moseley, a miner who had made himself so comfortable in the pub that he decided he wouldn't go to work that day. His wife stormed out, crying that she wished the Bull's Head would fall on him and bury him. As she passed an old tree in the yard, the pub's roof did indeed fall in, demolishing the upper storey, but leaving Samuel unhurt. Henceforth, the tree was known as the Wishing Tree and held in great awe. The pub was rebuilt in 1927, but closed in 2007. The **Wheatsheaf** was one of the town's oldest inns, dating from the 16th century, but was rebuilt in 1834, acquired by the Bloxwich Brewery in 1901 and later passed to Wolverhampton & Dudley Breweries. Nearby were the **Queen's Head** (1851), another popular meeting place for miners, but rebuilt in 1973, and the **Carriers Arms** (1849), closed in 1928.

In High Street, the **King's Arms** existed in 1778, when the Amicable Friendly Society was founded, but the pub was closed in 1984. **The George** dated from 1828, but is now a shop, whilst the **Prince of Wales** dates from 1861, but was rebuilt in 1928 and survives today. In 2015, Wetherspoon's spent £1.9m converting the derelict Grosvenor Cinema into the **Bloxwich Showman** (see below). Continuing towards Leamore, the **Lamp Tavern** was originally part of a farm, first licensed in 1828, and until recently was a Holden's (Dudley) pub. Nearby, the **Spread Eagle Hotel** was kept by the Somerfield family from 1828 for almost a century, but was rebuilt in 1932 and closed by 1970.

In Wolverhampton Road, the **Turf Tavern** has been described as "the last truly unspoilt terraced pub left in the country". It's listed as a historic building (Grade II) and included in CAMRA's inventory of historic pubs. Known locally as Tinky's, it's been run by the Wilkes family since 1881 and retains many original features, including a Victorian bar back, quarry tiles, seating, etched windows and outside gents' toilet, with a small brewhouse, lock factory and pigsties in the yard. A few doors away is the **Spotted Cow,** dating from 1849, which had a model brewery in the yard when William Roberts (Brownhills Brewery) bought it for £8,500 in 1900.

In Elmore Green Road, the **Romping Cat** is a Victorian street-corner local of 1849. It changed its name from the Sandbank Tavern in 1957, to maintain the local tradition that there should always be a pub of that name in Bloxwich, in memory of Sir Gilbert Wakeringe. He was a 16th century landowner and sheriff of Staffordshire, whose coat of arms included three golden lions. The pub retains its traditional three-room layout, complete with an original bar counter, smoke room, tiling, etched panels and sliding window for the Outdoor Department. It's a listed building (Grade II) and also included in CAMRA's inventory of historic pubs.

The **Blue Pig** was originally a home-brew pub dating from 1818, but was demolished in 1931 to make way for Bloxwich library. Nearby, the **Thatched House Tavern** dated from 1861 and was known locally as The Thatch. In the early days, it was a popular cockfighting venue, but was converted into a shop in 2017. Not far away, the **Spring Cottage** is another former Brownhills Brewery pub of 1859, rebuilt in 1904. It retains many original features, including a Victorian bar back and glass advertising panels. In Victorian times, the cellar was used as a temporary jail for prisoners, and is allegedly haunted by one of the miscreants.

In Reeves Street, the **Hatherton Arms** (1880) was once known locally as the Painters after long-serving licensees Horace & Eleanor Painter (1932-1964). The **Sir Robert Peel** in Bell Lane originally dated from 1849 and was recently refurbished. In Stafford Road, the **Royal Exchange** existed in 1845 and is Grade II listed. It was owned by Bloxwich and Highgate Breweries, and has a brewery at the rear.

At Wallington Heath, the **Old Kings Arms** prospered as a coaching inn on the turnpike road between Walsall and Churchbridge in the late 18th century. During this period, a young lady was murdered while staying here, which led to a legend that she haunted the inn. By 1902, it was a private residence and from 1904 was the Convent of St Paul of Chartres. At Little Bloxwich, the **Beacon Way** in Stoney Lane was originally the Nag's Head, believed to be 400 years old and first licensed in 1828, but rebuilt in 1965.

Apart from home-brew pubs, there were a few breweries in Bloxwich. In 1898, J.W. Brookes established the **Bloxwich Brewery** in Elmore Green Road, but this was taken over by Butler's (Wolverhampton) in 1923. In High Street, Edward Ingram operated the **Victoria Brewery** in the 1880s, which was later taken over by J & J Yardley. The only brewery in Bloxwich today is the **New Invention** micro-brewery, behind the town centre off Pinfold, which brews distinctive craft beers. So although Bloxwich has lost many of its historic pubs, several attractive and lively pubs remain serving an excellent pint of beer.

A Showman in Bloxwich

Pat Collins first showed moving pictures at the Bloxwich Wakes Fair in 1900 as part of his funfair. He later set up the Showman's Guild, and became its longest serving president. He was also a local councillor, MP and Mayor of Walsall. He died in 1943, was buried at Bloxwich Cemetery and the Pat Collins memorial clock was later erected in Promenade Gardens. The Electric Palace Cinema was originally built here in 1912, seating 400 people, but showed its last film in 1921. Pat Collins then built the Grosvenor Cinema on this site, seating 1,200 people, which closed in 1959. This derelict building was later refurbished in 2015 at a cost of £1.9m by J.D. Wetherspoon, who named the pub the Bloxwich Showman in his memory.

BRIERLEY HILL

"When Satan stood on Brierley Hill and far around he gazed,
He said I never more shall feel at Hell's fierce flames amazed".
"And while I'm taking in the view, I'm feeling rather thirsty here,
So I might as well find a local pub and sample a decent beer!".

Brierley Hill is in the heart of the Black Country and is best known for its glass and steel making industries. Its name derives from the woodland clearing and hill where the briar rose grew. First recorded in 1785, the area had become heavily industrialised by the 19th century, with collieries, brickworks, claypits, glassworks and iron and steel factories. All this heavy industry was thirsty work and, over the years, more than 120 pubs and beerhouses served the town. However, much of the heavy industry has disappeared, including Round Oak steelworks, and now fewer than a dozen pubs remain.

The heart of Brierley Hill lies along the High Street, where there were once around 20 pubs. One of the oldest was the **Old New Inn,** where Joseph Weston brewed his own beer. Dating from before 1818, it originally had two rooms, the House of Commons and House of Lords, the latter where civic business was discussed, but it was rebuilt in 1925 and closed in 2007. The **Horseshoe** (1822) was another historic pub, with a large concert hall in the old marketplace where travelling theatres performed. This eventually became the Palace Theatre, but the pub closed in 1982. Opposite was the **Five Ways** (1867-1957), a Thomas Plant (Netherton) brewery pub. The **Star** (1822) was home to Brierley Hill Alliance FC, with stables, a concert room and gym used for boxing training, before it closed around 1940. In 1834, Thomas Meese built the **Bell** as a commercial hotel, with a fine bowling green. It was used for meetings of ratepayers and the Free Home Brewers Protection Society, but closed in 1924.

The **Red Lion** (1854) was rebuilt to designs of local Dudley architect, Albert Butler, in 1926. Mary Pargeter was the licensee from 1963-1981 and became the first Mayor of Dudley MBC in 1974. In 1989, it became a Holt, Plant & Deakin pub and still serves a nice pint, as does the nearby **Three Crowns** (1857), kept by Thomas and Mary Plant from 1908-1940. In October 2021, a new sports bar, the **Brier Rose,** opened in the High Street. The **Town Arms** (1865) was near the police station and where Brierley Hill Alliance FC was founded in 1887, but was demolished in the 1960s. George Pearson brewed his own beer at the **Spread Eagle** (1856) before it became a Batham's House in 1926, kept by Arthur Joseph Batham until 1944, but it was demolished in 1967.

The **Golden Eagle** (1849-1956) was home to the Court Leet and Frothblowers Society, but was also known for its frequent fights. Next door was the **Market Vaults** (1860), first known as the Board, but its licence was not renewed in 1918 since there were 23 other licensed premises within 500 yards! The **Turks Head** (1857) provided a waiting room for travellers at the tram terminus, where Thomas Guttery and John Glover sold *Home-Brewed Ales of the Highest Standard*. It was kept by local footballer, Ralph Jasper in 1959, but is now a restaurant. The **Mitre** (1870) was a Hanson's (Dudley) pub which closed in 1966, whilst the **Dog & Partridge** (1864) is now a restaurant. **The Exchange Vaults** (1851) was originally the White Horse and had its own concert room featuring "Extraordinary Attractions" and "A Splendid Array of Talent", before closing in 1940.

Opposite St Michael's Church, the **Old Bell** (1845) was another venerable home-brew pub, where Benjamin Elwell brewed his own beer. Local colliers quenched their thirsts here until it closed in 1906. Along Church Street was the **Plough** (1857), alongside Frederick Warren's small brewery. Local brewer J.P. Simpkiss bought the pub in 1926, and between 1979-2003, it was kept by ex-Royal Marine and local footballer, George Gallagher. In 2003, the pub was briefly renamed after him, before closing in 2010. Benjamin Elwell brewed his own beer at another old pub nearby, the **Old Whimsey** (1818), which became a private house in 1941. Opposite was the **Travellers Rest** (1858), a home-brew pub until 1906, with its Victoria Concert Hall, but it closed in 1990.

Continuing north along Dudley Road, there were over a dozen historic pubs, including the **Fortune of War** (1822-1939), home to the Brierley Hill Histrionic Society. The **Queen's Head** (1845-1995) was reopened as the Crystal Tavern by local boxer, Pat Cowdell in 1988, but later converted into a restaurant and nightclub. On the corner of John Street, the **Round Oak** dated back to the opening of the turnpike road to Dudley in the 1790s, but was rebuilt to the designs of Messrs Scott and Clark in 1939 and converted into flats in 1986. Opposite was the **Dudley Arms** (1870-1956), where Thomas Banks brewed his own beer. A few doors away was the **Royal Oak** (1849), a home-brew pub which had closed by 1927 (see below).

Opposite the former Round Oak railway station is the **Blue Brick,** originally the Commercial Inn, popular with Round Oak steelworkers. It seems to have started life as a 19th century house, first licensed in 1856, with its front elevation modified with faience tiling in 1929. Next door was the **Round of Beef** (1871-1966), a Hanson's pub kept by James Tom Garratt from 1948-1956. The **Dog & Lamppost** (1872), originally the New Inn, was another Simpkiss pub, kept by Fanny Ward from 1913-1938 and Don Vasey from 1977-1990. At the **Britannia** (1861-1936), William Wassall was charged with wilfully damaging a pork pie in 1869 and fined 5s!

The **Saracen's Head** (1854) was popular with pigeon fanciers, but became a shop in 2013. From 1887-1940, Alfred Tandy and his family kept the **Miners Arms** (1864), where he ran a soup kitchen for striking miners in 1912, but it became a fish and chip shop in 1997. In Wallows Street, John Preston brewed his own beer at the **Woodman** (1871), which became a builders merchants in 1992, not far from the **Royal Exchange** (1871-1940).

In Mill Street, the **Alma** (1861) was kept by the town's oldest licensee, publican schoolmaster Benjamin Whittinslow, who read the newspapers to customers. Brierley Hill Cricket Club was founded here, but the pub was rebuilt in the 1930s, renamed the Teaser (one of a team of glassmakers) and later became a restaurant. A few doors away, the **Kings Head** (1868) is a traditional Black Country two-bay local pub, kept by local footballer, Fred Price between 1927-1932, and was also used for boxing training. **The Falcon** (1860) became a Hanson's pub in 1934, but closed in 1937. **The Swan** (1849) was acquired by Batham's in 1937, and was popular with pigeon fanciers, but closed in 1939. Sydney and Elsie Lane kept the **Waterloo** (1818) from 1942-1967, but it closed in 2014. At the bottom end of Mill Street, the **Cottage Spring** (1869) was rebuilt to designs of local architect Henry Jennings in 1900 and is now a vets.

In Bank Street, the **Bridge** (1860) was kept by Albert and Susan Hobson from 1907-1958, but became a restaurant in 2000. The **Rose & Crown** was originally two cottages, converted into a pub in 1854. It was a home-brew pub kept by Sarah and Robert Wood from 1904-1949, when it was acquired by Holden's (Dudley). The **Golden Cup** (1868) was originally called the Golden Cross, but had closed by 1924. In Moor Street, the **Swan** (1834-1958) was kept by home-brewers, Maria Higgs and Thomas Jeffries, and in 1854 was used for meetings to recruit workers for the Hudson Bay Company in Canada.

On the corner of Moor Street and Fenton Street, the **Lamp** (1861) was a former Darby's (West Bromwich) Brewery pub, which closed in 1973. At the other end of Fenton Street, the **Railway** (1851) was close to Brierley Hill railway station, but was converted into flats in 1999. In Albion Street, the **Albion** (1871) was another Darby's pub, which became offices in 1985. In Parkes Street, the **Bird in Hand** (1866-1940) was once a home-brew pub where John Partridge brewed his own beer and was kept by local footballer, Fred Price from 1932-1940, after he left the Kings Head. Just across the railway bridge in Moor Street were the **Cock** (1854-1937) and **Spotted Cow** (1872-1940), a home-brew pub where William Cartwright and his son brewed until 1935. Alongside Farmer's Bridge, the **Old Bush** (1834) was a Hanson's pub until it became a fish and chip shop in 2000.

Level Street passed through the huge Round Oak Steelworks, and not surprisingly the **Three Furnaces** (1818-1983) helped to quench steelworkers' thirsts. It was once owned by Edward Oakes who founded the Wordsley Brewery. On the other side of the road was the **Old Bush** (1834), another pub kept by footballer, Fred Price, but it was closed by 1994. Across the railway line was the **Queens Head** (1834-1940), where landlord Sam Insull kept monkeys, a sea lion and a bear, and often had a live snake down his shirt! At the **Fountain** (1864-1926), landlord Frederick Preston had a museum of nature and art and also exhibited obscene photographs.

At the **Fox & Goose** (1845-1940), landlady Theresa Gwilt was fined £50 in 1864 for using grains of paradise in her home-brewed beer! These were related to the ginger plant, giving the beer a black pepper flavour and illegally increasing its strength. At the time, Stipendary Spooner said that "Grains of paradise were most exciting, but had a very serious effect upon those who consumed beverages containing them".

Continuing along Brettell Lane to Silver End, we'd find the **Vine** (1857), kept by Richard Wassall and his family until 1920, before being converted into a fish and chip shop in 2009. Over the railway line in Bull Street is the **Bulls Head** (1845), which became a Black Country Ales' pub in 2008, but is currently closed. Back on Brettell Lane, the **Talbot** dates from 1822, became a Simpkiss pub in 1926 and is now known as the New Talbot. Close to the former Brettell Lane railway station is the **Old Crown,** dating from before 1822 and now listed as a historic building (Grade II). Harry Jeavons brewed his "Pure Home Brew'd Ales" here until 1932, but it's currently closed. Close by was the **Kings Arms** (1834), kept by the Webb family from 1845-1870, but closed in 1921. A few doors away is the **New Wellington,** originally dating from 1822 as the Wellington Arms. In 1919, the pub and its brewery were bought by J.P. Simpkiss for £3,000, and it became home to Simpkiss Brewery (see below).

We can't leave Brierley Hill without walking along Delph Road. At the top end is the iconic **Vine** (1836), better known as the Bull & Bladder, with its Shakespearian quotation on the façade and unspoilt interior (see below). Other surviving historic pubs include the **Black Horse** (1834), kept by Arthur and Susan Hobson from 1907-1958, and **Tenth Lock** (1866), originally the Delph Stores, kept by Sally Cartwright until 1955. The **Dock & Iron** (previously Duke William) dated from before 1822 and was home to George Elwell's Delph Brewery in 1876, but has recently been demolished. Unfortunately, the **Bell** (1849), a former Holt, Plant & Deakin pub at the bottom of Delph Locks, is currently closed.

Most of the area between Lower Delph and Church Street has been redeveloped with new housing, including distinctive tower blocks. In 1854, William Simpkiss, then a potter by trade, took over the **Potters Arms** in Potter Street, which had a small brewhouse. It was later kept by George Bullock and his family until 1941, but closed in 1955 (see below). The **Four Furnaces** (1841) was a Hanson's pub until it closed in 1939. In Hill Street, the **Rock Tavern** originally dated from 1860, but was rebuilt in 1911. It eventually became a music venue before being converted into a supermarket in 2001. The **Britannia** (1822) was a canalside pub in Lower Delph, but closed in 1939. In Turk Street, the **Vine** (1872-1912) was a home-brew pub with a small brewery which was kept by Benjamin Raybould and his family until 1896.

So, although Brierley Hill has lost most of its historic pubs, several remain, including Batham's iconic Bull & Bladder. Long may they prosper!

Brierley Hill – a brewer's paradise

Brierley Hill was home to several home-brew pubs, which became breweries in their own right. At the bottom of the Delph, in an area known as The Rocks, was the **Potters Arms**. In 1854, William Simpkiss bought the pub and passed it to his son, William Henry Simpkiss in 1861. He established a successful ginger beer and mineral water business here before acquiring the **Royal Oak** at Round Oak from Edward Smithyman in 1869. The site had a history of brewing beer, going back to 1797, and was close to a fast-growing population working in the local iron and steelworks, glassworks and brickworks. A few years later, Henry built a brewery behind the pub, but since he had little experience of brewing beer, immediately engaged 21-year-old Hercules Hazlehurst as head brewer. He was bought out by North Worcestershire Breweries (Stourbridge) in 1896, and the brewery then passed to Elwell & Williams who renamed it the Town Brewery. In 1934, it was bought by Julia Hanson & Sons (Dudley) and by 1967, had been replaced with a new fire station.

In 1919, Joseph Paskin Simpkiss bought the **Foley Arms** in Brettell Lane from Henry Bolton. This was an established home-brew pub, originally known as the Wellington Arms, dating from 1822. He began brewing in a small room at the pub (now the lounge), but in 1934, he built a new brewery behind the pub, named the Dennis Brewery after his son. After a partnership with Johnson & Phipps of Wolverhampton, the brewery and pubs were acquired by Greenall Whitley in 1985.

At the top of the Delph, the **Vine** (or Bull & Bladder, so named because it used to be a butcher's shop with an adjoining slaughterhouse) became the home of Batham's brewery. The pub had to be rebuilt due to mining subsidence and a new purpose-built tower brewery was built in 1911. The pub is memorable for its Shakespearian quotation – "Blessing of Your Heart You Brew Good Ale" (from *The Two Gentleman of Verona*). From its opening, the pub became a model of a good community pub, hosting many local organisations. Batham's other tag-line relates to the adjoining Delph Brewery – "The Birthplace of Genuine Beer". Interestingly, Batham's Bitter was not produced until the 1950s, when they leased two pubs in North Worcestershire, the Plough at Shenstone and the Swan at Chaddesley Corbett. The locals didn't much like the typical Black Country mild, so Batham's started to brew their award-winning bitter, which is now their flagship beer!

COSELEY

Coseley is one of nine villages making up the ancient Manor of Sedgley. It once had extensive mining areas, with many collieries, and industrial areas with foundries, brickworks and ironworks. This was thirsty work and, over the years, more than 100 pubs have served the area, but today, barely a handful survive.

One of the oldest pubs in Coseley was the **Painters Arms** in Avenue Road, first licensed in 1817. William Taft and his family kept this home-brew pub for nearly 50 years before it was bought by Holden's (Dudley) in 1928 for £2,375 and briefly kept by Edwin Holden. The Painters Morris & Holden's Golden Morris teams practised here and it was reputedly haunted by former barmaid, Jenny, before it was replaced by new housing in 2016. William Taft also owned the **Rolling Mill** in Highfield Road (1818), which closed in 1940. Probably the oldest pub still surviving in Coseley is the **Rising Sun** (1818) in Darkhouse Lane, another home-brew house where Daniel Rowley brewed his own beer.

The central area of Coseley is Roseville, focused on Castle Street. The **Old Chainyard** (1855) began life as the Red Lion, rebuilt in 1938 and renamed in 1991, which became a popular real ale tavern. Nearby, the **Royal Hotel** (1859) was a focal point for the local community and is another pub offering real ale. The **White Lion** (1868-2001) had a small brewery and was known locally as Webby's after long-serving licensees Bert and Dolly Webb (1937-1972). The **Apple Tree** (1871) was originally the Miners Arms, but was replaced with a new pub in Central Drive in 1961.

The Coseley Prize Band rehearsed at the **Old Bush** (1859-1940) in Ebenezer Street, whilst in School Street, the **Summerhouse** (1864-1961) was known locally as the Puzzle Garden after the maze in its grounds. In Ward Street, the **New Inn** (1868) had a small brewery run by Samuel and Sarah Timmins until 1944, when it became a Holden's pub. In Ivy House Lane, the **Ivy House** (1833) became a restaurant in 1987, before being demolished in 1992, whilst the **Horse & Jockey** (1849) was rebuilt in 1940, but closed in 2012.

Across the railway line, there were several pubs in and around Wallbrook. Richard and Clara Price kept the **Bush** (1833-1959) in Wallbrook Street from 1894-1940. Nearby, the **Union** (1833-1926) was a home-brew pub with its own pork butcher's shop, slaughterhouse and sausage machine. In 1889, landlord Nathaniel Attwood displayed the Greatest Living Novelty in the Midlands here – a four-legged duck! In Edge Street, the **Red Cow** (1871) was originally the Board, rebuilt later and converted into flats in 2016. **The Railway** (1851) in Chapel Street lasted until 1930, whilst the **Star** (1861) in Broad Street was rebuilt in 1965, but closed in 1998. In Church Road, the **Spread Eagle** (1833) was known locally as the Ten Legs before closing by 1940.

There was much heavy industry around Deepfields, including Cannon Industries factory. In Havacre Lane, the **Boat** (1824) was originally a coaching inn, popular with canal boatmen and close to Deepfields railway station. In 1869, stationmaster Joseph Plant was presented with 20 guineas for discharging his duties, and the pub was regularly used for inquests into deaths on the canal and railway and in local factories. Henry, Ann and Margaret Hardy kept the pub from 1972-1995, but it was demolished in 2008. The **Railway Tavern** (1848) was gone by 1928, whilst in Darkhouse Lane, the **Swan** (1841), surrounded by Cannon Works, and **Saddlers Arms** (1871) lasted until 1940. In Webb Street, the **Bulls Head** (1828) closed in 1926, whilst the **Rollers Arms** (1866-2014) in Foundry Street was reputedly haunted by two nuns. From 1904-1940, Ernest Holcroft brewed his own beer at the **Spread Eagle** (1851) in Ladymoor Road, but it closed in 1956, whilst the **Anchor Inn** (1828) was a popular canalside pub before it closed in 1957.

At Highfields Bridge, the **Boat Inn** (1863) was another popular canalside pub until it was demolished in 2002. In Rainbow Street, Benjamin Cole brewed his own beer at the **Ship & Rainbow** (1828), but it was rebuilt in 1959 and became the Rainbow Centre in 1997. In Skidmore Road, Edward Ward and Joe Adams brewed their own beer until 1969 at the **Old Bush** (1832), when it was leased by Holden's until closing in 2005. Known locally as Joey Adams, it was reputedly haunted by a male ghost who threw a glass around the pub!

In the west of Coseley, Joseph Nicholds was the most memorable landlord of the **Hop & Barleycorn** (1842) in Mason Street. He worked with Wombwell's Menagerie Band and composed religious songs, before the pub was rebuilt in 1957 and converted into housing in 2015. In Providence Road, the **Rose & Crown** (1845) closed shortly after 1950. In Upper Ettingshall Lane, William Hampton and John Sharkey brewed their own beer at the **Black Horse** (1841), which became a shop in 1928, whilst the **White Horse** (1849) became a restaurant in 2011. In Duck Street, the **Bird in Hand** (1850) was replaced by a new pub in Paul Street in 1959, which closed in 2002.

At The Coppice, the **Coseley Tavern** (1833) was another former home-brew pub where grocers John and Joseph Beardmore and David and Mary Millward brewed their own beer until 1933. In 1866, David Round exposed himself in the taproom and was jailed for 14 days! In Caddick Street, the **Druids Head** (1861-1971) was well known for landlord Joseph Joah Flavell's popular Bulls Blood home-brewed mild ale until 1970, and was the venue for the Black Country Society's first committee meeting in 1967. Nearby, Honor, William and Thomas Meddings kept the **Hurst Hill Tavern** (1848) from 1885-1940, but it was converted into housing in 2011, whilst in Clifton Street, the **Rifle Corps** (1860) lasted just a century.

At Hurst Hill, the Bryan family brewed their own beer at the **Queens Arms** (1865) until 1940, but it closed around 1965. In Gorge Road, William Tranter kept the **Old Gate** (1825) from 1915-1927, but it was rebuilt in 1937 and demolished in 2002. From 1927-1944, his son kept the **Miners Arms** (1851-1970), where he advertised *"Tranter's beer will keep you fit and help you do your little bit"* during the Second World War. Nearby, Thomas and Florence Slater and their son kept the **Gate Hangs Well** (1835) from 1938-1978, but it was rebuilt on the opposite side of the road in 1966 and became a shop in 2013.

James, Sarah and Jane Fellows brewed their own beer until 1925 at the **Horse & Jockey** (1854) at Cinder Hill, now in Robert Wynd. It was rebuilt on the opposite side of the road and became a Holt, Plant & Deakin pub in 1989. In Beacon Street, the **Talbot** (1835) was used by footballers for changing before it closed in 1957, whilst Richard Marsh and Job Butler brewed their own beer at the **Woodcross** (1857-1940) until 1935.

So, although Coseley has lost most of its historic pubs, a handful survive and offer a good range of local beers. Long may they prosper!

CRADLEY & COLLEY GATE

Cradley achieved prominence in the 19th century as a centre for nail and chainmaking, along with the surrounding collieries, ironworks and brickworks. All this heavy industry was thirsty work and by 1851, Cradley had 28 pubs and beerhouses serving 3,833 people. By 1901, the population had grown to over 6,700, with 20 inns and 42 beerhouses – one pub for every 108 people! Over the years, more than 60 pubs served the local community, but barely a handful remain today.

The centre of Cradley focused on the High Street (now Colley Lane), where one of the oldest pubs was the **Fish,** first recorded in 1829. Thomas Fox brewed his own beer here before it was taken over by Ansell's, but it closed in 1938 and was demolished in 1959. In the 1830s, John Attwood turned his butcher's shop into a beerhouse, known as the **White Horse.** After helping out at the pub, Daniel Batham became its landlord in 1882 and held the licence for 40 years, but the pub was demolished in 1971. Close by were the **Holly Bush** (1833-1964), home to Cradley FC, and **Robin Hood** (1835-1939), where Thomas Nock was found guilty of robbing and wounding John Penn in 1837 and transported to the penal colony of Port Macquarrie in Australia!

Mary Hingley, daughter of anchor and chainmaker, Noah Hingley, kept the **Black Swan** (1840-1939), whilst later, Samuel and Fanny Jones popularised the pub with entertainment, including Quadrille and string bands. In 1900, home-brewer Frederick Cutler bought the **Rose & Crown** (1849) for £1,730, which was more recently known as Potters, recalling licensees Alan and Lily Potter (1972-2015). In 1905, Frederick Cutler also bought the **Bridge** (1844) at the bottom of Bridge Street, but it was converted into offices in 1955 and later demolished.

In New Street were the **Lodge Forge** (1841-1910) and **Bell** (1859-1884), whilst nearby was the **Victoria** (1857-1923), where landlady Elizabeth Bennett was put on the blacklist in 1890 for being drunk in her own pub! The **Old Crown** in Intended Street (1860) was known locally as the Top Crown and was rebuilt in the 1940s before being demolished in 2008. The **Blue Ball** was another venerable tavern dating from 1822, giving its name to Blue Ball Lane. John Tandy brewed his own beer and horse-nailmakers regularly met here, before it was demolished in 1964.

At Lyde Green, the **Crown** (1854-1966) was known locally as the Blue Brick after the blue bricks on the frontage. Almost opposite is the **Vine** (1864), rebuilt in 1919 and kept by the Garrett family for nearly 50 years until 1982. At the bottom of Maypole Hill beyond Two Lanes End was the **Maypole** (1831-1955), popular for its auctions and May Day festivities.

Probably the oldest pub in Cradley was the **Old Mogul** in Mogul Lane, dating from 1775. Landlord Thomas Fellows offered bull-baiting and cockfighting here and it was Netherend FC's HQ until it closed in 1939. At Netherend, the **Horse & Jockey** (1858-1971) is remembered for its bowling green and long-serving landlord Reg Johnson (1935-1971), whilst the **Park Lane Tavern** (1868) was the home of a popular shooting club.

At Overend, the **Rising Sun** (1824-1925) was another venerable hostelry, known as the Sun Inn until 1878. Almost next door was the **Old Bull's Head** (1850-1995), kept by Joseph and Edith Garbett for almost 30 years until 1969. In Banners Lane, William and Amelia Palmer kept the **Black Horse** (1870) from 1915-1945, where Stourdell United FC was formed. The garret room was allegedly haunted by the ghost of servant girl, Lucy, and the Cradley XLCR brass band regularly played here until 1958. It was renamed Adventure in 2002, but replaced by new housing in 2012.

From the High Street, the land rises to Colley Gate and Windmill Hill. In Barracks Lane, the **Crown** (1870) became the Widders in 2007, recalling widowed landlady, Eliza Oliver.

Nearby, the **Malt Shovel** (1800-1891) was kept for over 80 years by Joseph Tibbetts and his family. In Furlong Lane, the **British Arms** (1829-1971) was a home-brew pub, whilst the **Duke William** (1871-1966) once displayed a pig with five legs!

In Colley Gate, the **Talbot Hotel** (1875) is still a prominent local landmark, listed as a historic building (Grade II). It was renamed the Chainmaker in 2001, but was converted into a children's play centre in 2015. Until 1937, Frank, William and George Oliver brewed here, with 18 tied houses (the brewery building still exists). In 1888, they displayed the largest pig in the world and in summer, Colley Gate Cricket Club played behind the pub. Daniel Mole and his family kept the **Gate** (1829) until 1900, originally known as the Colley Gate Inn, with a fine bowling green until 1998, but it closed in 2017.

In Windmill Hill, the **Little Chop House** (1833) started life 400 years ago as the White Lion, a stopping place for the *Tantivy* stagecoach plying between Stourbridge and Birmingham. In the mid 20th century, it was known as Stafford's after licensees George and Esther Stafford (1921-1967), but became one of Mad O'Rourke's Little pubs in 1985 and renamed the Little Chop House. Previously used as an undertakers, it's allegedly haunted by a young girl who died of scarlet fever in 1903. At the top of Windmill Hill, the **Round of Beef** (1844) is another of Cradley's oldest pubs, kept by Edwin Cox and his family for nearly 140 years until 1982. It served as Cradley's court room and coroner's office until 1922 and survived a threat of closure in 2015.

Two Gates Lane led out into the countryside and the surrounding collieries, named after the two gates used to stop sheep and livestock straying onto open farmland. The oldest pub was the **Old Two Gates Inn** (1828-1957), where landlord Thomas Edge bought a monkey and gave the pub its local name, the Monkey House. Further along Two Gates Lane, Henry Parish converted his old farmhouse into the **New Two Gates Inn** in 1849 with the **Vine** (1891) nearby, but both were replaced with new housing by 1992.

At the top of Why Not Street is the **Why Not** (1872), originally the Why Not Call and See. It started life as an early Victorian beerhouse and was used by thirsty miners from the nearby collieries. In 1878, it displayed the world's largest black Spanish Hen Egg weighing over 10½ ounces! In 1894, the pub was renamed after a winning Grand National race horse, and between 1993-2001, owners Juliet Trimble and Spike became something of a local legend. It still serves tasty meals and great beers.

One job is not enough

As well as looking after their pubs, many licensees had other jobs, in order to properly feed and clothe their often large families. Thomas Fellows (Old Mogul), Hezekiah Walker (Fish) and John Millward (Rose & Crown) were chainmakers, Jabez Adams (Bull's Head) was a rivet maker and Thomas Cemm (Bridge) made vices. Daniel and Fanny Mole (Gate) were blacksmiths, John Beasley (Black Horse) was a sword blade forger, Benjamin Beasley (Sun) made gun barrels and William Bunn and Benjamin Homer (Bell) were both shinglers in the iron trade. Several licensees were also butchers, greengrocers or shopkeepers.

CRADLEY HEATH

The centre of **Cradley Heath** focuses on the High Street, between Four Ways and Five Ways. Opposite St Luke's Church, the **Four Ways** (1857) was known locally as the Manchester House, with its music hall and small own brewery operated by William Nock. In the 1970s, it was home to Chris Jenkins' boxing academy before being demolished in 1987 after a lorry crashed into it. Next to the Empire Theatre, the **Holly Bush** was one of the oldest pubs in the town, dating from 1827. Originally a home-brew pub where Nehemiah, Richard and Jane Homer brewed their own beer, it was rebuilt by Atkinson's (Birmingham) in 1906 and closed a century later.

The **Heath Tavern** (1840) was first kept by chainmaker Tobias Hingley and known locally as the Boster, but was demolished in 2000. It was a cosy two-roomed pub serving Honest Plant's English Ales, where Mick Verracha used to park his tater cart outside, selling jacket potatoes, four a penny. A few doors away, the modern Wetherspoon's pub, **Moon Under Water,** opened in 1997. The **Bull's Head** (1858-1963) was another home-brew pub where Thomas Westwood, John Biggs, John Webb and Benoni and Samuel Buttery used to brew their own beer. The **Talbot** (1851) was known locally as the Big Lamp, due to the large lantern that hung outside, before it was damaged by mining subsidence in 1914 and became a shop in 1959. In 2021, a new micro-pub called the **Handle Bar,** operated by the local Fixed Wheel Brewery, opened in the former Presley's Bar.

There were several pubs grouped around Five Ways. The **Five Ways** (1833) is a prominent three-storey building which was once a commercial hotel with "Large Airy Bedrooms" and the "Finest Billiard Room in the District". Known locally as Charlie Wright's after a long-serving landlord who was renowned for his dogs, it became a shop in 2014. Nearby was the **Crown** (1850-1924), which also had a music hall where the Only Artiste that Turns Back Somersaults in Big Boots performed. At the top of Cradley Road were the **Old Cross Guns** (1849-1970), home to Joe Mallen and his Staffordshire bull terriers (see below), opposite the **Red Lion** (1865-1941), both of which are now shops.

A couple of well-known pubs stood at the top end of St Anne's Road, including the **Anchor Hotel** (1861-2003), originally the Royal Exchange, and **Bell** (1841-1999), home to local character, Benny Fiddler, which became the Cradley Sausage Works in 1988. In Spinners End, we'd find the **Bird in Hand** (1849-1972), a Simpkiss (Brierley Hill) pub, and **Bridge** (1870-1959), where landlady Mary Harris was put on the blacklist in 1884 for serving beer during prohibited hours.

In Lomey Town (now Lower High Street), the **Salutation** was another venerable hostelry dating from 1833. It had a music hall where Pietro Carle entertained audiences with his "Wonderfully Trained Pigeons", but the pub closed in 1956. Opposite, next to Christ Church, was the **Railway Hotel** (1864) where Thomas Parsons and Richard Province brewed their own beer. It was kept by Joseph and Beatrice Bennett from 1937-1962, before closing in 1970. Further along Lomey Town were the **Royal Oak** (1870-1965), **Swan With Two Necks** (1864-1994), now offices, and **Vine & Railway** (1851-1968), a popular railwayman's pub where Sophie Cartwright brewed her own ales.

In the back streets of Cradley Heath, we'd find the **Royal Oak** (1861-1990) in Bannister Street, known locally as Laney's after popular landlord James Lane (1937-1955). On the corner of Newtown Lane, the **Holly Bush** dates from 1833, was rebuilt in 1898 and became a popular music and comedy venue. Nearby in Holly Bush Street, the **Hand of Providence** (1851-1985) was kept by the Price family who were renowned for brewing their own strong beer, and was known locally as Posh's.

In Providence Street, we'd find the **Crown & Anchor** (1864-1928), while the **Swan** (1868) was home to the Aston family, who brewed their own beer until 1928. It was known locally as Jasper's after landlord Harold Jasper (1928-1963), before becoming a Holden's (Dudley) pub in 1983 and was later converted into apartments. In Prince Street, Esther Lane and Frank Tibbetts brewed their own beer at the **Reindeer** (1856), which was renamed Roost in 2008. In Tibbetts Gardens, the **Round of Beef** (1861) was once a Thomas Plant Steam Brewery (Netherton) pub, known for a short time as the Cheese, but demolished around 1990.

Corngreaves Road was home to the Corngreaves New British Iron Works and brickworks, and not surprisingly, several pubs served the thirsty workers. Sarah Yardley brewed her own beer at the **Chainmakers Arms** (1857-1965), known locally as the Chainees, whilst the **Queen's Head** (1849-1965) originally sold Bridgewater's Ales (Dudley Wood). In 1885, landlord Jeremiah Westwood was put on the blacklist for permitting gambling at the **Railway Tavern** (1869-1906), whilst the **Vine** (1865-1990) had a concert hall, where workers met when the Corngreaves Ironworks closed in 1895.

Close to the junction with Graingers Lane, the **Plough & Harrow** (1849) was sandwiched between a butcher's shop and a hairdressers and known locally as Billy Plough's. It's popular with real ale drinkers, having won several local CAMRA awards. The **Corngreaves Hotel** (1865) was a popular drinking haunt for workers at the ironworks, and was kept by the Cole family who were saddle makers and brewed their own beer until 1926. It was then kept by the Kirkham family until 1964, before being renamed the Black Country Inn in 1987 and closing a decade later.

Further along Graingers Lane, the **Beehive** (1849-1956) was used by performers at the Theatre Royal which used to stand opposite the pub. The **New Inn** (1859) was kept by local brewers, the Tibbetts family until 1919. Later, landlord Richard Llewellyn Province gave it the local name of Lew's, before it was demolished and replaced with new houses in 2017. The **Railway** (1868) was known locally as Bellyfield's after landlord and local brewer, Henry Bellfield (1910-1928). It was kept for a few years by Caleb Batham, but closed in 1956. Finally, in Toys Green, the **Jolly Collier** (1849) was popular with local miners, but was renamed the Garden House in 1986 and the Wizard & Glass in 2002, before closing in 2020.

So, although many of Cradley Heath's historic pubs have been lost, a handful remain serving a variety of excellent beers. Long may they prosper!

Cradley Heath – Home of the Staffordshire Bull Terrier

In Cradley Road, not far from Five Ways, the **Old Cross Guns** was first licensed in 1849. By 1921, it was in the hands of blacksmith, Joe Mallen, who had also worked as a chainmaker at William Griffiths' Triton Works. When he took the pub over, it was renowned for cockfighting and dog fights in the cellar. He kept the pub for nearly 30 years and was well known for his interest in Staffordshire bull terriers. He was keen to see that the breed did not die out, so campaigned relentlessly for it to be properly recognised. In fact, Joe won the first ever diploma for the Best in Show at Cruft's in 1936 with his dog "Cross Guns Johnson". Three years later his dog "Gentleman Jim" became the first champion Staffordshire bull terrier in the world. His nephew, Norman Plant, went on to establish the Cradley Heath Whippet Racing Club.

DARLASTON

Darlaston is thought to date back to the 8th century, but most pubs in the town were built in the 19th century, when thousands of people moved into the area, attracted by its plentiful employment in the iron and steel factories, collieries and claypits. There was also work in the older trades of making clocks, locks and gunlocks, nuts and bolts, buckles, stirrups and bridle-bits. In 1851, the town had some 20 pubs and 73 beerhouses serving 10,600 people, but by 1901, this had increased to around 150 pubs and 30 beerhouses in Darlaston and the wider Moxley area, of which around a dozen remain today.

Foremost amongst the oldest pubs in Darlaston was the **White Lion Hotel** at the top of King Street. It was one of the town's important coaching inns, where stagecoaches called en route to Birmingham. It's a Grade II listed building, but was converted into flats in 1997. On a wet night in 1743, the notorious Darlaston mob stopped here for refreshment before chanting "Church and King" and dragging Methodist preacher, John Wesley, before the local magistrates. The pub had a bowling green and a small brewery, where the old malthouse was used for meetings of the Darlaston Board of Health. It was also a courthouse until the town hall opened in 1887.

At the lower end of King Street, George Bayley's horse-drawn omnibuses left the **Waggon & Horses** (1818) for Birmingham and Wolverhampton in 1845. Nearby, the **Dog & Partridge,** first licensed in 1818, was known as the Coffin Handles because of its brass door fittings. It also had a gym for training boxers, but was demolished in 1962. Opposite and next to the **New Inn** (1868-1936), the **Queen's Head** (1834-1960) had a concert hall and was a regular meeting place for nut and bolt makers.

In Church Street, the Foster family kept the **Bell** in the early 18th century. They were one of the richest families in town and lived at a fine Georgian house not far from the pub. In 1835, the pub was bought by Thomas and Obadiah Howl, who also operated a stage-coach service to Birmingham and Wolverhampton. In 1851, James Pritchard bought the pub and established the Darlaston Brewery nearby to supply several other pubs. The brewery was acquired by William Butler & Co. (Wolverhampton) in 1946 and the pub was demolished shortly afterwards. Other old pubs in Church Street included the **George** (1841), home to Darlaston Football Club in the 1890s, and the **Red Lion** (1818), both closed in the 1960s. In 1822, William Wilkes kept the **Duke of Wellington,** which became the **Green Dragon** in 1834 after protests about the 1830 Beerhouse Act. Nearby, in Bell Street, is the **Vine,** dating back to 1834.

Facing The Leys in Bilston Street, the **Bradford Arms** was originally three separate buildings dating from the 18th/19th centuries, and was known locally as the Frying Pan (see below). Nearby in Cramp Hill, the **Old Crown** dated from 1818, but was demolished in 1939.

In High Street, the **Dartmouth Arms** (1841) was known locally as the Blazing Stump and was popular for darts, but it was demolished to make way for road improvements in the late 1960s. Nearby, Silas and Annie Edwards kept the **Seven Stars** from 1928-1951, whilst the **Rose & Crown** (1868-1926) was popular with cyclists, and the **Bull's Head** (1834-1982) had a winning darts team in 1942.

In Pinfold Street, the **Three Horseshoes** (1868) was a former home-brew pub, but was taken over by William Butler's brewery in 1961 and converted into flats in 2011. Facing the Bull Stake was the **Old Castle,** a commercial hotel dating from 1845, where the Rotary Club met. Landlord John Stokes made gunlocks in his workshop, but it was demolished in 1968 to make way for Darlaston Library. The **Black Horse,** dating from the late 18th century, was a traditional spit and sawdust bar, with spittoons. It was also home to the town's horse racing fraternity, as well as landlord Thomas Newton's nut and bolt workshop. On the opposite side of Pinfold Street were the **Bird in Hand, Union** and **Noah's Ark,** dating from the 1830s, but all long gone. Along Walsall Road, John Corns and his family kept the **Horse & Jockey** from 1834-1861, whilst the **Old Engine** (1871) in Bull Street is now a restaurant.

On the corner of Catherine's Cross, the **Staffordshire Knot** (1871) is a fine example of a Victorian pub, whilst the **Nelson** (1818) was a popular darts pub, demolished in the 1990s. On the corner of Moxley Road, the **Duke of York** (1818) was replaced by a rest home in the 1980s. In Foundry Street, Harry Humpage kept the **Lamp** from 1935-1962, with its gas lighting and trestle tables, and served roast potatoes and sandwiches. When he called time, he would personally finish any leftover drinks and wouldn't stand for any bad language. The pub was replaced nearby with the **Aladdin's Lamp,** which was converted into housing in 2014.

At Darlaston Green, the **Boat** (1818) was a popular canalside inn for local workers, but was rebuilt in 1935 and closed in 2006. The **Nags Head** (1818) was also a popular drinking haunt for nearby factory workers, whilst the **Why Not** (1871) became a Davenport's pub. Joseph Yates kept the **Scott Arms** in Blockall from 1834-1881, which was a meeting place for nut and bolt makers and the Ancient Order of Shepherds. In 1880, John Green had a small brewery behind a beerhouse in Blockall, until it was replaced by the Olympia Cinema in 1912. In Bush Street, John and Elizabeth Aldridge kept the **Old Bush Inn** from 1828-1851. They not only brewed their own beer, but also made money by buying up adjoining pieces of land and selling building plots (hence Aldridge Street), but the pub was demolished in 2007.

Many landlords had a second occupation as well as running a pub. Martin Perry Foster was a respected licensee who kept the **Spread Eagle** in Cramp Hill for over 50 years from 1881. He had a family of eight children, and boosted his income by making files in his workshop behind the pub. Samuel Canlett, landlord of the **Swan** (Victoria Road) was also a butcher, slaughtering pigs in the back yard, hanging joints of meat upstairs (the original meat hooks are still there!) and selling pork and bacon in a room next to the bar.

So, although many of Darlaston's oldest pubs have been lost, several interesting historic pubs survive, serving a range of fine beers.

Into the Frying Pan

The **Bradford Arms** in Bilston Street was originally a home-brew pub, dating back to the 1830s as the Hatherton Arms. It was renamed in 1871, and then kept by William and Rachel Howells from 1901-1923, by Edward Ted Perks from 1936-1952 and by Arthur and Rose Mills from 1950-1976. It was known locally as the Frying Pan, since a huge frying pan was kept on the hearth for local workmen to cook their dinners. In the early 1900s, regulars organised a Sunday night "Fryin' Pon Club", where members wore a special badge and needed a password to enter. Each week, the chairman wore a hat and chain around his neck from which was suspended, inevitably, a small frying pan. Anyone who lit their own cigarette or lifted their beer glass with their right hand was fined, with the money going to local charities. The original pub was demolished in 1982 and replaced next door with a new Frying Pan.

DUDLEY – HOME-BREW PUBS

Dudley is well known as the home-brew capital of the Midlands, with over 150 pubs once brewing their own beer until they were taken over by larger commercial breweries. Most of Dudley's home-brew pubs dated back to the early 19th century, but some go back to the 1600s.

One of the oldest recorded home-brew pubs in Dudley town centre was the **Old Woolpack Inn** in Castle Street, established in 1622. By 1861, Isaac Aulton was advertising his Prime Home-Brewed Ales and, as a cooper, the pub had beer barrels instead of tables. It closed in 1960 after being bought by Hanson's (Dudley). In Hall Street, the **Seven Stars** was another ancient inn, first licensed in the reign of Charles I (1635). Brewing continued until it was taken over by Deakin's Manchester Brewery in 1904, which later passed to Ansell's (Birmingham) and closed in 1960. Nearby, the **Britannia** was another home-brew pub dating from the 17th century, until it was acquired by Frederick Smith (Aston) in 1936 and closed in 1961.

In High Street, the **Old Bush** was established before 1752, where James Cartwright's family brewed from 1805-1871. It was one of Dudley's coaching inns and later became a meeting place for Chartists and radicals, before closing in 1929. The **Windmill** in Stafford Street was first licensed in 1777, but closed by Ansell's in 1957. James Jackson's family brewed at the **Brewers Arms** in Fisher Street from 1780 for almost a century, but it was taken over by Peter Walker (Warrington) around 1900 and closed in 1931. In 1786, the **Dudley Arms Hotel** replaced the Rose & Crown (1717) in High Street, and became the town's principal coaching inn and commercial hotel. Brewing ceased in 1898, when it was taken over by John Rolinson's Five Ways Brewery (Netherton), but was demolished in 1968 to make way for a Marks & Spencer's store.

In Upper High Street, the **Plume of Feathers** was a home-brew pub from 1792, when a milestone to London (122 miles) stood outside. In 1931, it was owned by Sarah Hughes, George Hughes was the licensee/brewer and was also the grandfather of John Hughes of today's Sarah Hughes' Brewery at Sedgley. It was one of Dudley's last home-brew pubs to close in 1961. In Castle Street, Edward Jewkes brewed at the **Green Man** from 1793, but it closed in 1975. The alleyway adjoining the pub (Green Man Entry) was reputedly haunted by the ghost of a man wearing old-fashioned working clothes and a cap.

There was a **Saracen's Head** in Stone Street in the 18th century, named to commemorate the Crusades, but the current building dates from 1808. The **Freemasons' Arms** was added later, when it became their local headquarters, it was also a meeting place for non-conformists. It was a well-known coaching inn, known locally as The Napper, and is now Grade II listed. From 1835-1850, it was kept by John Mantle, Julia Hanson's father, and some say that Hanson's Mild was first brewed here. Brewing ceased in 1881 and the pub became a Hanson's house in 1923.

In Tower Street, the **Malt Shovel** dates back to Georgian times when it was known as the Lord Wellington. In 1926, it was the scene of a brutal murder, when 14-year-old Jimmy Bayliss was found battered to death in his bed, and he still haunts the pub as the Blue Boy. It was a home-brew pub until it was taken over by Wolverhampton & Dudley Breweries in 1940 and it's now an independent real ale tavern.

In 1819, Robert Garrett was brewing at the **Blue Gates** in Church Street. When kept by Janet Yates in the 1930s, the beer was served in platter mugs, often by popular barmaid, Nellie Walliscroft. In New Street, the **Town Hall Tavern** was a home-brew pub from 1819, originally known as the Marquis of Granby, a general who enabled retired soldiers to become publicans in the 18th century. The **Castle & Falcon Hotel** in Wolverhampton Street dated from 1820, and by 1899 was renowned for "Dando's Home-Brewed Mild & Bitter Ales".

In 1820, Joseph Pitt brewed at the **Royal Oak** in Salop Street until it was bought by W. Butler Co. (Wolverhampton) in 1945. In New Street, the **Old Priory** is another haunted home-brew pub dating from 1820, but by 1911, Wild Willy Wilkinson had taken over. He was not only a brewer, but also a former circus knife thrower who sharpened stiletto blades behind the bar!

In Castle Street, the **Angel** dated from 1820, but by 1915 it was kept by Edward and Elena Jones, the parents of Doris (Ma) Pardoe of the Old Swan, Netherton. The **Old Hen & Chickens** also dated from 1820, but was rebuilt in 1934 and closed in 1982. The **Shakespeare** was one of 13 pubs in Stafford Street, originally dating from 1820, but rebuilt in 1870. It was a home-brew house until acquired by Rolinson's in 1906, and until recently, retained many original features. In Upper High Street, the **Three Crowns** also dates from 1820, but was rebuilt in 1927.

In Church Street, the **Royal Exchange** dated from 1828, but by 1857 had gained a reputation under landlady Sarah Wroe, who was fined 7s 6d for "permitting notoriously bad characters to meet there" including "seven notorious prostitutes". In 1873, town councillor, Solomon Crow brewed at the **Peacock** (1819) in Upper High Street until it was bought by Hanson's in 1895. The **Three Swans** in High Street dated from 1839 and was the only pub in Dudley to be destroyed by enemy bombing in 1940. Other home-brew pubs first licensed in the early 1800s included the **Blue Boar** (Stone Street), **Crown** (Crown Street), **Horseshoe** (Hall Street), **Malt Shovel** (High Street), **Castle** and **Swan** (Castle Street) and **Duke of York**, **Talbot** (Shrewsbury Arms) and **Fox** (Wolverhampton Street).

In 1900, the **Bird in Hand** in New Street was advertised as the oldest licensed house in Dudley "with home-brewed ale on tap". It certainly dates from before 1819, but was soon taken over by Hanson's and closed in 1927. In Stone Street, the **Two Bulls Head** (1819) was originally a home-brew house, but was taken over by W. Butler & Co. in the 1940s. Thomas Marsh brewed at the **Struggling Man** in Salop Street from 1828 until it was taken over by Atkinson's (Birmingham) in 1898.

In Wolverhampton Street, the **Vine** (1828) was a home-brew house until it was taken over by Holt's (Birmingham) in 1946, but was also renowned for its sheep's trotters, porter and whelks. In New Street, the **Court House** (1854) was originally a home-brew house until it was taken over by Hanson's, and remains a popular Black Country Ales' real ale pub.

Many will remember the **Gipsies Tent** in Steppingstone Street. Dating from 1841, it was bought by Thomas Millard in 1867 and remained in the family's ownership for over a century. In 1886, he built the Little Model Brewery and when he died in 1899, his widow, Harriet took over, followed by her son, Harry. It passed to brothers Bert and Don Millard in 1951 (both teetotallers), who continued brewing until 1961, but the pub eventually closed in 1980.

It's a pity that the town has lost all its original home-brew houses, but at least we can still have a decent pint in some of the remaining pubs.

DUDLEY – PUBS RECALLING FAMOUS PEOPLE & LOCAL TRADES

From the late Middle Ages, pubs (or ale-houses, taverns and inns) needed to identify themselves in some way at a time when most people were illiterate. So simple signs evolved, ranging from a crooked piece of wood, holly bush or tradesman's sign, to a type of heraldic sign borrowed from religion or aristocratic coats of arms. There are probably upwards of 17,000 different signs for pubs, the most popular of which are the Red Lion, Crown and Royal Oak.

Dudley was no different, with 13 pubs called the **Crown** (or Crown & Anchor, Crown & Cushion, Rose & Crown or Three Crowns), eight pubs named the **Royal Oak** and three pubs called the **Red Lion**. But there were also 13 pubs named the **Jolly Collier, Colliers Arms** or **Miners Arms,** and seven pubs named the **New Inn, Hearty Good Fellow** or **Vine**.

Two pubs had the generic name of **Kings Head,** with one **King & Queen** in Stafford Street (1856-1990). **King Edward VII** was remembered in High Street (1851), but was replaced by the Criterion Cinema in 1912. **King William** was recalled in Holly Hall (1835), along with the legendary **King Arthur** in Priory Road (1939-2012). Two pubs were named the **George,** in High Street (1822-1911) and Holly Hall (1835-1865).

Two pubs were named the **Queens Head,** including those at Kates Hill (1868-1938) and Holly Hall (1835-1865). The **Victoria** at Holly Hall (1868-1918) and Woodside (1860-1879), along with the **Victoria Arms** at Queens Cross (1916-1914) and **Victoria Vaults** in Hall Street (1870-1907), recalled the long-reigning monarch.

Princes were not forgotten, with the **Prince of Wales** in John Street (1870-1934) and Harts Hill (1864-1870). His **Plume of Feathers** was recalled at pubs in Upper High Street (1792-1961), Russells Hall (1984-2010) and Kates Hill (1862). Less is probably known about the **Prince of Prussia,** who was a member of the German Royal House of Hohenzollern, based in Brandenburg, and whose name was recalled at a pub in New Street (1861). In Stafford Street, the **Duke of Sussex** (1835-1916), known locally as the Pokey House, probably referred to Prince Augustus Frederick, the sixth son of King George III, rather than the current holder of that title.

Several pubs in Dudley were named after military figures and battles. In Wolverhampton Street, the **Duke of Wellington** (1846-1975) was a home-brew pub which recalled the national hero who defeated Napoleon at Waterloo in 1815 and later became Prime Minister. The battle itself was recalled at the **Waterloo** in Church Street (1830-1870). The **Duke of York** in Wolverhampton Street (1819-1986) recalled probably the best remembered holder of that title who commanded the English army in Flanders in 1794-1827. However, the popular song misrepresents the facts, since the Duke was only 31, had 30,000 men, and there were no hills in the area where he was fighting!

In New Street, the **Town Hall Tavern** was a home-brew pub from 1819, originally known as the **Marquis of Granby,** a general who enabled retired soldiers to become publicans in the 18th century. The **Saracen's Head & Freemasons Arms** in Stone Street is one of the oldest pubs in the town centre, dating back to at least 1775, where Julia Hanson's father allegedly first brewed his mild ale. Its name recalls the battles in the Crusades, which were also reflected at the **Turks Head** in Bath Street (1873-1927), New Street (1854-1898) and Shaw Road (1872-1908), along with the **Grand Turk** in New Street (1840-1910) and Queens Cross (1854-1961). The **Alma** in Hall Street (1835-1975) recalled the site of an important battle in the Crimean war.

Famous politicians were also remembered in Dudley. The **Sir Robert Peel** in Salop Street (1851-1965) recalled the founder of the modern police force who went on to become British Prime Minister in 1834 and 1841. In Wrens Nest Road, the **Washington** (1937-2006) recalled George Washington, the first US president.

The landed gentry are not forgotten in Dudley. In Wolverhampton Street, the **Shrewsbury Arms** is another old pub, dating from before 1818 as the Talbot, which is known locally as the Cow Shed. It was once haunted by Old Joe, associated with the adjoining farm or slaughterhouse. Its name recalls the Earl of Shrewsbury, a local landowner whose family home is at Wanfield Hall, near Kingstone in Staffordshire and who also owned Alton Towers. Baron Somers of Worcestershire was a prominent politician and local landowner, whose name was recalled at the **Somers Arms** in Salop Street (1828-1851) and at Kates Hill (1841-1865).

The Earl of Dudley was central to the development of the town over several centuries. His name was recalled at the **Dudley Arms Hotel** in the Market Place, one of the town's principal coaching inns and commercial hotels dating from 1786, but demolished in 1968 to make way for a new Marks & Spencers store. The Earl of Dudley and Baron Ward were also recalled at the **Earl of Dudley's Arms** in Wellington Street (1860) and **Ward Arms** in Birmingham Road (1927-2001).

As in most towns, homage is paid to writer William Shakespeare. In Dudley, he's recalled at the **Shakespeare** in Stafford Street (1835-2013) and New Mill Street (1835-1881), along with the **Shakespeare Head** in Hall Street (1819-1881). In 1818, Lord Byron wrote a poem about Ivan Mazeppa, who became leader of the Ukraine, whose name was recalled at the **Mazeppa** in Campbell Street (1850-1931).

Seven pubs in Dudley were named the **Hearty Good Fellow,** including those in Flood Street (1860-1934), Maughan Street (1861-2012) and Woodside (1873-1938). Its name recalls a ballad sung in the 1860s: *"I am a hearty good fellow; I live at my ease, I work when I'm ready, I play when I please; with my bottle and glass, many hours I do pass, sometimes with a friend, sometimes with a lass".*

Not so long ago, Dudley was in Worcestershire and the county's cricket team always played a few matches at the town's cricket ground. The **Cricketers Arms** in King Street (1819-1922) was one of the oldest pubs in the town centre, originally known as the Horse & Jockey. Until 1933, there was also another Cricketers Arms in Tipton Road, at Dudley Cricket Club's ground.

Horse racing was recalled at the **Salamander** in Salop Street (1960-2000), named after the winner of the 1866 Grand National. The **Sweet Turf** at Harts Hill (1864-1966), known locally as The Middle, and **Turf Tavern** in New Hall Street (1845-1865) also recalled this sport. In King Street, the **Nags Head** (1835-1916) was a commercial inn, previously known as the Harmonic Tavern, where landlord George Morris ran the "largest funeral carriage establishment in the Midland Counties".

Other sports were recalled at the **Hare & Hounds** in Birmingham Street (1819), which was closed when the bus station was extended in 1957, and at Bramble Green (1957-2003), along with the **Fox & Dogs** in Market Place (1841-1871).

Local landmarks are recalled in Castle Street, at the **Castle** (1828) and **Castle House** (1850-1954), known locally as the Little Castle, along with the **Castle & Falcon** in Wolverhampton Street (1820-1975). The **Wrens Nest** geological feature was recalled at pubs in Priory Road (1934-2006) and Shavers End (1819-1892), whilst the limestone caverns are recalled at the **Caves** in Wrens Nest Road (1957).

Dudley was one of the birthplaces of the Industrial Revolution and grew into an industrial centre in the 19th century, with its iron, coal and limestone mining. Its population grew rapidly during this period, from around 10,000 in 1801 to over 45,000 a century later. The town began to be dominated by the iron and steel industry, along with brickworks, glassmaking, textiles and leather working. Not surprisingly, many of the town's pubs recalled these local trades and industries.

Coal mining was reflected at eight pubs called the **Jolly Collier,** including two at Holly Hall, along with the **Colliers Arms** in High Street. Four pubs were called the **Miners Arms,** including those in High Street (1820-1964) and Salop Street (1835-1970). Pubs named the **Engine,** such as that in King Street (1818-1860), usually referred to colliery pumping engines, as did the **Wonder** in Church Street (1864-1928). The **Whimsey** in King Street (1835-1872) and Woodside (1841-1995) recalled a machine for drawing coal and carrying workers in the local collieries.

Iron and steel foundries began to be established in the 19th century, and are recalled at the **Old Foundry** in King Street (1830), previously the Coach & Horses, rebuilt in 1936 and renamed in 1997, and **Three Furnaces** in New Dock (1856-1965). Other parts of the process were recalled at the **Hammer** in Stafford Street (1871-1977). More specialised trades were recalled at the **Anvil Makers Arms** in Constitution Hill (1867), **Moulders Arms** in King Street (1867) and **Shinglers Arms** in Harts Hill (1867-1952). Other metal-working trades were remembered at the **Smiths Arms** in Hall Street (1850) and **Whitesmiths Arms** in King Street (1835-1870), which recalled workers in tin or other light metals.

There were many other trades and industries in Dudley reflected in the names of its pubs. They included the **Coachmakers Arms** in Stafford Street (1850-1976) and **Glasscutters Arms** in the Minories (1830). A currier helped to dress, colour and finish tanned leather hides, a trade recollected at the **Curriers Arms** in Hall Street (1819-1867). There were also several brickworks around the town, recalled at the **Brickmakers Arms** at Holly Hall (1874-1934). Two pubs were also called the **Masons Arms,** in Salop Street (1828-1881) and at Queens Cross (1850).

Butchers were particularly plentiful in the town, reflected at the **Butchers Arms** in Hall Street (1854-1867) and Kates Hill (1862). Their products were recalled at the **Round of Beef** in High Street (1850-1884), an old licensed inn and eating house where a sign read: *"If you be hungry or dry, or your stomach is out of order, there's some relief at the Round of Beef, for both these disorders".* The **Shoulder of Mutton** at Dixons Green (1851-1973) reflects the dish of the same name which was popular in many inns and taverns.

Dudley was the capital of the home-brewing trade, so it's not surprising that several pubs reflect this. James Jackson's family brewed at the **Brewers Arms** in Fisher Street from 1780 for almost a century, but it was taken over by Peter Walker (Warrington) around 1900 and closed in 1931. There was a similarly named pub in Stafford Street (1860-1919). Two pubs were named the **Barrel,** in High Street (1861) and Upper High Street (1819-1915), along with the **Little Barrel,** also in High Street (1869). The **Bottle & Glass** is the on-site pub at the Black Country Living Museum, formerly a Wordsley Brewery pub, reconstructed brick-by-brick in 1982 from its former site in Brockmoor. It's allegedly haunted by a man with a round face and glasses and a small boy, Issac Male, who drowned in the canal.

The **Malt Shovel** in High Street was also a home-brew house, which lasted a century until 1920, whilst the one in Kates Hill closed in the 1960s.

Railways were important in the growth of the town and were recalled at the **Railway** in Trindle Road (1871-1996) and Woodside (1875). Other pubs included the **Railway Vaults** in High Street (1861-1975) and **Railway Tavern** in Bond Street (1850-1868). The Great Western Railway was remembered at the short-lived **Great Western** in King Street (1868-1870) and the **Refreshment Rooms** at Dudley's Great Western railway station. The **Station Hotel** in Birmingham Road (1878-2021) was opposite this station, enlarged and modernised in 1936 and it is home to the ghost of a lecherous landlord. There was another **Station** in Shaw Road (1870-1978), near Netherton station. Rail traction was recalled at the **Locomotive** in Portersfield (1862-1901), Trindle Road (1911-1973) and Vicar Street (1861-1975).

Perhaps surprisingly, few pubs reflect the presence of canals, where were also important in the town's development. The sole examples were the **Anchor** in High Street (1884) and **Boat** at Woodside (1870-1934). However, someone who enjoys watching boats and other activities on canals is sometimes referred to as a **Gongoozler,** a name used for Dudley Canal & Tunnel Trust's on-site pub along Birmingham New Road, near the Black Country Living Museum.

The days of the old coaching inns were recalled at the **Coach & Horses** at Scotts Green (1835-2007) and Holly Hall (1835-1862), along with the **Old Coach & Horses** in Stourbridge Road (1830). A more basic form of transport was remembered at the **Waggon & Horses,** in Hall Street (1819-1914), Oakeywell Street (1851-1865), Stourbridge Road (1820-1987) and Woodside (1862-1877). The **Old Waggon & Horses** in Stourbridge Road (1830-1994) was known locally as the Duck Hole.

In the early days, Dudley prospered from the surrounding agricultural areas, with local pubs recalling some of those trades. They included the **Old Farm** in Harts Hill (1864-1975), **Plough & Harrow** in Hall Street (1872-1907) and **Barley Mow** in Constitution Hill (1850-1993). Farm animals were not forgotten, at the **Bulls Head** in Hall Street (1819-1909) and **Two Bulls Heads** in Stone Street (1819-1975). The **Hen & Chickens** in Castle Street (1820-1982) was rebuilt in 1934 and is remembered for its popular jazz club. The **Dun Cow** in Wolverhampton Street (1850) and Dixons Green (1861-1872) recalled a monstrous beast that went on a murderous rampage until it was slayed by the legendary Guy of Warwick.

The woollen trade was remembered at the **Old Woolpack Inn** in Castle Street, one of the oldest recorded pubs in Dudley town centre, established in 1622.

Forestry trades were recalled at the **Foresters Arms** in Fisher Street (1872-1932) and **Woodman** in Wolverhampton Street (1869-1882). Beekeeping was a popular hobby, recalled at the **Beehive** in Stafford Street (1861-1919) and Tinchbourne Street (1851-1965), originally known as the Red Cow.

So, Dudley had many pubs named after famous people and local trades. Few survive today, but those that do have some happy memories to recall.

GORNAL

I'm sure we're all familiar with the rhyme asking:

*"Who put the Pig on the Wall at Gornal to see the band go by?
Was it: Billy the Boy, Jimmy the Go, Billy on Th' Ob or The Pokey Mon..."*

Upper and Lower Gornal were originally part of Sedgley Manor. Gornal was famous for its home-brewed beer, with recipes handed down from generation to generation. Nearly every pub brewed its own beer before the commercial breweries took over. It was thirsty work when the Industrial Revolution came to Gornal, with collieries, claypits, brickworks and quarries, including Gornal's distinctive yellow sandstone.

Many pubs dated from the mid 1850s, but some have much earlier roots. Over the years, around 25 pubs served Upper Gornal, mainly grouped along Kent Street and Clarence Street, with almost 40 in Lower Gornal and Gornalwood. Now barely 15 remain, but they include some fine real ale pubs.

Sited astride the old turnpike road running from Dudley to Wolverhampton, **Upper Gornal** was always more accessible than the more isolated settlements of Lower Gornal and Gornalwood. Between Jews Lane and Moden Hill, there were over a dozen pubs, virtually one on every street corner.

One of the oldest pubs in Upper Gornal is the **Britannia,** a former home-brew house dating from 1780. One of its earliest landlords, Henry Perry, was a butcher who had a slaughterhouse behind the pub, and later, Louisa Perry continued as one of the few women butchers in the country. The pub was kept by the Perry family for over 100 years, and was popularly known as Sally's or Old Sal's after long-serving landlady, Sally (Perry) Williams, who kept the pub from 1942-1991. Philip Bellfield reopened the brewery in 1995, but ceased brewing when Batham's (Brierley Hill) took over the pub in 1997. The pub had a makeover in the 1920s and retains many original features, including handpulls on the wall, a mirrored bar-back, wooden panelling and etched windows, and is included in CAMRA's national inventory of historic pubs. Since it's also haunted, ladies tend to go to the toilets in pairs because of apparitions seen there, including an old lady dressed in black. Dogs are also afraid of the cellar. Some say that one of the pub's finest moments was when Nigel Farage called in during his 2014 election campaign!

A few doors away was the **Shakespeare,** dating from 1854 and originally the Painters Arms, but converted into takeaways in 2000. Further along Kent Street was the **Pig on the Wall,** originally the Miner's Arms dating from 1841 and later the Bricklayer's Arms. It was also known as Hammond's after licensees Annie and William Hammond who kept the pub between 1913-1974, and was home to the Painter's Morris team. After a fire in 1987, it reopened as the Pig on the Wall under John and Pat Green, and was not only the first pub in Gornal to have a 1.00am licence, but also had six hotel bedrooms. Many will remember this lively pub which was sadly closed and replaced by McDonalds in 2002.

At the junction with Jews Lane was the **Green Dragon,** dating from 1826, with its pigeon club and popular dances, but converted into a restaurant in 2006. Other historic pubs in Kent Street included the **Limerick** (1851), which became a Co-op store in 1909, and **Lion** (1859), originally named the Exhibition Inn where Ada Cartwright brewed, but closed in 1963. From 1858-1937, Edward and John Bodenham kept the **Royal Oak** (1839-1972), whilst the **Three Horseshoes** (1832) was originally known as the Horseshoe Inn until 1913, but closed in 1921. The modern **Spills Meadow** pub, opened in 1976, is no replacement for these historic pubs.

At the top end of Clarence Street is the **Jolly Crispin,** a former 18th century shoemaker's house named after the patron saint of shoemakers, St Crispin. It became a pub in 1831 and has plenty of history. In 1845, Joseph Penn was convicted of manslaughter here and was transported to Tasmania. It was a home-brew pub until Simpkiss (Brierley Hill) took it over in 1940. Until recently, it was the taphouse for Fownes Brewery, before they moved their micro-brewery to Quarry Bank. It remains a popular free-house, winning CAMRA awards, with Fownes' "Crispin's Ommer", other guest beers and regular "tap-takeovers". Almost opposite was the **Cottage of Content** (1848-1998), now a restaurant.

Not far away was the **Horse & Jockey** (1833-1986), which was popular with local nailmakers and remembered for the foaming tankards served during the Sedgley Wakes in the adjoining field, with free roast beef and landlord Jack Millard's rabbit in port wine! Nearby, the **Leopard** also dated from 1833, with the Sedgley Brewery next door. Landlord Lawrence Lol Abbis kept the pub until 1962 and knew everything about dogs, pigeons, ferrets and game, but it was replaced with housing in 2015.

In the 1830s, Ruiton folk were well known for selling white sand, ground from Gornal stone in the local windmills. They also bought salt from Droitwich and Cheshire and sold it from their distinctive wagons across the Black Country. Several historic pubs supported their trade. Next to the Wesleyan Chapel in Duke Street, the **White Lion** dated from 1833, but was gone by 1913. Towards the top end of Vale Street was the **Good Intent,** originally a row of houses dating from 1820 and converted into a pub in 1851. It was kept by Harold and Gemma Guest from 1937-1976, but sadly closed in 2010. Further along Vale Street, the **Bull & Butcher** (1845) only survived until 1913, and further down Holloway Street, the **Crown** (1841) was converted into offices in 2011.

In Hill Street, the **Duke William** (1833) was one of six beerhouses within 500yds, which was losing money and closed in 1928. A few doors away, the **Durham Ox** (1864) was named after a huge two-ton beast which toured the country in the early 19th century, but was converted into a house in 1994. In Windmill Street, the **Old Mill** (1852) recalls the 17th century Ruewardine (Ruiton) windmill. In the 1880s, it was kept by William Parrish who also owned the Junction Inn, a local colliery and several racehorses. It was home to the local Band of Hope and once had a small brewery run by William Naylor until 1940. It was bought by Holden's (Dudley) in 1981 and it's now a popular local pub, run by Sam Vasey and Charlotte Smith.

The oldest pubs in **Lower Gornal** date from around 1820. One of the oldest is the **Bush** in Summit Place, which is reputedly haunted by the ghost of former landlady, Nancy Hale, wearing a Victorian dress. In 1989, it became a Holt, Plant & Deakin pub and still serves a good pint. **Straits House** was originally home to Alexander Gordon, a benevolent Methodist wines and spirits merchant. It became a pub in 1960, but was converted into apartments in 2008. In the centre of Lower Gornal, the **Five Ways** dated from 1851 and is a listed building (Grade II). Joseph Waterfield brewed his own beer here before it was taken over by Hanson's (Dudley), but it became a funeral directors in 1998. In Lake Street, the **Swan** (1869) was originally the Miners Arms, but closed in 1956. It was known locally as David Hyde's after landlord David Hyde (1900-1934), who also owned two sandstone quarries.

On the corner of Dibdale Lane, the **Black Bear** (1830) was originally the Horse & Jockey, built on the site of an old burial ground. Known locally as the Bonk, Edwin Alfred Holden, founder of Holden's Brewery, was born here on a foggy night in 1907. It reopened in 1983 as the Black Bear, recalling a 19th century print of a dancing bear in Sedgley bull ring, and served its own Black Bear beer brewed by Kinver Brewery. Nearby, in Humphrey Street, the **New Inn** (1835) was known locally as the Sunshine, but was replaced by new housing in 1995.

It was kept by the Waterfield family for over 50 years until 1915, and later by William ("Billy on th' Ob") Jones (featured in the Gornal rhyme about the pig). In Grosvenor Road, the **Red Cow** (1835) is a thriving community pub, kept by Florence Floss Lodge from 1975-1996 and was once known as the tavern in the graveyard.

In Ruiton Street, the **Waggon & Horses** existed before 1823 and was kept by John and Elizabeth Lodge from 1939-1966. It was a regular venue for miners' meetings and boxing matches, but closed in 2008 and later converted into a house. Almost next door was the **Cross Keys** (1834), known locally as the Clinic, but it was replaced by houses in 2001. Across the road is the **Chapel House,** first licensed in 1834 and originally named after the Gornal Ranters (Methodists) who met here. It's reputedly haunted and the cellar was once used as a local jail. In 1900, brewer Charles Evans renamed it the Miners' Arms, and Holden's bought it in 1954 for £3,240. Until 1972, it was kept by local character, Absalom ('appy) Horton, and reopened as the Chapel House in 2013.

One of the oldest pubs in Gornalwood is the **Old Bull's Head** in Redhall Road, dating from 1834. Known locally as the Top Bull to distinguish it from the Bull's Head in Himley Road, it was rebuilt in 1900 and was next door to Emanuel Bradley's Brewery. It was HQ for Lower Gornal FC from the 1890s, but it's reputedly haunted by three ghosts of times past, including a man in the cellar, a grey lady and a lady in red who hung herself from the rafters of the old brewhouse after being jilted. In 1984, it reopened as a Holt, Plant & Deakin pub, but since 2004 it's been the taphouse for Black Country Ales, who have expanded the old brewery behind the pub. Further up Temple Street, the **Fountain** (1851) was kept by Thomas and Ida Griffiths from 1914-1972 and reopened in 2018 with Bill Redwood in charge of another popular real ale tavern.

In the heart of Gornalwood is the **Red Lion,** dating from 1842 and the venue for miners' meetings. It was known locally as Pokey's after landlord Thomas Pokey Malpass who replaced his hand, lost in an accident, with a steel hook (probably the Pokey Mon in the famous Gornal rhyme). Former collier and Netherton publican, Thomas Booth, rebuilt and expanded his Red Lion Brewery here until it was taken over by Hanson's in 1942. In Abbey Street, the **Junction** (1868) was another pub reputedly haunted by a small grey miner who disrupted the cellar, but it became a shop in 1991. The **White Chimneys** (1852-1983) was originally the Rose & Crown, where riots took place during the 1874 elections. In New Street, the **Queen's Head** (1858) was converted into a house in 1930, whilst the **Pear Tree** (1867-1992) was known locally as the Stuffed Whippet and was a venue for local miners and pigeon clubs. One of the landlords, John Greenway, was a local inspector of mines and Eli (Ayli the Tree) Jones brewed here from 1916-1936. The **Woodman** (1849) is a friendly community pub in Wakelam's Fold, where local miners, Methodists and the bowling, pigeon and bull terrier clubs met. It's also reputedly haunted by a mysterious old man with two mischievous children. In Straits Road, the **Fiddler's Arms** was originally a farmhouse, which became a pub in 1857, but was damaged by fire in 1995 and again in 2021. Not far away, the **Bricklayer's Arms** (1830) was home to landlady Betty Hickman (married to a sailor) and her 22 children, but it was converted into a house in 1907 and later demolished.

In Summit Place, the **Limerick** dated from 1849 and was a popular meeting place for local miners and its bull terrier club. Rebuilt after a fire in 1917 and kept by William Bradley from 1939-1961, it was demolished in 1999. On the corner of Himley Road and Cinder Road, the **Five Ways** (1845) was known locally as the Widder's, after landlady Emily Marsh, and now serves Batham's beer. On the opposite corner, the **Bull's Head** (1835) was known locally as the Bottom Bull and had a short life as one of Mad O'Rourke's Little pubs (Steak 'n Pie Factory) in 2009-2012, before becoming a restaurant in 2015.

Much has been said and written about the **Glynne Arms,** just over the border in Himley. Named after local landowner William Glynne, it was known as the Siden House and more recently called the Crooked House. Originally a farmhouse dating from 1765, it became a pub in 1830 and suffered from mining subsidence, resulting in walls, doors and windows at crazy angles. It was allegedly haunted by at least two ghosts, including a former landlord and parlour maid, Polly. I'm sure the tourists enjoyed watching the marbles rolling uphill and drinking the Tilted Tipple house beer and, who knows, they may have even seen the ghost of barmaid Polly. Sadly, it was destroyed by fire and demolished in August 2023.

So, although many of the historic pubs in Upper & Lower Gornal have disappeared, several remain, offering a wide range of beers, many of which are from local breweries.

Advertisement for the Real Ale festival at the Old Bull's Head, Lower Gornal

GREAT BRIDGE

Great Bridge lies in the heart of the Black Country, straddling the border between Tipton and West Bromwich. Its name derives from the Old English "greot" meaning grit or gravelly stream, along with the first bridge over the branch of the River Tame that runs through the town centre. The Industrial Revolution brought many collieries, brickworks, tube works, foundries and factories, and later, Italian immigrant, Giuseppe Bonaccoorsi, established his ice cream business here in 1948. Much of the centre of the town, including most of the old pubs and hotels, was lost when new roads were built. Over the years, more than 100 pubs served the people of Great Bridge, along with Toll End and Horseley Heath, but today, barely a handful remain.

The heart of Great Bridge has always been the busy marketplace, overlooked by the **Limerick Inn.** The original building dates from 1824, with its name possibly recalling the Irish navvies who built the canals. Edward Durham brewed his own beer here, and later it was known as the Wrexham after Peter Walker's Wrexham Ales. It was a popular meeting place for local colliers and ironworkers and, in 1861, hosted the Great Norfolk Giant – Robert Hales, the tallest and heaviest man in Europe at the time, 7'6" tall and weighing 33 stone! Popular landlord Arthur Cumberbatch kept the pub for 40 years until 1943, and it was renamed the Lounge Bar in 2007.

Close by, on the corner of Mill Street, is the **Nag's Head,** originally dating from 1872, but rebuilt to a design by local architect, George Wenyon, for Holder's (Birmingham) in 1907. In 1998, it was renamed the Fusilier, after Corporal Joseph Davies VC, who saved the lives of eight comrades during the Battle of the Somme in 1916. It returned as the Nag's Head in 2003, but closed in 2009. Just opposite was the **Leopard** (1852), where Joseph Williams brewed his own beer and kept whippets and rabbits, but it was demolished in 1975.

Just on the other side of the great bridge was the **Stork Inn,** dating from 1851, with a fine bowling green. James Jim Partridge kept the pub from 1936-1954, but it was replaced by a supermarket in 1985. Close by was the **Waggon & Horses,** the oldest pub in the area, dating back to 1764, when it was the town's premier commercial hotel and coaching inn. It later held dog shows, boxing and wrestling matches, but closed around 1958. Over the years, there were several other pubs and beerhouses in this part of Great Bridge, including the **Lion** (1874-1956), known locally as "Lucas's" after landlord Charles Lucas (1911-1947), and **Red Lion** (1858-1912), with others further along Great Bridge Street towards Swan Village.

In Brickhouse Lane, the **Rose & Crown** originally dated back to the 1700s. From 1887-1950 it was kept by two long-serving landlords, George Sheldon and Frank Corbett, but was demolished in 1956. At Brickhouse Bridge is the **Beehive,** dating from 1868 and a popular music venue.

From the marketplace, New Road was crossed by two railway lines, with two separate stations, one serving the South Staffordshire (Dudley-Walsall) line which opened in 1850, and the other on the Great Western Railway from Swan Village which opened in 1866. Several nearby pubs included the **Old Bush** (1828-1939), **Griffin** (1853-1976), **Railway** (1854-1985), known as the Fourpenny Shop, and **Railway Tavern** (1861-1961) in Eagle Lane, known as Joe Be Late's after landlord Job Henry Laight.

Further along New Road, towards Toll End, the **Tipton Tavern** (1825) was destroyed in an air raid in May 1941, killing six people and leaving landlord Roger Preece trapped in the cellar, giving the pub its local name, Roger's. Rebuilt in the 1950s, it was renamed the Hallbridge Arms, Comedian and Pearl Girl, but it became a day nursery in 2015. A few doors away is the **King's Arms** (1835), a popular pub for the local cricket club, pigeon fanciers and British Legion, but it was rebuilt as a new pub in 1987.

Around the corner in Horseley Road is the **Rising Sun,** originally dating from 1836, but rebuilt by Butler's (Wolverhampton) in the early 1900s, retaining a fine etched mirror advertising their beers. Herbert Standley kept the pub from 1955-1977. He had an aviary and often offered his customers free "gray pays and bacon". In 1999, it won CAMRA's National Pub of the Year award and became a Black Country Ales' pub in 2013. Further along Toll End Road is the **Dewdrop** (1855) and **Waggon & Horses** (1871), originally a local Darby's Brewery pub and, from 2004, home to the Toll End Brewery, a four-barrel micro-brewery. Not far away were the **Old Crown** (1828-1989) and **Cottage Spring** (1828-1975).

Along the road in Horseley Heath, there were another 20 or so pubs, almost one on every street corner. Amongst the oldest was the **Prince Regent** (1825-1991), which once displayed a large stuffed ape, originally belonging to William Perry (the Tipton Slasher)! The **Golden Ball** (1828-1927) was another popular meeting place for local miners, whilst the **Port 'n Ale** (1841) was originally the Star, with its own brewery. It was popular with pigeon fanciers and still serves a nice pint, as does the **Horseley Tavern** (1855) and **Royal Oak** (1841). The **Old Court House** in Lower Church Lane (1864) was once owned by Premier Ales (Stourbridge), but closed in 2021. On the corner of Providence Street was the **White Rose** (1856-1972), whilst the **Moulders Arms** (1871-1875), **Grinders Arms** (1863-1937) and **Fitters Arms** (1881-1920) recalled local trades.

There were other venerable hostelries along Sheepwash Lane, the oldest being the **Dartmouth Arms,** originally dating from 1791. Its name recalls the local Legge family, who became the Earls of Dartmouth and played an active part in the life of West Bromwich, endowing schools and engaging in other philanthropic activities. Known locally as the Old Coal, it was rebuilt in 1915, but closed in 1946 and later became offices and flats. From 1953-1971, popular landlady Lilian Shakespeare kept the **Old Crown** (1865), which was home to Great Bridge Celtic FC and the local angling club. It became Zions Bar in 2017, but it is now closed. Next door, the **Cop Hall Inn** (1835-1959) had a fine bowling green. At Sheepwash Bridge, the **Tame Bridge** started life as the Seven Stars in 1859, but was rebuilt in 1928, renamed in 1990 and remains a popular riverside pub.

Just off Whitehall Road in Greets Green, Charles Darby founded **Darby's Dunkirk Brewery** in 1894 at the **Dunkirk Inn,** originally Dunkirk Hall, dating from 1660. When the brewery was sold to Mitchells & Butlers in 1951, it had over 100 tied pubs, many in Great Bridge, West Bromwich and Tipton. Not far away in Whitehall Road, the **Royal Oak** (1854) lasted until 2012, whilst Fred Leeson kept the **Britannia** (1845-1987) from 1953-1974, and became Mayor of West Bromwich in 1957-1958.

There were more pubs and beerhouses in the backstreets of Great Bridge, including the **Queen's Head** (1865-1997) in Horton Street/Cophall Street and **Royal Exchange** (1871-1966) in Fisher Street, but all have now gone. In fact, of the 100 or so pubs serving the area over the years, less than a dozen remain today.

And finally, you may want to know where the statues of two lions on the new roundabout came from – the old Roman Mosaic Works at Burnt Tree Island!

HALESOWEN

The history of **Halesowen** dates back over 1,000 years. In 1086, the Domesday Book records the town as being larger than Birmingham. From 1177, it became known as Halas Owen, when King Henry II gifted Halas Manor to his sister, Emma, the wife of David ap Owen, the Prince of Wales. By 1220, the Abbot of Halesowen Abbey had established a market and by 1272 Halesowen had become a separate borough. At this time, the town was in a largely rural area, although there are early references to coal mining at Coombs Wood in 1307 and ironworking in 1312.

Pubs and beer were never far away in Halesowen's news. In 1270, fines were imposed for brewing beer too weakly, or giving short measure, or selling too cheaply. Between 1293-1307, 111 different sellers of ale were brought before the manorial court for offences relating to the brewing and selling of ale, including William Simond on 24 occasions. In 1468, the borough of Halesowen licensed and regulated five common brewers:

"One brew in the street between the Church and the end of town leading towards Cradeley, and in the High Street one brew, and from Laconstoon by the High Cross up to Cornebowe one brew, and from the said Cornebowe by the High Cross up to Laconstoon one brew, and in the street called Birmyngeham one brew, under penalty of each one 6s 8d wherof 40d therof shall be levied to the use of the lord, and 40d to the use of the Parish of Hales. And so in this manner that all brewers shall brew alternately from week to week, so that there may be five of new and five of old."

From the 14th century, Ale Conners (tasters) were appointed to check the quality and measurement of ale sold. In 1477, one of Halesowen's Ale Conners had the appropriate name of William Beare. Licensing hours were also specified in a local law of 1429 which decreed that *"no man after the ninth hour, afternoon, shall use any alehouses in the town"*. In 1570, the sale of ale in the town was further regulated by fixing prices for its sale:

"All brewers that brew ale to sell shall brew good ale and wholesome for a man's body at 3d a gallon and 1d a gallon to be warranted by the ale taster. And that they do not sell by the cruse or cup but by the pewter pot of a lawful size in pain of 3s 4d."

The earliest reference to specific pubs is found in the Rent Roll for Halesowen Abbey in 1500, which recorded two inns in the abbey's possession. One was the **Lyttelton Arms,** then situated in High Street, which was so named after the manor was sold to John Lyttelton in 1558, and by 1648, it was owned by Sir Thomas Lyttelton. The other was the **Red Cow** in Kenelmstowe, a farmhouse near St Kenelm's Church, Romsley. The hamlet of Kenelmstowe itself was thought to have been almost wiped out by the Black Death in 1349.

One of the ways the church raised money for repairing its buildings was by brewing and selling Church Ale. At Whitsuntide in 1505, Halesowen's Norman parish church raised £3 13s 4d through such an event. Church Ale was banned by Oliver Cromwell, but enjoyed a brief revival under Charles II and fell out of use by 1700. The brewing of Bride Ales was also popular. The bride, on her wedding day, would sell her ale to the participants. However, local regulations stipulated that *"No person that brew any wedding ale to sell shall brew above 12 strikes of malt at the most"*.

By 1755, there were over 30 recognised alehouses, most of which brewed their own beer. By the end of the 19th century, around 30 retail brewers were recorded, mainly based at inns and pubs in the town. They included several local brewing families, such as Tom and Harry Cresswell (Talbot & Old Royal, Islington and Hare & Hounds, Hasbury), George and William Grainger (Royal Oak, Birmingham Street and Star, Little Cornbow) and Edward and Samuel Lowe (Bell, Gorsty Hill). Halesowen's commercial brewing companies were rather short-lived and all are long gone. Hodgetts & Cooper brewed in Church Street between 1884-1892 on a site near the Malt Shovel, which was taken over by Carr & Co. in 1895. By 1906, they were in receivership, but continued trading until 1915 when the business was put up for sale. Joseph Cooper set up the New Road Brewery in 1895, which was later used by J. Bloomer & Sons until 1939. He also owned the Globe Inn (Peckingham Street) and Fox Inn (Little Cornbow). There were also eight maltings in the town to supply these breweries and home-brewers.

From the late 1800s, most pubs in Halesowen were owned or operated by brewers from outside the area. They included Atkinson's, Ansell's, Mitchell's & Butler's, Dare's & Davenport's, Frederick Smith and Edgbaston Brewery (Birmingham), Banks's & Hanson's (Wolverhampton & Dudley), Thomas Plant (Netherton), Home Brewery (Quarry Bank), Cheshire's (Smethwick), Showell's (Langley), Twist's (Walsall), Joules (Stone), Darby's (West Bromwich), Penn Brewery (Wolverhampton) and Ind Coope & Allsop, Burton Brewery & Bass Brewery (Burton-on-Trent).

Life was not always smooth-running in Halesowen's pubs. Over the centuries, the most common charge against licensees was keeping the pub open during prohibited hours and permitting drunkenness and illegal gambling, for which fines were often imposed. Other offences included disorderly conduct, fighting and riots, failing to leave the premises, robbery, theft and assaults on landlords, which also resulted in fines, imprisonment or even transportation!

Few licensees made their living just from being publicans. For example, Thomas Siviter, landlord of the Cock Inn in 1840, was also the manager of Halesowen Gasworks, whilst in 1873, a later landlord, George Yardley, ran the bus service to Birmingham. At the George Inn, William Moseley was both a butcher and a publican, whilst George Moseley at the Globe was not only a publican, but also a farmer, butcher and maltster. At the Anchor (Gorsty Hill), Jethro Hemp was the local hangman, hence the pub's nickname of the Throttler, whilst later landlords, John and James Adams operated the market garden behind the pub. At the New Inn, Giles Melley was also a grocer, whilst Henry Grainger at the Royal Oak was a fruiterer and used donkeys to carry the fruit. At the Plume of Feathers, Aaron and Moses Rose were not only maltsters, but they also owned a nearby gun-barrel factory, and even sold guns at the pub for 4s each! The machinery at Rose's factory was driven by water from New Pool where, in 1845, a large paddle steamer offered aquatic excursions and refreshments. Boaters and canoeists could also row along the canal to the Black Horse pub in the summer.

Halesowen's earliest recorded pub was the **Lyttelton Arms,** then sited in High Street. Until the mid 19th century, it was the town's premier inn and an important meeting place for local dignitaries and turnpike trustees, public meetings, inquests, excise offices and property auctions. Even Princess Victoria stopped here to change her carriage horses. The original Lyttelton Arms was demolished in 1845 and rebuilt as a private house. This became a greengrocers with a beerhouse licence, named the **Old Lyttelton Arms,** but was demolished around 1955. Meanwhile, in 1845, a new **Lyttleton Arms** had opened at the junction with Birmingham Street, which remains today as Pick's, recalling long-serving landlord, William James Pick, who kept the pub from 1905-1942.

Many old inns and taverns were clustered around the Bull Ring, including another of the town's earliest pubs, the **Crown Inn,** referred to in a conveyance of 1584. It was in the hands of the Stokes family for almost a century until 1860 and was rebuilt in 1883. After it closed in 1938, it was used as solicitor's offices and was demolished in 1962. Just opposite, the **Talbot** was another ancient inn, bequeathed in William Attwood's will of 1651, but closed by 1701. It then became a shop, button factory and then butchers, before being demolished in the 1960s.

Around the corner in Peckingham Street was the **Dog & Duck,** part of two houses dating from 1685. In 1827, Walter Woodcock sold it to George Moseley, who changed its name to the Globe Tavern, but it became a shop and was gone by 1967. In the same street, the **Golden Cross** was an ancient inn with good stabling and a music hall, first mentioned in 1746, but it was rebuilt in 1911 and became the Cosy Corner Cinema. The **Half Moon** dated from 1809 and was renamed the Talbot in 1896, but closed in 1910 after the Justices decided the town had too many licensed premises and became a hairdressers. Next to Church House in Church Street was the **Plume of Feathers,** first licensed in 1756 and later run by Aaron and Moses Rose, but it lost its licence due to structural defects and was replaced by shops and offices (Church Street Chambers) in 1892.

Probably the oldest surviving building in Halesowen that's still a pub is the **Loyal Lodge** of Free Givers in Furnace Hill, a Grade II listed building, with a plaque confirming its date of 1736. Originally a branch of the Grand Institute of Masons (local Freemasons), it became a pub in 1835, in the hands of Reuben and Samuel Parsons, and was later owned by Thomas Plant's Brewery (Netherton), Ansell's and Holt, Plant & Deakin. It's sited at the bottom of Furnace Hill, just across the river from Lord Lyttelton's Hales Furnace, established by 1642. Here, ironmaster Richard Foley was an active Royalist who supplied Prince Rupert with 1,900 pike heads during the Civil War. The pub was also the finishing point for Sammy Pigiron Whitehouse's famous walk, carrying a hundredweight of pig iron for 4 miles from Netherton in 1921.

Between 1727-1782, new turnpike roads were built, including a new road between Halesowen and Colley Gate. This led to the opening of several new pubs along the route, including the **New Inn** opposite the Finger Post (Whitehall Road) in 1762. It was not only used as an Inland Revenue excise office and a venue for meetings, inquests, property sales and auctions, but also where landlady Betty Taylor established Halesowen's first Friendly Society in 1806 (New Union Society). It was also a staging post for the "Independent", "Nimrod" & "Tantivy" stagecoaches plying between Birmingham, Stourbridge and Kidderminster. It closed in 1955, transferring the licence to the Huntingtree, and was demolished in 1960.

In Forge Lane, the Connop family owned the **Bridge Inn** in 1773, when the Bromsgrove-Dudley turnpike road was diverted. It was renamed the Railway Inn in 1896, but was closed by 1939. At the end of Hagley Street, Walter Woodcock owned the **Bull's Head** in 1784, which was the headquarters of the town's pigeon club. It was rebuilt around 1900 and replaced by a block of shops (Churchill House) in 1962.

During the early 19th century, Halesowen developed rapidly as a result of the Industrial Revolution and the coming of the canals, making nails (including horseshoe nails), screws, gun barrels, shovels, chains and other iron production. By 1822, more taverns had opened, including the **Olde Queens Head** in Birmingham Street, once a home-brew house and later owned by Davenport's (Birmingham), which remains one of the town centre's oldest surviving pubs. Also recorded in 1822 is the **Leopard** (High Street) where, in 1900, landlord Fletcher made a bet that he could sing in the lion's den at the African Menagerie in Hagley Road. He succeeded, confirming that "music hath charms to soothe the savage beast"! However, its licence was revoked in 1906 and it was converted into two cottages, then replaced by the Municipal Bank around 1940, and is now a betting shop.

On the corner of Stourbridge Road, the **George Inn** was first licensed in 1822, and is now a Grade II listed building, but is currently closed. On the corner of Church Lane, the **Malt Shovel** was also first licensed in 1822, but was closed by 1935, became a private house and is now a car park. In Little Cornbow, the **Fox** dated from 1834, was a popular cider house until the late 1960s, and is now used as offices. Along Gorsty Hill, two pubs survive – the **Anchor** (now Lighthouse), first licensed in 1834, and the **Bell** (now Bell & Bear), which has its origins in an Elizabethan farmhouse, first licensed in 1841.

As Halesowen expanded after 1835, the **Hare & Hounds** (Hasbury), **Stag & Three Horseshoes** (Halesowen Road), **Royal Oak** (Manor Lane), **Swan** (Long Lane) and **Waggon & Horses** (Stourbridge Road) opened, although most have since been rebuilt. There has been a **Fox Hunt** at Hayley Green for centuries, the first licensee being recorded in 1834, and the current pub, built in 1990, is actually its third incarnation. The **Black Horse** (Manor Lane) existed before 1840 to slake the thirst of miners from the colliery on the other side of the Dudley Canal and boatmen before and after they had experienced the murky delights of the 2¼ mile-long Lapal Tunnel to Selly Oak. Early landlords, like Joseph Heath, were also coal merchants.

By 1845, several more inns and taverns had opened in and around the town centre, including the **Red Cow** (Great Cornbow), **Star & Garter** and **Royal Oak** (Birmingham Street). Next to the gasworks at the bottom of Great Cornbow, the **Cock Inn** (formerly Pool Inn) was a home-brew house in 1840 and later renamed the Vine, but was demolished for road improvements in 1978. In Birmingham Street, the **Old Lion** was also known as the White, Red and Brown Lion over the years, but was gone by 1912. At Hasbury, the **Nelson, Sawyers Arms** and **White Lion** had also opened, followed in 1846 by the **Waggon & Horses** (Long Lane).

By 1849, new pubs included the **Vine** (Blackheath Road) and **Plough** (Rumbow), the latter becoming a popular cider house before closing in 1963. In Little Cornbow, Benjamin Grove ran the **Star Inn** from 1850, followed by William and George Grainger, but it closed in 1965 after being bought by the Borough Council. It then became a coffee bar but was demolished around 1970. Other pubs opened during this time included the **Samson & Lion** (Stourbridge Road), **Woodman** (Bromsgrove Road), **Talbot Inn** and **Old Royal** (originally the Nailforgers' Arms) (Islington) and **Rose & Crown** (Hasbury).

The **Townsend Stores** on the corner of Church Street was first licensed in 1854, rebuilt in 1901, but demolished around 1973 for road improvements. In 1855, the **Shenstone Hotel** opened at the bottom of Mucklow Hill, with Moses Rose in charge. It became an important venue for meetings, including the Court Leet, inquests, dinners and other events, but closed in July 1966 after a lorry ran away down Mucklow Hill and crashed into it; it was later demolished.

By the 1860s, the opening of Coombs Wood Steelworks, Walter Somers' Forge, local collieries (like Hawne, Coombs Wood and Witley) and other factories like James Grove's horn button factory, brought more industry and jobs to the area. This led to the building of more houses and pubs in and around the town, boosted by the opening of the railway line from Old Hill in 1878 and its extension to Longbridge in 1883. Indeed, dinners were held to celebrate the opening of these railways at the New Inn (1878) and Shenstone Hotel (1883). By 1919, there were over 100 coal mines in and around Halesowen, along with several forges, tanneries and factories. During this time, hotels and inns like the Lyttleton Arms, George Inn, New Inn and Shenstone Hotel, acted as the social and commercial hubs of the town, whilst some of the older inns were also posting houses, served by the horse-drawn coaches running between Birmingham and Kidderminster.

During this period, many more pubs opened, including the **Beehive** (Hagley Road). This was a popular pigeon-fanciers' pub kept for nearly 80 years by the Withers family, but was rebuilt in 1960 and became a supermarket in 2018. One of the first landlords used to throw buckets of water onto the steep road in front of the pub on frosty nights (known as Nathan's Slether), so that horses couldn't get a grip, causing the carters to stop for a drink! It was also reputedly haunted by the landlord's wife, Hannah Withers, who appeared in the upstairs window.

Other new pubs included the **King Edward VII** (originally the Heart in Hand, but renamed to celebrate the King's coronation in 1902) and **Whitley Hotel** (Stourbridge Road), **Shelton**

Inn (Belle Vale), **Red Lion** (Hagley Road), **Traveller's Rest** (Long Lane) and **Cross Guns** (Birmingham Street). In Gorsty Hill, the **Old Dun Cow** was licensed before 1867, but was converted into a house in 1963. By 1870, the **Ashley Hotel** (now Windmill's End; Long Lane), **British Arms** and **Royal Oak** (New Street), **Acorn** (Cockshed Lane), **Stores** (Malt Mill Lane) and **Black Horse** (Illey) had opened. In Dudley Road, Samuel Salt, known as the Nailer's Poet, lived at the **Forge** before it became a pub in 1871. In 1994, it was renamed the Shoveller's Arms, followed by the Boilermaker in 2002, it then reverted back to the Forge in 2003, before being converted into offices in 2012. In Attwood Street, just off Stourbridge Road, Thomas Marriott owned an off-licence, which became the **Hawne Tavern** in 1874.

In the countryside along the Hagley Road, the **Gipsy's Tent** was first licensed in 1876, but the pub was rebuilt in 1938 and later renamed the Badger's Set. This pub has several ghostly associations, with visions of a gentleman in a tweed jacket and Bella in the Wych Elm, along with other ghosts of a Civil War Cavalier, a woman in white, a figure in grey and a phantom hound along the adjoining main road! In 1882, the **Victoria** opened in Malt Mill Lane, but was rebuilt in 1939, before closing in 2014 and becoming housing. In 1897, the **Waggon & Horses** (Stourbridge Road) was rebuilt as an M&B pub and retains some original fittings, including a Victorian bar back and wooden seating.

Between 1850-1900, 35 new pubs had been established, but 17 had disappeared, and by the turn of the century, there were 53 licensed pubs and 20 beerhouses serving Halesowen. In 1905, the **Clock** (Nimmings Road) opened, first known as the County Inn – it was renamed the Nimmings Tavern in the 1960s and the Clock in 1982. The first licence was granted to a public house trust which favoured temperance in drinking. This was in response to the Salvation Army and Temperance movement who saw drink as one of the chief evils of the time. The licensing justices also considered that there were too many licences in proportion to the population (one pub for every 206 people) and attempted to reduce the number of pubs in the town. This led to fewer licences and the closure of several historic pubs, including the Star & Garter, Leopard and Golden Cross.

In the 1930s, the **Nelson** (Hagley Road), **Royal Oak** (Manor Lane) and **Stag & Three Horseshoes** (Birmingham Road) were rebuilt, followed in 1938 by the **Fairfield** (Fairfield Road). Unfortunately, its first landlord, Colonel Albert Prickett, died two weeks after serving his first pint. By this time, a further 19 pubs had been lost. In 1951, Seth Somers, chairman of Walter Somers, forgemasters, established **Somers' Sports & Social Club** at The Grange (Grange Road), a Grade II* listed building dating from 1707. Originally home to the Lea family, it housed German and Italian prisoners of war during the 2nd World War. In 1955, the **Huntingtree** (Alexandra Road) opened in the former residence of the Grove family, which more recently was renamed the Button Factory, but has now reverted to its original name. Between 1955-1980, several new housing estates were built, with more new pubs, including the **Maypole** (Bassnage Road), **Lutley Oak** (formerly Arian's/Lutley Mill) (Stourbridge Road), **Full Moon** (Hurst Green Road) and **Cobham Arms** (Howley Grange Road). Some pubs were rebuilt, including the Fox Hunt and Hare & Hounds (Hasbury). However, during this period, the Borough Council purchased and demolished many old buildings in and around the town centre as part of its redevelopment plans, resulting in the loss of several historic pubs, including the Cross Guns, Old Lyttelton Arms, Star Inn and Bull's Head.

In 1999, **Benjamin's** opened in a former Methodist church in Birmingham Street (1868), named after local Mayor, ironmaster and Liberal MP, Benjamin Hingley, who laid the foundation stone. A year later, a new Wetherspoon's pub opened in the town centre, the **William Shenstone,** named after the famous landscape gardener and designer of The Leasowes. Halesowen's first micropub, the **Crafty Pint** (Wassell Road), opened in 2016, followed a year later by **Shell-ter** (Nimmings Road). There's also a new brewery taproom at the **Fixed Wheel Brewery** in Long Lane.

Over the centuries, around 90 pubs have served Halesowen, but we have lost over 70% (64) of them! The oldest remaining pubs in the town centre are the **Olde Queens Head** and the **George Inn** (1822), and the **Lyttleton Arms** (1845). The **Loyal Lodge** (Furnace Hill) is probably the oldest building (1736) that has been a pub for nearly 200 years. Many pubs have closed and been demolished as a result of road improvements or redevelopment, and some have been replaced by shops or new housing. A few remain unoccupied and others have been converted into offices or residential accommodation. Around 25 pubs remain, clocking up over 2,500 years between them! And the prize for the shortest-lived pub must go to the **Husky Dog** on the corner of Hagley Road (on the site of the Red Lion), opened in 1976 and lasting just 10 years! Several pubs have also won local CAMRA awards in the last few years, including the Waggon & Horses (Stourbridge Road), Hawne Tavern (Attwood Street), Crafty Pint (Hasbury) and Swan (Long Lane). Long may they prosper!

The Bell & Bear, Gorsty Hill, Halesowen, courtesy Bill Hazlehurst

HILL TOP & HARVILLS HAWTHORN

The area in and around Hill Top and Harvills Hawthorn has a long and distinguished history. **Hill Top** is one of the oldest settlements surrounding West Bromwich Heath, lying astride the London-Chester turnpike road of 1727, but soon developed with collieries, foundries and ironworks, aided by the coming of the canals and railway. **Harvills Hawthorn** was originally known as Harvill's Oak (1531), recalling Heronville and the lords of Wednesbury, whilst Golds Green and Golds Hill owe their existence to benevolent ironmaster, John Bagnall. All this heavy industry was thirsty work, and over the years, the area was served by more than 60 pubs, but only a handful remain today.

The oldest pub in the area is probably the **Sow & Pigs,** dating from the 1770s. Once a home-brew pub kept by Thomas Griffiths and Joseph Wesley, it was acquired by Hanson's (Dudley) for £1,500 in 1938. Until recently, Two Crafty Brewers brewed their own beer here, and now it's a popular music venue and Indian grill bar.

In Black Lake, George Lyman brewed his own beer at the **New Talbot** (1871) until it passed to Hanson's in 1921 when it was rebuilt. It was kept by Norman and Ivy Harding from 1953-1968, but closed in 2020. On the corner of Church Lane, the **King Edward VII** (1870-2006) was originally the Britannia, but was renamed to celebrate the King's coronation in 1902. Almost opposite was the **Roebuck** (1860), whilst further along Church Lane is the **Queens Head** (1870), kept by George, Annie and Bert Sperring from 1904-1951 and rebuilt in 1949.

In Old Meeting Street, not far from St Andrew's Church, is the **Halfway House,** originally dating from 1881 as the George, but rebuilt in 1937 as a Darby's Brewery (West Bromwich) pub. When the Prince of Wales visited the area in 1923, he recognised landlord Jack Martin as a stoker who served with him in Hindustan. In the back streets, the **Great Western** (1872) in Chapel Street was once a home-brew pub where an inquest was held in 1881 into the death of shoe-maker Henry Crow, who choked eating a piece of cooked beef! It became a Cheshire's Brewery (Smethwick) pub, kept by Albert Reece from 1913-1930, but closed in 1960.

Back in the heart of Hill Top, the **Springmakers Arms** (1868) was once a Holder's (Birmingham) pub, but closed a century later. On the corner of Hawkes Lane, the **Hen & Chickens** is another venerable hostelry dating from 1818, but later rebuilt. In New Street, the **Globe** (1861-2010) was originally the Struggling Man, kept by Samuel and Jane Stanley from 1904-1931. In 1910, Samuel was accused of stealing a pigeon from Arthur Deakin and was ordered to return the bird and pay the costs of the court hearing. Nearby, the **Golden Pheasant** (1861-1932) was once a Frank Myatt Brewery (Wolverhampton) pub.

The area around Hawkes Lane has largely been redeveloped. The **Bulls Head** (1853) was originally the Moulders Arms, but since it adjoined a butchers shop, was renamed in 1892 and kept by Herbert Pritchard from 1908-1931. A few doors away were the **Grapes** (1871-1903) and **British Oak** (1858), kept by Amos Jones from 1914-1941, opposite the **Swan** (1868-1915). In the back streets were the **Vine** (1871), kept by William Innes from 1955 until it closed in 1967, **Railway Tavern** (1871-1922), kept throughout by Benjamin and Elizabeth Ludlow, and **Bird in Hand** (1864-1966), which only had nine licensees during its 100+ year life.

Back on the High Street, the **Box Iron** (1801-1911) was another venerable tavern, whose first landlord, John Siddons, held the licence for over 40 years. He also made saddle pistols and was brother to Joseph Siddons who founded the nearby Hill Top Foundry. In 1868, the inn sign showing a large gilded box iron was removed by rioting supporters of Wednesbury's first Liberal MP, Alexander Brogden.

A few doors away, the **Stores** (1871) was once a Wordsley Brewery pub, but was closed by 1907. The **Three Crowns** dated from 1818 and was the centre of village life, hosting dinners and political, miners' and football club meetings. Once another Holder's pub, it closed in 1969, and its licence was transferred to the new **Dovecote** (1971), previously named Flash Harry and Hillcrest, a few doors away. In Barncroft Street, Enoch and Eleanor Dabbs kept the **Brown Lion** (1872-1921) until 1906.

Witton Lane was home to the **Junction** (1858), kept by Harry Bladon from 1904-1948, but converted into a supermarket in 2008, and **Golden Lion** (1835-1938). The **Three Horseshoes** originally dates from 1864, was rebuilt for William Butler (Wolverhampton) in 1908 and is now a fine Black Country Ales' real ale pub. At the junction with Jowetts Lane, the **Gough Arms** originally dates from 1849, passed to Hanson's in 1929 for £2,152, and was later rebuilt in Art-Deco style.

In Crookhay Lane, the **Cottage Spring** (1850) was bought by Bent's Brewery (Stone, Staffordshire) for £3,628 in 1929, and was kept by George and Jane Ferguson from 1936-1966 and rebuilt in 1960.

The steep hill of Holloway Bank was home to the **Hop Pole** (1872-1955), acquired by Darby's in 1934, and **Miners Arms** (1868-1907), another Wordsley Brewery pub. Close to Wednesbury Bridge was the **Globe** (1855-1982), once a Highgate Brewery (Walsall) pub, and **Fountain** (1818), an old coaching inn, known locally as the Fountain in th' Hole, rebuilt in 1936 and closed in 2009.

Harvills Hawthorn lies beyond the Great Western railway line, where several pubs served the thirsty workers. The **Spring Cottage** (1858) was rebuilt on the site of the Old Crown (1818) in 1961, but was demolished in 1999. The **Samson & Lion** (1872), once another Bent's Brewery pub, became a fish and chip shop in 1994, whilst the **Royal Exchange** (1870) closed in 1977.

Dial Lane was home to the **Hawthorn** (1835), which became a Holt, Plant & Deakin pub in 1989, but was converted into housing in 2012. Nearby were the **Shoulder of Mutton** (1870-1908) and **Britannia** (1858), a Banks's (Wolverhampton) pub, allegedly haunted by Ebenezer the ghost, rebuilt in 1962, but converted into function rooms in 2012.

Golds Green and Golds Hill were centred on the quaintly-named Puddingbag and Pikehelve Streets, around the old colliery and canal bridge and not far from Brickhouse Colliery and Golds Green Colliery and Slag Works. Bagnall Street was home to the **Navigation** (1869-1911), once owned by Flower's Brewery (Stratford-on-Avon), **Miners Arms** (1868-1907), another Wordsley Brewery pub, and **Three Furnaces** (1834-1913). In Pikehelve Street, the **Britannia** (1853) was sold for £1,500 in 1900 and became a Darby's Brewery pub, kept by William, Medelina and Sumaria Heath from 1853-1922. It was later known locally as Merther's after landlord John Bill Merther, who ran it from 1937 until it closed in 1957.

In Old Row, close to the canal, the **Boat** (1871-1937) was a home-brew pub ran by Thomas Burgess, Dan and John Bishop, Joseph Jones and Herbert and Florence Francis. In 1881, ironworker John Burgess was charged with attempting to blow up the pub because he wouldn't be served!

Although the area around Hill Top and Harvills Hawthorn has changed dramatically and has lost most of its heavy industry, a handful of interesting and historic pubs remain. Long may they prosper!

KATES HILL & TIVIDALE

Kates Hill saw chaotic scenes in 1684 when Parliamentarians used the area as their base in the Civil War against King Charles I. As a result, some roads recall famous parliamentary figures such as Oliver Cromwell and Robert Peel. It's even said that Oliver Cromwell fired his cannons at the Royal garrison at Dudley Castle from Cromwell Street!

The area began to be developed from the 1830s to accommodate people moving into the Black Country who were seeking work in the many factories and coalpits. After 1915, its rural surroundings changed when hundreds of new houses were built, including Dudley's first council houses, and more redevelopment took place in the 1950s-1970s. Kates Hill has changed dramatically since the early 20th century, yet still retains several pre-1900 buildings, including St John's Church, although almost all of its 40 pubs are long gone.

Probably the oldest pub in Kates Hill is the **Bush Inn** in Buffery Road, next to Buffery Park. Originally built in 1828, it was rebuilt in 1905 by local architect, Frank Lewis, for Netherton brewer, John Rolinson, and kept by Frederick and Doris Pardoe (of Old Swan, Netherton fame) in the 1920s. Another venerable tavern was the **Sailors Return** in Cromwell Street (1835-1955), apparently named after a sailor who was murdered in Tower Street in the 19th century. It was once a Diamond Brewery (Dudley) pub, established in Cromwell Street by Joseph Plant in 1899. But it may also be remembered for the time in 1855 when barmaid, Mary Ann Mason, was shot through the mouth with a horse pistol by admirer, Joe Meadows, while she was flirting with miners in the bar!

Also in Cromwell Street, the **Dog & Partridge** (1850-1961) was a home-brew pub where local women used to drink in the entry alongside the pub! On the corner of Hill Street, the **Junction** (1860) was a popular Hanson's (Dudley) pub until it closed in 1941. In George Street, the **California** (1854-1937) was originally a home-brew pub known as the Jolly Collier, where John Bowen brewed his own beer, but it later became part of a school playground.

In High Street, landlord Sam Sherwood used to train boxers in his gym at the **Loving Lamb** (1841-1950), next to the **Bird in Hand** (1845-1965). Not far away was the **Leopard** (1856-1937), where Isaiah Aston brewed his own beer until it was bought by the Diamond Brewery in 1926. Nearby were the **Seven Stars** (1872-1929), **Royal Oak** (1830-1909) and **Golden Lion** (1819-1854), home to Joseph Gwinnult's lemonade, seltzer and soda water factory.

The **Star & Garter** (1841-1902) was once owned by Kates Hill Brewery, established by Samuel Salt at the **Malt Shovel** (1862-1965) in St John's Street. This brewery had a chequered history, being first established by Henry Cox & Co. in 1820 as the Dudley New Brewery and rebuilt in 1830. It passed to Samuel Salt in 1862 who brewed here until 1895. In 1902, it was sold to John Foley, who then sold it to Thomas Plant (Netherton) in 1910. Not far away, the **Jubilee** (1880-1937) also became part of a school playground.

William Whitehouse brewed his own beer between 1888-1906 at the **Freebodies Tavern** (1830) in St John's Road, which was later home to Samuel Wright's small brewery. Unfortunately, in 1880, landlord Lamech Harper committed suicide by hanging himself. The pub was rebuilt in 1976 and closed in 2008. The nearby **Fir Tree** (1872) was demolished in 2005, whilst the **Queen's Head** (1868-1938) was once a Rolinson's Brewery (Netherton) pub, as was the **Acorn** (1851-1933) in John Street.

In Brewery Street, the **Ivy House** dates from 1850 as a home-brew pub and more recently became a Black Country Ales' pub, but is currently closed. In Cross Guns Street, the **Cross Guns** (1835) was once a Diamond Brewery pub, but closed in 1959. At Cawney Hill, the **Cromwell Grove** (1830) had pleasure gardens which were replaced by a water reservoir in 1920. In Brown

Street, the **White Swan** (1867) was closed in 1933, whilst the **Four Ways** (1852) was a home-brew pub until it was acquired by Wolverhampton & Dudley Breweries in 1941.

Nearby, at Waddam's Pool, near the Bean Cars' factory in Hall Street, George England established the **Dudley Brewery** in 1823. But after several other owners, it passed to George Thompson in 1881, who ran the nearby **Victoria Brewery** at the Victoria Vaults, also in Hall Street. In 1890, both breweries became part of the newly-formed Wolverhampton & Dudley Breweries.

Continuing down the hill along Bunns Lane, we'd soon reach **Tividale.** This area was largely developed from the mid 19th century along the main road from Dudley-Oldbury and became a centre for iron and brick manufacturing, although most of the collieries were worked out by 1914. The community was effectively split by the Birmingham New Road, constructed in 1927, after which more development and housing estates took place. Around 30 pubs once served this community, but less than a handful remain.

One of the oldest pubs was the **Gate Hangs Well** in Tividale Road. Dating from 1818, it had a sign which read: "The Gate Hangs Well and Hinders None; Refresh and Pay and Carry On". It was kept by Benjamin and Caroline Whitehouse from 1911-1940, and later, landlord Eynon Evans, who used to play Tommy Troubles in the 1940s radio show, *The Welsh Rarebit*, held free-and-easy nights before the pub closed in the mid 1970s. Nearby, at the **Albion** (1881), William Cooper was fined 10s for stealing seven bottles of stout in 1903, whilst Arthur Harper was fined £6 12s in 1956 when he headbutted and kicked pianist, John Bond, in the face at a pre-wedding reception! At the **Plough** (1860-2011), landlord William Woodhouse was fined 10s in 1879 for being drunk in charge of a horse and trap.

In Dudley Road West, landlord Samuel Brookes of the **Britannia** (1845-1924) was fined £1 5s in 1882 when he drove his horse and trap through a Salvation Army parade in Dudley and assaulted Elizabeth Mayfield. The **Wonder** (1845) was kept by Thomas Harris and his family until 1882 and once had a hotel next door, whilst Ernest Stanton kept the **Ash Tree** (1860-1983) from 1936-1961. The **Miners Arms** (1860) became a fish and chip shop in 1938, whilst the **Pear Tree** (1835) closed in 1908. The **Seven Stars** (1860) closed in 1966 and the **Brown Lion** (1832) only lasted until 1904.

Closer to Burnt Tree, **Sawyers** (1988-2018) was based at the former Roman Mosaic Tile Works and later became a carvery. The distinctive mosaic was lost, but the lion statues ended up on the roundabout at Great Bridge! The **Burnt Tree Tavern** (1861) was closed by 1912. In the back streets, the **Royal Oak** (1861-1922) in Gate Street was originally called the Engine and was a popular prize-fighting venue, whilst the **Vine** (1866) in Hopkins Street was demolished in 1978.

Regent Road was home to the **Hangman's Tree** (1961-2005), built on the site of Oakham Colliery, and **Red Lion** (1939-2007), known locally as the Green Tap due to its green tiled roof. Drinkers are now served by the new **Tivi-Ale** micro-pub, opened in 2018. In City Road, the **Barley Mow** (1864-2009) was originally Bagnall's farmhouse, whilst the **Huntsman** (1956-2006) is now an Indian restaurant.

KINGSWINFORD & WALL HEATH

Kingswinford was once a rural village, relying on agriculture. Swinford Manor (*Suinesford*) existed in the 10th century and was known as Swinford Regis in 1579, gaining its prefix due to royal ownership. Some suggest that the "ford for the King's swine" derives from the villagers' dependence on pigs!

Coal mining was first recorded in the area in 1291 and more coal, sand and ironstone pits were sunk from the 1600s. Being on the western fringe of the Black Country, Kingswinford was not unaffected by the Industrial Revolution, with the Earl of Dudley's Pensnett mineral railway and collieries to the north around Himley, along with brickworks, collieries and factories to the east towards Dudley. By the end of the 20th century, much of the area had been built up with new housing estates, but many historic buildings remain, including several old inns and taverns. Over the years, around 50 pubs served the area, and almost 20 remain today.

The historic centre of Kingswinford is around the "Cross", or "Townsend", where the main roads to Stourbridge, Wolverhampton, Dudley and Swindon meet. Standing guard is the **Cross Inn,** dating back to 1750 and a Grade II listed building. Originally owned by glassmaker Diana Briscoe, it was an important coaching inn on the routes to Stourbridge, Wolverhampton and Tipton. It was regularly used for meetings, dinners, auctions, inquests, boxing and billiards matches, and was also the venue for the Court Leet, pigeon fanciers and local suffragettes. It also had a skittle alley, bowling green and tennis lawn. Originally a home-brew pub, it became a Showell's (Langley) house in 1896, passed to Ansell's in 1963 and became one of the chain of Holt, Plant & Deakin pubs in 1987. It's now been refurbished as a popular Wetherspoon's pub, complete with specially commissioned glass artwork.

A few doors away along High Street is the **Bell,** a former home-brew pub originally dating from 1842, but rebuilt in 1990. On the corner of Cottage Street is the **Cottage,** initially dating from 1851 as the Cottage of Content. It was kept by Joseph and Martha Brettle for over 40 years until 1964, but was rebuilt in 1966. It was known locally as the Pump, because the first public water supply came from a pump outside the pub. It also had a bowling green, a symphonium and was the headquarters of Kingswinford Wanderers FC.

On the corner of Water Street, there were two old inns dating from 1849. The **New Inn** closed in 1937, whilst the **Old Crown** had a boxing ring, stables and bagatelle club, but was demolished in 1925. The **Union Inn** (1860) in Water Street is a former Rolinson's (Netherton) pub, where landlord Joseph Vickers was also a hairdresser for 30 years until 1962. Opposite The Village is another venerable tavern, the **Old Court House,** built by the Earl of Dudley around 1775 as a public house and meeting place for the manorial court from 1781-1850. Now a Grade II listed building, it was a popular pub, but is currently closed.

Back at The Cross, along Market Street is the **Market Hall Tavern,** a former home-brew pub dating from 1866, where local churchwarden, Cliff Chambers, was a popular landlord and brewer in the 1950s. Nearby, the **Swan Inn** originally dated from 1864, but in 1956 the licence was transferred across the road to Greenfield House, previously the home of Geoffrey Chance (of Chance Brothers).

In Summer Street, the **Leopard,** a backstreet local dating from 1864, was once a Simpkiss (Brierley Hill) pub, kept for over 25 years by the Gordon family until 1980. At the end of Broad Street is the **Park Tavern,** dating from 1871 and originally a Thomas Plant's (Netherton) Brewery pub. Along Swindon Road, **Summerhill,** a fine Georgian house and once the Briscoe's family home, is now a Harvester restaurant. Back on the main road, the **Portway** (1861) was originally known as the Halfway House until 1889.

The settlement of Mount Pleasant (or California) grew up in the mid 19th century, and was focussed on the Methodist Chapel (1858) with two surviving pubs. On the corner with Cot Lane is the **Mount Pleasant Tavern,** dating from 1857 and another former Rolinson's pub, which once had a popular bowling green. Further along Mount Pleasant is the **Woodman** (1857), rebuilt in 1939 and now home to the Sommai Thai restaurant.

To the north of The Cross is the **Old Bridge Inn,** dating from 1845, noted for its fine home-brewed ales and now a Black Country Ales' real ale pub. In 1898, landlord Walter Edwards displayed the Largest Pig Alive here, whilst in the 1950s, landlord Thomas Pearce delivered coal from the adjoining coal wharf. Crossing the route of the former Pensnett mineral railway and turning into Stallings Lane, we find the **British Oak.** It was originally built in 1684 as Philip Foley's farmhouse for Old Stallings Farm on Pensnett Chase. It became a pub in 1845, when early landlords were still farmers, but was rebuilt in 1974.

In the early days, **Wall Heath** was a separate village in the green borderland of the Black Country, but many residents worked at the nearby collieries, forges, brickworks and rolling mills. In 1605, it achieved some notoriety due to the involvement of Stephen Littleton of Holbeche House in the Gunpowder Plot. But, with its tearooms and inns, Wall Heath soon became a weekend playground for Black Country families. In the 1930s, there was even a lido in a former sandpit at the Kingfisher Club, which remained a popular resort for families in the 1950s.

One of the oldest pubs is the **Wall Heath Tavern,** dating from 1842 and known locally as the Top House or Railway, since it was next to the mineral railway. In its early days, cockfights were held here, and in 1991 it became a Holt, Plant & Deakin pub, and it's still a popular local hostelry. A few doors away, the **Seven Stars** dated from 1834, but closed in 1912 and is now a shop. Outside the **Prince Albert** (1849), landlord John Solari installed Wall Heath's first petrol pump, but in 1937 the licence was transferred next door to the former Laurels. Opposite is the **Horse & Jockey,** built in 1861 by Frederick Hackett, its first landlord, apparently with his winnings from riding the winning horse in the Mile Flat Stakes at the Yew Tree!

In Albion Street were the **Drillman's Arms** (1861-1908), recalling miners who drilled the rock and lit the explosives, and the **Albion Inn** (1858-2014), now converted into housing. The **Yew Tree** dated back to 1849, and was another popular venue in Enville Road, with dancing in the ballroom and in the extensive pleasure gardens, running track, whippet racing, bull-baiting and whist parties. Kept by Alexander Mason for over 45 years until 1956, it was sadly demolished in 1995. Nearby, the **Waggon & Horses** (1845) eventually became a nightclub, but was replaced by housing in 1997.

Several interesting historic pubs remain in Kingswinford and Wall Heath, serving a range of excellent beers, many from local breweries. Long may they prosper!

LANGLEY

In the 16th century, **Langley** formed part of the largely rural Manor of Walloxhall, but it soon merged with Oldbury. It became home to several major industrial firms, including Chance's chemical and alkali works and Albright & Wilson's phosphorus works, along with other iron and steel foundries, engineering and chemical works, collieries, claypits and brickworks, as well as Parkes' Classic Confectionery factory. A handful of breweries also supplied the local pubs which served the thirsty workers.

Langley Green is the oldest part of Langley, but the main focus is along High Street, with its shops, pubs, institute, picture theatre and park, dominated by the chimney of the phosphorus works. On the corner of Five Ways stands the **Crosswells,** originally a home-brew house dating from 1849, where William Wincott and Stephen Duffield brewed their own beer until it was taken over by Showell's Crosswells Brewery in 1890. After it was rebuilt in 1924, Albert Cotterill kept the pub until 1951, when it's remembered for its Saturday night "free and easies". In 1984 it opened as one of the first Holt, Plant & Deakin pubs, based on the nearby micro-brewery.

In High Street, the **Fountain** (1862) was another Showell's pub, which became Langley's post office in 1910. In Trinity Street, the **New Market Tavern** (1881) was yet another of Showell's pubs, first kept by William and Harriet Ashley, who were also grocers, and later by Robert Read. Facing Holy Trinity Church is the **Coal Shed,** originally the Queen's Head dating from 1845, but known locally as the Model, with its windows advertising Frederick Smith's Aston Model Brewery. It was home to Langley's Homing Pigeon Society and was renamed the Model in 1968, but became the Coal Shed in 2018. Not far away in Park Lane was the **Eagle** (1858), once a Holder's (Birmingham) pub, kept by Robert Read and his son from 1914 until closing in 1940.

In Station Road, at Uncle Ben's canal bridge (named after a local pawnbroker), was the **Bridge.** This started life as the New Inn in 1861 and was another Showell's pub. It was also the headquarters of the local cricket, bowling and cycling clubs. In 1984, it became the base for the new Holt, Plant & Deakin micro-brewery and was renamed the Brewery Inn, but became the Finings & Firkin when it was sold to the Firkin Group in 1997. Renamed the Bridge in 2011, it was demolished in 2013 and replaced by new housing.

In Langley Green, next to St Michael and All Angels Church, the **Old Cross** is probably the oldest pub in the area, dating from the late 18th century and first licensed in 1845. Originally a home-brew pub, its first landlord, Thomas Goode was a pig farmer and cattle dealer (did he have a "Good Life"?), whilst another early landlord ran the local smithy. It became a Cheshire's (Smethwick) pub, kept by Fred and Martha Darby from 1906-1948, and once had a popular bowling green. Opposite was the **Royal Oak,** dating from before 1844 as the Red Lion and once another Holder's pub. It was rebuilt in the early 1900s, and kept by Fred and Gertie Butler until 1941, but it has now been converted into flats. Closer to the railway line, the **Railway** (1870) was originally a home-brew pub, but had a much shorter life, closing in 1910, whilst in Henry Street, the **Beehive** (1881), another Showell's pub, closed in 1923.

In Tat Bank Road, opposite Wellesley Road, was the **Albion,** next to Henry Swain's Albion Brewery. In 1987, it was renamed the Cottage, after a fatal stabbing, and became the New Cottage Indian bar and grill in 2017. In Vicarage Road, the **Merrivale** opened as one of the "Fewer and Better" Mitchells & Butlers' pubs in 1938. At that time, this mock Jacobean building was described as a new architectural feature and one of the best hotels in the area, but unfortunately it was seriously damaged by fire in 2017.

In Titford Road, the **Navigation** (1845) was a canalside home-brew pub where William Comley and Charles Etheridge brewed their own beer until it was taken over by Showell's in

47

1905. In 1931, it was rebuilt as the New Navigation in a Tudor-revival "improved" style to designs by local architects, Scott & Clark, and is now a Grade II listed building retaining some original features. Remembered for its weekend ox roasts, it was renamed more recently as the Navigation.

November 1927 saw the opening of the Birmingham-Wolverhampton New Road, cutting through the fringes of Langley, with several new roadhouses built along its route. One of the most well known was the **Hen & Chickens,** originally dating from 1871, where Jane and Silas Whitehouse and Captain Rose brewed their own beer until it was taken over by Showell's in 1914. It was rebuilt in the popular roadhouse style and eventually passed to Ansell's. Fondly remembered for the romances started in its ballroom, opened in 1961, it became a popular restaurant in 2000. Another similar roadhouse, the **Wernley,** was built further along the New Road in 1933 for Mitchells & Butlers in a Jacobean-revival reformed style, with a bowling green, by noted Birmingham pub architects Wood, Kenrick & Reynolds; it is a Grade II listed building.

Finally, on the other side of Causeway Green Road is the **Old Dispensary,** a micro-pub recently opened in a former pharmacy, but now dispensing prescriptions of a different kind – an ever-changing range of cask and craft keg beers.

Langley was also home to several local breweries. Walter Showell established his **Crosswells Brewery** here in 1870, using water from an ancient medicinal spring (Well of the Holy Cross – the trade mark). His beers were available in many local pubs, not only in Langley, but further afield. He also built the nearby Langley Maltings (see below), but the brewery was taken over by Samuel Allsopp (Burton-on-Trent) in 1914, along with its 194 tied houses, and it eventually became part of a distillery now making Langley gin. David Millerchip Sadler also used the same spring water at his nearby **Dog Kennel Brewery** in the 1880s. In 1877, S.N. Thompson and William Webb established the **Arden Grove Brewery** in Junction Street, but it was bought by Charles King in 1887 who sold it to J. Nunneley (Burton-on-Trent) in 1894. In 1871, Henry Swain & Co. established the **Albion Brewery** at the Albion pub in Tat Bank Road, but this was taken over by Showell's in 1915.

Many will remember the **Holt, Plant & Deakin** brewery, set up by Ansell's in 1984 at the New Inn (renamed the Holt's Brewery Tap) in Station Road. Each week, they brewed 5,000 gallons (40,000 pints!) of their famous Entire beer here until 1997, when the brewery and almost 50 pubs were sold to the Firkin chain.

The sad tale of Langley Maltings

Langley Maltings (also known as Showell's Maltings) originally dated from 1870, but were rebuilt in 1898 by Arthur Kinder & Son for Showell's Brewery. They comprised two parallel three-storey ranges of malting floors with six kilns at the eastern end. They were one of the last maltings to use the traditional floor malting method, whereby grains of barley were doused with water, spread over the floor, then turned regularly to ensure even germination. Local barley was used in the malting process, first brought by canal and then by railway and road. There was some rebuilding after a fire in 1925, and in 1944, the maltings were bought by Wolverhampton & Dudley Breweries. The maltings finally closed in 2006, but were seriously damaged by arson in 2009. They were saved from demolition in 2012, but in 2018, the Victorian Society included Langley Maltings on its list of the top 10 most endangered buildings and they have an uncertain future.

LYE

The township of **Lye** is situated midway between Stourbridge and Halesowen. It derives its name from the Saxon word for "lea", signifying untilled land or pasture. A map of 1625 showed the area as "Ye Lye", and local people have always referred to it as The Lye. A picture on the wall of the Windsor Castle pub showed all the pubs in Lye and Wollescote in 1900 – "*A total of 69 pubs and clubs, 55 within half-a-mile square!*" It was researched and drawn by local publican, Len Pardoe, who looked after the Old Peartree pub in The Hayes.

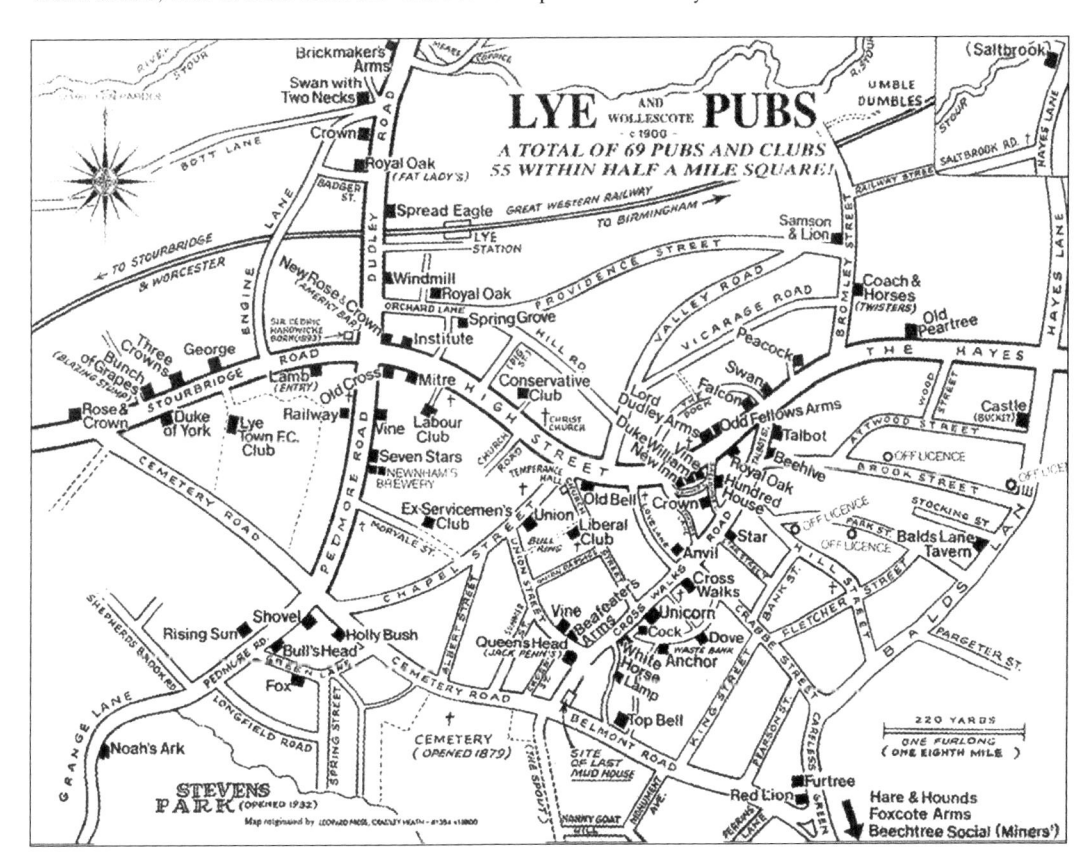

In the early days, life in Lye was uneventful, except when Prince Rupert used nearby Wollescote Hall as his local HQ in 1643 during the Civil War. But by the end of the 1650s, gypsies and squatters began to inhabit The Waste, an area of uncultivated land half-a-mile from the main centre of Lye around The Cross. In 1699, there were over 100 crude clay-built houses in this shanty town, the origin of Lye's other local name – Mud City. The Lye Wasters, as they were known, were hard working, but didn't integrate with the local community, who regarded them as uncivilised, lawless, uncouth and a Godless lot. One reported them "a dirty, squalid, immoral, lecherous, drunken, thieving bunch of heathens", whilst others thought them "a tribe of people of diminutive size, innocent of the usage of civilised life, who spent their time making nails".

In 1762, the Birmingham-Stourbridge turnpike road was constructed through The Waste, and the 1781 Enclosure Act enabled some of the squatters to become landowners. However, in 1800, Birmingham ministers declared that the inhabitants "were proverbial for their ignorance and vice" and that "there is no more rude or uncultivated spot in the whole of the British Isles".

Others saw Lye as a wild and barbaric place, with an early poem describing the place:

Lye, Lye Waste & Careless Green,
The three worst places ever seen,
A red brick church and a wooden steeple,
A drunken parson and wicked people.

In 1790, Revd James Scott, a Unitarian minister from Netherend, was a civilising influence on The Waste and built a Presbyterian chapel in 1806. Later, in 1813, local benefactor Thomas Hill helped establish the Anglican church, which became the parish church (Christ Church) in 1843. In 1818, John Wesley held meetings and by 1822 a Wesleyan chapel had been built at Lye Waste. The Unitarian Church, with its distinctive tower at the eastern end of the High Street, was built in 1861 on the site of Revd Scott's original chapel; the Methodists and Salvation Army were also influential. In 1782, the first Waste Bank School was founded by Thomas Hill, who also built another school in 1813. The Lye National School was opened in 1840, followed by new schools in Orchard Lane and Cemetery Road in 1882. However, by 1872, Lye remained the poorest area in the Stourbridge Poor Law Union.

At that time, the major occupation was nailmaking by hand, but when this was threatened by foreign competition and mechanisation from the 1840s, there were nailers' strikes and riots. Folkes' iron forge dated back to 1699, and later, other industries started to develop, first with Thomas Perrins' chainmaking factory built at Careless Green in 1770, along with factories making hollow-ware, including buckets and baths, anvils, stained glass and horseshoes. This latter trade grew after 1880 when local man, Henry Wooldridge, invented the frost cog – a device fitted into the horseshoe to prevent the horse from slipping in frosty weather; horseshoes are still made and exported from the town to this day. By 1863, Lye was known as the "Bucket Capital of the World" due to its galvanising and metal manufacture. These other trades, including coal mining and factory work, paid considerably more than home nailmaking and this led to its decline; by 1891 the number of nailmakers had declined by nearly 80%. By 1832, on the fringes of Lye, the presence of superior fireclay seams also led to the manufacture of firebricks, furnace linings and ornamental and building bricks. Examples can be seen clearly in buildings such as Centre Building at Lye Cross (1901), Rhodes Buildings (1881) and Bank Buildings (1901) in the High Street. Coal mining also took place locally and, in 1875, a banquet was apparently held in a dining room hewn out of the solid coal at the Earl of Dudley's Lye Cross mine!

Public transport included the railway from Birmingham to Stourbridge, with a station at Lye which opened in 1863. Local buses were popular and a tram line from The Hayes to Stourbridge opened in 1902 but closed in 1930. The cemetery was opened in 1879 and Lye's first public park (now Stevens' Park) was established by local industrialist Ernest Stevens in 1932. From 1897, the Lye and Wollescote Urban District Council began to tackle slum clearance, introducing modern water, drainage and sewerage systems, and opening a new library in 1935. Between 1900-1914, properly surfaced streets were provided (using the council's new steam roller), the first gas street lamps appeared in 1898 and electricity cables were laid in 1904.

However, although some of the old slum dwellings were cleared, many pubs and other social facilities were lost. Further major redevelopment took place in the 1960s (including demolishing the last mud hut), centred on the area bounded by High Street, Talbot Street, Cross Walks, Union Street and Chapel Street. In 2002, the Lye (one-way) bypass was opened. Until recently, Lye was known as the Balti Capital of the West Midlands, with no fewer than 10 Balti restaurants in the High Street. Famous people of Lye have included actor and Hollywood film star, Cedric Hardwicke, who was born in 1893 and died in 1964, and local MP, Wesley Perrins who died in 1990.

Against this background, many pubs and bars were established, firstly as home-brew alehouses. Much of the money earned in local industries was spent and gambled in the pubs (sometimes using tokens), and by 1866, there were some 53 pubs serving around 7,000 people. Many had their own cricket, football, bowls and darts teams, pigeon clubs and domino leagues. Some were still home to bull and badger-baiting, bare knuckle bouts and bear, cock and dog fighting well into the last century. In 2010, J. Jasper quoted a doggerel penned by a visitor to Lye in 1866, who took a trip around the town referring to virtually every one of the 53 pubs then existing! Today, barely a handful of them remain in and around the town. We'll reflect on George Wooldridge's poem *The Beauties of Lye Waste*:

I walked till a publick house came into view
When I called and got some good ale it is true
I sat myself down, 'twas the sign of the Swan
And I vow that the landlord's a pleasant old man

So let's take a walk around Lye in 1900 and see what we could find, especially in terms of pubs. We start our journey at the old centre of Lye, at the crossroads at Lye Cross. On the north-western corner is the distinctive **Centre Building,** designed by local brickworks manager, Owen Freeman. It was once Elisha Cartwright's clothing shop, and was the first to have outdoor electrically illuminated signs, and is now an Indian restaurant and bike shop. On the opposite corner was the equally impressive **New Rose & Crown,** with its fine terracotta frontage with a rose and crown on top of the corner pediment. Plenty of coloured and engraved glass, bright tiling and dark wooden panelling inside this Banks's pub, built in 1903 and replacing an earlier pub which Cromwell had fired at! But it was also known as the Merica Bar because of the brass footrail around the bar counter and the thick brass hitching rail around the outside walls for tying up horses. Echoes of the American Wild West in sleepy Lye! It was replaced by modern shops in the 1960s.

On the opposite corner was the **Old Cross,** popularly known as Polly Brooks, who was a long-serving landlady (1914-1928); she also brewed her own beer and owned a large fruit and vegetable business a few doors away. Bull-baiting once took place in front of the pub, which was closed and demolished in March 1935, and replaced by single-storey shops. The south-western corner is now occupied by the **Windsor Castle,** a former printworks, which only became a pub in 2004. Once the home of Sadler's Brewery, it was the base for the new Printworks Brewery, established in late 2019.

A century ago, the **High Street** was a thriving thoroughfare, with shops of all descriptions, many family-run businesses, tailors, drapers, milliners, ironmongers and hardware shops, intermingled with butchers, bakers, grocers, fruiterers, greengrocers and fishmongers, and of course, pubs. Memorable shops included Mr Webster's Ye Olde Antique Shoppe near Lye Cross and Meshak Lavender's tailors shop which specialised in hunting gear – just what did they hunt in Lye? Pharaoh Adams' butchers was always well stocked with meat hanging outside the shop, whilst "Woodcraft" is an ironmongers dating from 1866, one of the oldest businesses in the High Street. Lye's first Co-operative store was established in 1861, and unusually specialised in ironmongery and industrial goods, including hand-made horse nails!

Walking along the High Street, the first notable building on the left was the **Working Men's Institute** (the Stute), built in 1856. This was the scene of rioting in 1874 during elections when the Riot Act was read from a nearby doorway for the last time in England; after closing in 1960, Lloyds Bank occupied the site. Opposite would have been the **Mitre,** a Mitchells & Butlers pub dating from 1862, which was originally a home-brew pub and issued its own tokens. Closed in 1974, it's now a chemist's shop, and only Mitre Road remains to recall the pub. A few doors down was The Vic Picture Theatre, designed and built in 1913 by local man, Hugh Folkes, demolished in the 1960s and replaced by a new Spar supermarket. Down an alleyway was the Lye **Labour Club,** now demolished.

Past the Congregational Chapel (dating from 1827 and now a mosque) and a bank, on the opposite side of the road beyond Pig Stink Alley (now Clinic Drive) are the Rhodes Buildings, designed by Owen Freeman and built in 1881 by local brickmaker, Thomas Rhodes; note the distinctive banded terracotta brickwork and inscriptions: "Be not slothful" and "Diligent in business". The **Lye Conservative Club** lay down an alleyway at the side of these buildings, and is now a car park. Next, set back from the main road, is the impressive Christ Church, dating from 1813, now minus its spire which was removed in 1985.

Opposite the Bank Buildings, on the south side of the High Street, is the junction with Chapel Street. Next to the shed housing the town's fire engine, complete with polished bell, would be the new library, opened in 1935 by Cecil Hardwicke, opposite the police station. Around the corner in Church Street was the Temperance Hall, dating from 1874, partly funded by a festival held in Hagley Park in 1870 and built to counteract drunkenness and provide civilised entertainment. It later became a concert hall and cinema, closed in 1956 and was finally demolished in 1967.

Fronting the High Street, snugly wedged between the old bank and Collin's fruiterer's shop, was the **Old Bell.** Known locally as the Bottom Bell (to distinguish it from the Top Bell in Belmont Road), in the early years it was a home-brew pub that was run by the Brettell family for more than 80 years. Afterwards, the licensee was David Millward, a contemporary cricketing companion of Cecil Hardwicke. Another Banks's pub, it closed in 1974 and was rebuilt shortly afterwards, but closed again in 2011 and became a community hall. Opposite was the luxurious 1,100-seat Clifton Cinema, designed by Roland Satchwell in 1937, which closed in 1965 after showing its last films, Jerry Lewis' *The Patsy* and *Robinson Crusoe on Mars*! It became Woodworth's toy shop and is now an indoor market hall.

Along the southern side of High Street between Connops Lane and Talbot Street was a concentration of pubs, none of which survive today. In close succession were the **New Inn, Duke William** and **Vine.** Some of these were originally home-brew pubs, but most closed in the late 1930s; the Vine is now a newsagents. A little further along, the **Royal Oak** dating from 1835 was once a Butler's pub and briefly owned by Batham's (Brierley Hill), but was closed and demolished in 1958.

On the opposite side of High Street, past the distinctive Unitarian Church and backing on to The Dock (so called because horses used to have their tails docked there!) was another grouping of pubs. These included the **Lord Dudley Arms, Oddfellows Arms, Falcon, Swan** and **Peacock,** some of which were Hanson's (Dudley) pubs, but were all gone between 1928 and the 1960s. The Lord Dudley Arms was perhaps best known for the famous Victorian writer, Sabine Baring-Gould, who visited the pub to collect information for his novel, *Nebo the Nailer*, set in Lye and published in 1902.

A walk up **Talbot Street** would have revealed yet more hostelries, all of which are long gone. We'd first come to the **Talbot** and **Beehive,** followed by the **Star.** Some of these pubs were owned by the North Worcestershire Brewery, based in Stourbridge, which was taken over by Wolverhampton & Dudley Breweries in 1910. Just around the corner in Skeldings Lane, in an area once known as Slack Mound, was the **Crown Inn.** Opposite was the **Hundred House,** dating from 1871, which was originally a home-brew pub run by Frank and Florence Pardoe, but was taken over by Banks's and demolished in 1968.

Continuing along Cross Walks Road, there was another group of pubs, now all long gone. On the corner of Love Lane was the **Anvil,** originally a home-brew pub dating from 1871 and taken over by Hanson's. Landlord A.H. Cook issued tokens from here in the 1870s and Harry Cook sponsored the Lye Bowling League in 1931. Opposite was the **Cross Walks Inn,** an Ansell's pub run by the Hayes family from 1881. Further up the road were the **Unicorn, Cock** and **White Horse,** with the **Anchor, Lamp** and **Dove** behind in Waste Bank. The Unicorn started out as a Thomas Plant Brewery (Netherton) pub, but only lasted until 1911, whilst the White Horse was demolished and rebuilt in the late 1960s, but closed in 2006. The other pubs were gone by the 1930s.

On the corner of Union Street was the **Queens Head,** known locally as Jack Penn's, after one of the landlords whose family kept the pub for over 50 years. A home-brew pub from 1914-1950s, it was also home to the local pigeon club, but closed in the 1960s. Behind the pub was the **Cross Walks Brewery,** dating from 1914, but closed in 1956. Apart from supplying beer to the Queens Head, it also supplied the Holly Bush (Cemetery Road). Opposite was the **Beefeaters Arms,** another home-brew house dating from 1861, but closed in the 1920s, and the **Vine,** a Hanson's pub, which lasted a similar time. At the bottom of Union Street in Chapel Street was the **Union,** originally an Atkinson's/Ansell's pub, but closed in October 1939. Around the corner in Church Street was the **Lye & Wollescote Liberal Club** (M&B), that opened in July 1906.

At the top of the hill in Belmont Road, we've already mentioned the **Top Bell,** originally dating from 1865. It was a home-brew pub where, in 1873, 70-year-old Richard Knowles ate some pancakes and died "by the visitation of God"! This former Ansell's pub was rebuilt in 1987 and reopened by boxer Pat Cowdell; it was formally renamed the Top Bell in 1998. On the corner of Careless Green was the **Red Lion,** a home-brew pub dating from 1860, which was taken over by Hanson's, demolished and rebuilt, but finally closed in 2007. Close by was the **Firtree,** whilst on the corner of Wynall Lane is the **Hare & Hounds,** originally dating from 1829, but still serving Banks's beers and home to the local clay pigeon shooting club. Walking back along Balds Lane, we'd have seen the **Balds Lane Tavern,** a home-brew house dating from 1871 and known affectionately as the Sawdust Hotel. It was rebuilt in 1911 and 1970, but closed in 2014. On the corner of Attwood Street was the **Castle,** another home-brew pub dating from 1881 and one of the Simpkiss Brewery (Brierley Hill) pubs. Known locally as The Bucket, it was closed and demolished in 1987.

At the bottom of Hayes Lane near the River Stour was the **Saltbrook Inn,** dating from 1871. In the early days, landlord Joseph Pearson brewed a powerful beverage here called Salty Dick's, using water from the local brook. Formerly known as the Saltbrook End Tavern, it was renamed the Dewfall Arms and Ye Olde Saltbrooke before closing in 2009. Back in The Hayes was the **Old Peartree,** a M&B pub closed and demolished in 2009. Around the corner in Bromley Street were the **Coach & Horses,** kept for many years by the Taylor family and known locally as Twisters, and the **Samson & Lion.** North of the High Street in Orchard Lane were the **Spring Grove** (serving beer from the Wordsley Brewery) and the **Old Royal Oak,** a Hanson's pub dating from 1862, but demolished to make way for the new bypass.

Back at Lye Cross, we take a walk down Dudley Road, once part of the old Saltway from Droitwich to Dudley. First, on the right-hand side was the **Windmill,** a former Hanson's pub, now a restaurant. Just across the railway bridge was the **Spread Eagle,** dating from 1845, whilst further down the hill were the **Royal Oak** (affectionately known as Fat Lady's and closed in 1940), the **Crown** and **Swan with Two Necks,** which was rebuilt in the 1920s and is now a restaurant. At the bottom of the hill was the aptly-named **Brickmakers Arms,** a former home-brew house opposite the local brickworks, once kept by a member of the Batham family, Caleb Batham. It was taken over by Banks's and once used as a Coroners Court, but closed in 1964.

A walk along Stourbridge Road also reveals a handful of old pubs. First, on the left-hand side was the **Lamb** (locally known as the Entry), whilst beyond Engine Lane we'd see the **George, Three Crowns** (a M&B pub dating from 1829, once the home of the local aquarium society), **Bunch of Grapes** (known locally as the Blazing Stump), opposite the **Duke of York** and **Rose & Crown.** Finally, a walk up Pedmore Road sees the **Railway Inn,** opposite the **Vine.** A few doors down was the **Seven Stars,** next to **Herbert Newnam's Brewery,** which was first established in 1895. He brewed a particularly potent Premier Cuvee pale ale (12%), with the tag line "Treat it with respect". Across the junction with Cemetery Road is the **Shovel,** formerly Malt Shovel, dating from 1835, refurbished in 1970 and reopened in 1984 as a free house.

Further along Pedmore Road was the **Rising Sun,** opposite the **Bull's Head** (a former M&B pub, rebuilt in 1960, closed in 2009), beyond which was the **Noah's Ark,** a Banks's pub where long-serving landlord, Harry Holmes also owned a chemist on the High Street. Back around the corner in Green Lane is the **Fox,** once a home-brew pub where Harry Perry brewed potent ale in the 1900s and also reared the heaviest pig in England! Finally, in Cemetery Road, not far from Mr Jones' pikelet bakery, is the **Holly Bush,** an old established pub owned by Jack Penn's Cross Walks Brewery, which was occasionally used for inquests and was also home to the local pigeon club. For many years, George Bromley was the landlord who also owned a paint shop in the High Street.

So, we've covered all the pubs that used to exist in Lye in 1900 and seen what's there today – a shadow of its former self – just six pubs open instead of nearly 70 that existed in 1900.

NETHERTON

The first references to **Netherton** go back to 1420, when it was referred to as *Nederton*, meaning lower farm, and it gained a market charter granted by King Charles II in 1684. It was once a quiet North Worcestershire village on the ancient road from Dudley to Halesowen. But by the late 1800s, it was something of a development zone, with the town expanding and industries booming, from chainmaking to industrial boilers and ships' anchors. By the 1900s, there were more than 100 pubs and alehouses serving the town and its wider area, with several breweries and over 40 home-brew alehouses. Most of these pubs and breweries have long gone, and today, barely a handful of pubs remain in and around the town.

Probably the most well-known pub in the town centre is the **Old Swan** in Halesowen Road, originally dating from 1835, but rebuilt in 1863. It's affectionately known as Ma Pardoe's (or more correctly Mrs Pardoe's) after long-serving landlady, Doris Pardoe. Frederick and Doris Pardoe moved into the pub in 1932 and she continued to keep it after her husband died in 1952 until 1984, when she died, aged 85. The pub has long been a home-brew house and was one of only four home-brew pubs remaining in the country when CAMRA's first Good Beer Guide was published in 1974. Now Grade II listed, it's included in CAMRA's National Inventory of Historic Pubs, notably for its interior, with its iconic front bar and enamel-panelled Swan ceiling, Victorian servery with engraved mirrors, free-standing stove with flue and old weighing machine. Current landlord, Tim Newey, strives to maintain the traditional character of the pub; the pump clips don't display the beers on offer, they're listed on a board behind the bar. Brewing still continues to this day and, as the sign still proclaims, "The Ales brewed at this establishment are the purest in the Borough".

The marketplace is overlooked by the Public Hall and Free Library dating from 1894, once home to Dudley CAMRA's Winter Ales Fayre. It's also home to the replica Titanic anchor, originally made locally at Noah Hingley's foundry. There were several pubs around the marketplace, including the **Castle Inn** (1835) on the corner of St John's Street. By 1921, it was known as the Castle Hotel, but was demolished and replaced by the **Mash Tun** in 1967, which itself was replaced by apartments in 1999. Just behind the pub was Thomas Plant's Steam Brewery, founded by William Round in 1837 and bought by Thomas Plant in 1875

Also around the marketplace were the **Sampson & Lion** (1842), closed in 1952, and **Cottage Spring,** once the oldest pub in town. In 1836, William Round, an illiterate butty collier, built two cottages here, knocked them together and opened this beerhouse in 1838. His son, Samuel, went on to brew his own beer here, before it was acquired by Thomas Plant in 1881. In 1967, the pub was demolished and replaced by the Mash Tun. In nearby Raybould's Fold alley, the **New Inn** (1862) was a former home-brew pub, which closed in the 1960s.

At the top end of High Street, the area known as Sweet Turf was overlooked by the **British Oak** (1855), a former home-brew house that was closed by 1941. It was kept by Frederick and Doris Pardoe in 1931, before they moved to the Old Swan. Nearby was the **Spread Eagle Hotel** (1835), which was popular with miners and Netherton Rovers Cricket Club, but demolished around 1963.

Between High Street and Hill Street there were many pubs, whilst just off Simms Lane, Brewery Street gave a clue to some of the small breweries which had existed nearby. On the corner with Simms Lane was the **Golden Lion** (1880), a former home-brew house closed in 1957. On the corner of Halton Street is the **Crown,** a modern pub built in 1983. On the corner of St James' Street was the **Old Cottage,** another former home-brew house dating from 1864, but closed in 1910. Throughout that period, it was in the hands of brother and sister, John and Abagail Hampton, who were apparently an "odd couple", with John brewing the beer and Abagail looking after the pub. When serving a beer, Abagail would light a tallow candle and go down into the cellar to draw a can of ale from the barrel, and measure it before pouring it into your glass, returning the residue to the barrel.

On the corner of St John's Street was the **Queens Head** (1891-1959), kept by Francis and Bertram Billingham until 1940, with a small brewery at the rear. On the corner of St James' Street, the **Royal Exchange** (1854) was popular with local miners, but closed in the 1960s. In the nearby Nocks Fold alleyway, the **Church** (1835) closed in 1927. On the opposite side of Hill Street was the **Old Bell** (1835-1960), whilst on the corner of Spittles Fold was another **Crown** (1864), closed in 1961. On the corner of Hampton Street was the **Old Pack Horse** (1868), where Richard Rolinson brewed at the Netherton New Brewery until it was destroyed by fire in 1895. It was acquired by John Rolinson in 1900 for £3,100, who moved his Five Ways Brewery here in 1910. In 1996, the pub was renamed Oasis, but was converted into housing in 2009.

Continuing along Netherton's saintly streets, on the corner of St Andrew's Street was the **Five Ways Inn,** originally a home-brew house established in 1835 by Thomas Pendlebury. By 1881, John Rolinson had built the Five Ways Brewery behind the pub, but it was closed in the 1970s. Nearby, in Harrisons Fold, the **Bull's Head** was first recorded as a home-brew house in 1830 and kept by Thomas Round between 1906-1935. The **Travellers Rest** (1855) was gone by 1946, whilst the **Miners Arms** (1880) became offices in 1983. In St Thomas' Street, the **White Horse** (1873) was once owned by the Home Brewery (Quarry Bank), but closed in 1939.

In St Andrew's Street, Albert Prestidge kept the **Bird in Hand** (1855) from 1910-1946, but it closed in 1968. Nearby were the **Blue Pig** (1862), built by Joseph Homer and kept by his family until 1906, but demolished in 1997, and **Bricklayers Arms** (1852-1906). The **St Andrew's Tavern** dated from 1750, with its gin and pony pit, but was converted into houses in 1855. On the corner of Griffin Street and Castle Street was the **Wheelwrights Arms,** with its own brewery, established in 1870 by Samuel Houghton, It was kept by brewers, Joseph Davies and Sarah and Thomas Siviter from 1885-1942, and later rebuilt, but was demolished in 1996.

Continuing northwards along Cinder Bank, opposite William Smith's Netherton Brewery, we'd find the **Crown Inn** (1841-1960), where Netherton & Woodside Building Society was founded in 1848. On the corner of Swan Street, the **Hope Tavern** (1852) was rebuilt in 1899 after a major gas explosion damaged the pub and killed three regulars who were playing cards. Known locally as the Blue Brick, it used to be the "roughest, toughest alehouse in the area", and once had a splendid Victorian interior. Thomas Danks and his family kept the **Jolly Collier** (1820) until 1901, but it was later extended and became a house in 2002.

In Swan Street, the **Prince of Wales** (1870) was closed a century later. On the corner of Baptist End Road, the **White Swan** (1830) was kept by home-brewer, James Roe and his family from 1880-1939. After becoming a Holt, Plant & Deakin pub in the 1980s, it was later renamed Turner's, after long-serving landlord, Tommy Turner (1954-1980).

Returning to the Market Place, at the junction with Cradley Road was the **Junction Inn** (1870), rebuilt in 1905 for North Worcestershire Breweries, which later became a drop-in centre for the elderly. **The Dolphin** (1871) was kept by Elizabeth Gower and her family until 1956, but was demolished in the mid 1970s. Continuing along Halesowen Road, the **Old Crown** (1854-1957) had its licence transferred to the **Moot Meet,** a modern Ansell's pub, opened in 1957, but closed in 2008. At Bishton Bridge, landlord William Bishton operated a packet pleasure boat to Birmingham every Sunday from the canal wharf behind the **Crown** (1835-1904).

Next to Noah Hingley's ironworks on the corner of Washington Street was the **Loyal Washington** (1850-1955). The first landlord was William Washington, a timber merchant who became the first local councillor for Netherton. He belonged to that branch of the family who remained loyal to the British Crown, and had his glasses stamped with the crossed flags of the Union Jack and the stars and stripes of the Washington family, which formed the original flag of the USA. Further along the street was the **Trust in Providence** (1854-1912), where Edwin Holden (of brewery fame) met his wife, Lucy, who was the daughter of brewer Benjamin Round.

At the **Star** in Primrose Hill (1860), landlords plied their trades while keeping the pub and brewing beer. First landlord, Zacheus Spittle was a stone calciner, whilst William Bannister, who took over the pub in 1872, was a chainmaker. George Chatham and George Bywater brewed at the brewery behind the pub, but it closed in 1917 because "the premises were ill conducted".

Nearby in Chapel Street, the **Bird in Hand** (1840-1970) was home to William Onslow's Primrose Hill Brewery and kept by James Kenrick's family from 1900-1959. The **Brickmakers Arms** (1835) was rebuilt in 1923, but closed in the 1960s. George Bywater and Wilfred Simms brewed their own beer at the **Colliers Arms** (1864) before it closed in 1952. The **Red Lion** (1855) was a Hanson's pub, which was closed in 1934.

In Cradley Road, the **Blue Bell** (1781) was one of the oldest pubs in the area, kept by Hannah and Septimus Griffiths from 1851-1905 and by Thomas and Sarah Harris until it closed in 1939. The **Bridge** (1876) was kept by brewer William Hotchkiss before being demolished in 1918. The **Elephant & Castle** originally dated from 1854, but was later rebuilt and became one of the Holt, Plant & Deakin pubs, kept briefly by the Old Swan's Tim Newey in 1987. The **Golden Cross** (1850-2006) was rebuilt in 1938, whilst the **Providence** (1870) was closed by 1920, and the **Reindeer** (1861) lasted until 1938. The **White Swan** (1845) was known locally as the Round Steps and was affected by mining subsidence in 1912, but was demolished in 1997.

In Northfield Road, the **Loving Lamb** Inn was once a vicarage that became a pub in 1855. When it was being rebuilt during the Second World War, customers used to drink in a large wooden building behind the pub, but it closed in 2004 and was converted into housing. The **Britannia** (1835) stood at the entrance to the Wakes Ground and supplied water to the fairground showmen, but was closed in 1970. The **Red Lion** (1870) was kept by Daniel Ashman until 1931, was later rebuilt and kept by West Bromwich Albion footballer, Joseph Joe Smith.

Famous athlete, 'Jumping' Joe Darby was born at Darby End in 1861 and no doubt visited some of the pubs there. The **Rose & Crown** in Withymoor Road (1839) was a home-brew pub kept by the Bird and Dunn families. Rebuilt in 1901, it was acquired by Holt's (Birmingham) in 1930, but was converted into flats in 1984. Luke Walker, the first landlord of the **King William** (1849), was a well-known bare-knuckle fighter (Netherton Collier). The pub was kept by Daniel and Arthur Batham between 1901-1926, was rebuilt in 1956, but demolished in 2007. Around the corner in Cole Street, the **Gate Hangs Well** (1830) was known as Father Bennett's after long-serving landlord, Benjamin Bennett (1904-1938). In Belper Row, the **Red Cow** (1871) used to be a cockfighting venue, but closed in 1960, whilst the **Hand of Providence** (1845) closed in 1923.

At Windmill End, one of the most unusual pubs was the **Dry Dock.** Originally the Bull's Head (1842), it was once known locally as Reuben's after long-serving landlord Reuben Kirby (1931-1958), but closed in 2013. In 1985, it became one of Colm O'Rourke's Little pubs, famous for their Desperate Dan cow pies, but this pub had the added quirk of having a bar servery made out of an old canal narrowboat! Joseph Tilly and his family kept the **Wheatsheaf** (1849) until 1904. It was known locally as Ocker's when Thomas and John Parkes (his nickname) kept the pub, until it was rebuilt in 1955. The **Old Bush** (1842) and **White Horse** (1869) both closed in 1913.

Nearby, at Bumble Hole, the **Fox & Goose** (1835) was next to the canal bridge of the same name, but was closed by 1941, whilst the **Malt Shovel** (1841) was another popular cockfighting venue, closed in 1957. The **Dog & Duck** (1855) was a canalside pub closed in the 1930s, whilst the **White Lion** (1841-2015) was later rebuilt and converted into housing. In St Peter's Road, the **Boat** (1850) was originally known as the Navigation and Boatman's Inn, but became a printers in 1987.

Dudley Wood Road was home to the **Victoria** (1845), where James Bartlett and George Bridgewater brewed at the small brewery here until 1950. George Bridgewater and Joseph Sidaway later helped to set up Cradley Heathens' speedway and greyhound track, which was replaced by housing in 2002. In Bowling Green Road, the **Cottage Spring** (1871) was rebuilt in 1955. In Saltwells Road, the **Woodman** (1938) opened when the surrounding housing estates were built, whilst the **Bunch of Bluebells** (1957) became a Holt, Plant & Deakin pub in 1987. In Hockley Lane, the **Yew Tree** (1954) was demolished in 2015.

Finally, we mustn't forget the **Saltwells Inn,** which originally dated from 1809 when it was owned by the Earl of Dudley; it was rebuilt in 1939 (see below).

Not far away is **Mushroom Green,** a chainmaking community, which was saved by the Black Country Society and preserved by the Black Country Living Museum, complete with an original chain shop. There were once a handful of beerhouses serving this hamlet, including the **Cottage** (1830) and **Jolly Miner** (1849), but they'd all gone by the early 1900s.

So, although Netherton has lost many of its historic pubs, several remain, including the iconic and possibly unique, Old Swan. Long may they prosper!

A Spa near the bar

In 1823, the enterprising landlord of the **Saltwells Inn,** Thomas Holloway, decided to launch his local saline springs onto the fashionable spa market. The spring had been known for its healthy waters since Dr Robert Plot wrote about it in 1636. Customers of the inn would visit the nearby Saltwells Spa, which was used as a cure for rheumatism, sciatica and gout. In 1833, Samuel Lewis noted that *"Lady-wood is a valuable spring, called the Spa Well, in high estimation for its efficacy in cutaneous disorders and complaints arising from indigestion"*. It's even said that the waters were taken by William Perry (the Tipton Slasher) and by footballers from Aston Villa and West Bromwich Albion. Unfortunately, they didn't seem to work for landlord George Flavell, who hobbled around with gout and always kept a shotgun within reach. Once, a customer trod on his foot and he shot the clock on the wall to pieces, remarking that "next time, it'll be thy dial as guz west"! Unfortunately, mining activity polluted the waters and prevented further use. But the surrounding area now forms part of the nationally-acclaimed Saltwells Nature Reserve, the first to be recognised for the importance of its geology, including Doulton's Claypit, once used by Doulton's pipeworks, just outside Netherton.

OLDBURY

Oldbury was an ancient rural settlement (*Ealdanbyrig*) that began to grow during the Industrial Revolution. From the 1770s, coal mining and ironworking were established at Rounds Green, along with canals, brickworks and foundries. By the 1840s, new chemical and glass factories came along, such as Chance's and Albright & Wilson. But after a century of rapid unplanned growth, Oldbury was bursting at the seams and public services were wholly inadequate to serve the expanding population. Things began to improve when the Urban District Council was formed in 1894, providing a clean water supply and new housing. All this industry was thirsty work and led to the growth of pubs and beerhouses from the 1820s onwards. Over the years, more than 180 pubs have served Oldbury and the wider Langley area, of which around 20 remain today.

The centre of the town focused on the marketplace, home to some of the oldest pubs and hotels. On the northern side, the **Old Talbot Inn** dated from 1759, and was kept by popular landlord, William "Old Bill" Marigold, but it closed in 1960 and was later demolished. Across the marketplace was the **Talbot Hotel,** dating from 1829. This was the town's premier hotel and coaching inn, where the Earl Grey coach called, and was a flagship for Showell's Brewery (Langley). In 1887, Oldbury Town FC was founded here and the Manorial Courts met here until 1923. It was also the headquarters of Oldbury Cycling Club and the local Conservative Party, which resulted in broken windows during one Victorian election campaign! Unfortunately, the hotel was demolished in 1970, when many old buildings were swept away as part of the redevelopment of the town centre, including the **British Lion** in Talbot Street (1861-1978).

Probably the oldest building used as a pub is the **Court of Requests** in Church Street, now a Grade II listed building. Opened in 1816 as Oldbury's courthouse, it became the town's police station in 1855 and later the public library. The prison regime was particularly severe, ordering that "no kinds of provisions, ale, spirits or drinkables be taken to prisoners, except a loaf of bread weighing 1lb for each person per day". After a £1.25m refit in 2012, it was converted into a Wetherspoon's pub and retains the original courtroom and prison cells.

Almost next door is the **Waggon & Horses,** originally dating from 1789 when it was owned by prize-fighter, Issac Perrins. In 1890, it was replaced by a purpose-built pub for Holt's Brewery (Birmingham) in a typical brick and terracotta style, with a polygonal turret and Holt's squirrel emblem. Many original features remain, including wall tiles, copper-clad ceiling (now painted over), bench seating, bell pushes and etched windows. It's also a Grade II listed building, included in CAMRA's national inventory of historic pubs.

Birmingham Street was a hive of activity, with many shops, banks (including Lloyd's first bank branch in 1864) and pubs. One of the oldest pubs was **Ye Olde Bull's Head,** dating from 1793, but rebuilt in 1900 and closed in 2013. From 1894-1904, Thomas Bedworth brewed his own beer here, noted for purity, and then it passed to Nathaniel Sadler, of the eminent Sadler family. In 1884, Pricilla Little was fined 10s and given 14 days hard labour for being drunk and disorderly here.

Occupying a focal point in Unity Place, the **Junction** dates from 1861, is listed Grade II, and was known locally as the Wrexham, when it served Peter Walker's Wrexham ales. Jack Judge was a regular here and sold fish from his cart outside the pub. Jack lived next door to the **Malt Shovel** in Low Town (1845-1962), where he regularly sung with pianist Harry Williams and may have written his famous *Tipperary* song here. He died in West Bromwich in 1938, aged 65. Other old pubs such as the **Beehive** (1871), **Brown Lion** (1829), **Crown & Anchor** (1829), **King's Arms** (1850) and **White Lion** (1829) are long gone. Further along Birmingham Road, the **Perrott Arms** (1845) lasted until 1993, but the **George** (1870) and **British Queen** (1870) survive, the latter being the brewery tap for John Jordan's ales and stout until 1913.

There were several old pubs in Halesowen Street, including the **George & Dragon** (1829-1962), a popular home-brew pub before being acquired by Atkinson's (Birmingham) in 1903. The **New Inn** (1862-1963) was popularly known as Such's after long serving licensees, William and Sophie Such. There was a violent murder in 1828 at the **Whimsey** (1828-1957), when the Sergeant of the Court of Requests was stabbed by William Billy Sugar Steventon, who was later publicly executed. In Church Street, the **Red Cow** (1829-1962) was home to Richard Williams, an agent for David Sadler's ale and a porter from the Dog Kennel Brewery (Langley). Nearby, the **White Horse** (1829) sold Oliver's Pure Pale Ales (West Bromwich), but was gone by 1961.

Along West Bromwich Street were the **Sycamore** (1839-1938) and **New Cart & Horses** (1829-1912). Just beyond the **Spring Cottage** (1845-1908) was the **Duke of Malakoff** (1865-1906), kept by Frenchman Edward Idoine with his wife and seven children. The pub was named after Marshall Pélissier, commander of the French army who helped to end the Siege of Sebastopol in 1855 during the Crimean War (not a lot of people know that!)

In Rounds Green, the **Bird in Hand** dated from 1760 and was kept by the Hadley family until 1894, it was closed in 1956. William and Hannah Hadley also brewed their own beer at the nearby **Bell** (1823-1956). Further along Brades Road, the **Brades Tavern** (1870) survives as an Indian restaurant.

The local Sadler family owned the **Windsor Castle** from 1862-1927, including John Sadler (the Grand Old Man of Oldbury). Nathaniel Sadler soon established his brewery here and, at its height, when Thomas was in charge, they were supplying another 10 pubs. But brewing ceased in 1927 and the pub closed in 1956. In 2004, John and Christopher Sadler recalled their family's brewing heritage by opening the Windsor Castle Pub and Brewery at Lye, which became home to Sadler's Peaky Blinder ales and was the base for the Printworks micro-brewery. Benjamin Sadler was well known for his collection of stuffed beasts and other natural curiosities, which he transferred to the **White Swan** in Church Street in 1884. This pub survives, now on the opposite side of the road after rebuilding in 1984 to make way for the new council offices.

In Dudley Road East, the **Blue Ball** dated from 1834, and was kept for many years by Fred Growcott. It had a bowling green and quoits club, and was the HQ for Brades Park FC, but closed in 1984. Around the corner in Junction Street, the **George** (1845) and **Jolly Collier** (1845) both survive. The **Fountain** in Albion Street (1850-2008) was sometimes known as the Pretty Fleur. In 1913, a young soldier, Thomas Fletcher, shot himself here and accidently killed his sweetheart, Lily Wharton, the landlord's daughter. He was later hanged at Worcester.

So, although Oldbury has lost most of its historic pubs, a few remain to serve a wide range of excellent beers. Finally, remember that you can't leave Oldbury town centre without crossing water – there are plenty of canals!

OLD HILL

Old Hill is a long-established settlement along the turnpike road from Dudley to Halesowen. The Industrial Revolution saw the town expand, with collieries, brickworks, sawmills and iron and steel foundries, along with its local trades of nailmaking and Eliza Tinsley's chainmaking factory. All this heavy industry needed pubs for workers to quench their thirsts and, by 1901, there were more than 50 pubs and beerhouses serving a population of 11,600. Now, barely a handful remain.

Old Hill was originally centred at The Cross, where one of the town's oldest pubs was situated. Dating from before 1820, **Ye Olde Cross** was first kept by the Tromans family until 1865 and later by Edward Ted Finch (1945-1972). It was a coaching inn, with a fine bowling green, and a meeting place for nailers and brickmakers. One of its more infamous patrons was Jed Black, the master of the local workhouse. In 1983, it reopened as Samuel's, but was destroyed by fire in the late 1990s. On the opposite corner, the **Royal Exchange** (1851) was known locally as the Glasshouse, and was kept by Harry and Ann Cooksey from 1887-1927, but was gone by 1987.

Another venerable tavern was the **Gate Hangs Well** in Halesowen Road. Originally a home-brew pub first licensed in 1829, it was kept by Horatio James and his family until 1916, before being taken over by Darby's (West Bromwich) Brewery in 1941. It was demolished in 1990. The **Beehive** was a popular beerhouse from 1881, which became an off-licence in 1919 and later a shop. Further down was the **George Hotel** (1879), a popular Banks's pub, which had a jazz theme when it was renamed Satchmo's in 1998. It then became a shop in 2012. A few doors away, the **Spring Meadow** (1890) has recently been refurbished and reopened in 2021. William Foley and his family kept the **White Swan** from 1867-1924 and brewed beer at their Swan Brewery, but it was demolished in 1965. Opposite is **Wheelie Thirsty,** Fixed Wheel Brewery's new micro-pub, opened in 2019.

In Garratts Lane, the **Fox Hunt** (1841) was originally the Fox & Hounds, a home-brew pub, popular with miners and pigeon fanciers, but converted into housing in 2010. Nearby, Albert Sidaway kept the **Duke William** (1841-1990) for many years, which was the HQ of Old Hill Pigeon Club. Until 1912, he also kept and brewed beer at the **British Oak** (1851-1960), as did Joseph Foley in the 1890s at the **Queen's Head** (1871-1965).

In Station Road, the **Crown Inn** was previously a farmhouse owned by the Wright family, and was first licensed in 1834. Originally a home-brew pub kept by Lucy Tibbetts and Jeremiah Laister, it was a popular venue for cockfighting and local miners. Opposite, Samuel Darby and Eliza Gadd kept and brewed at the **Horseshoe** from 1849-1905, but it closed in 1996. Along Waterfall Lane, the **Three Furnaces** was originally the home of Simeon Bennett, the owner of Bennett's Brickworks, and became a home-brew pub in 1861. In 1896, landlord John Foley was unfortunately killed by a train when he fell from the platform at Handsworth station. It had a fishing club which used the nearby mines pool, but became a house again in 2014. Further along Waterfall Lane is the **Waterfall,** originally the Vine from 1841 and then variously the Oak, Royal Oak or Oak Tree. It was renamed the Waterfall in 1987, bought by Holden's (Dudley) Brewery in 2004 – it remains a popular real ale tavern.

Along Station Road, the **Boat** existed in 1831 and was a Hanson's (Dudley) canalside pub, popular with boatmen, but was converted into housing in 2015. Further along Station Road and approached by a hump-back canal bridge, was the **Sportsman & Railway.** Originally the farmhouse of Slack Hillock Farm, it was first licensed in 1852 as the Sportsman. In 1913, it was renamed the Sportsman & Railway when it was bought by George "Abner" Harris, a footballer who played for Aston Villa and West Bromwich Albion (1899-1908). It remained in the Harris family until 1968, when it was renamed the **Wharf** by Premier Ales (Stourbridge) in 1985. It closed in 2005 and was later demolished after fire damage.

In the back streets of Old Hill, a surprising survivor is the **Riddins Tavern** (1870), a popular Banks's pub which originally overlooked Riddings Colliery. Nearby, the **Blue Ball** (1857-2008) served local factory workers, and the **Pack Horse** (1827-1965) was a home-brew pub where John Tibbetts brewed. In Elbow Street, the **King's Head** (1861-1972) was known locally as Rasher's, recalling landlord Ted Slater who kept pigs and goats in the back yard. The **Old Engine** existed in Waggon Street before 1857 and lasted until 1939. In Cherry Orchard, the **Pear Tree** (1860-1968) was known locally as Freddie's, after long-serving landlord Wilfrid Freddie Pritchard. It featured in Philip Donnellan's classic 1958 BBC TV documentary, *Joe, the Chainmaker*. Nearby were the **Prince of Wales** (1860-2014), the **Cherry Orchard** (1855-1965) and the **Old House at Home** (1861-1958), all swept away in the redevelopment of the area. The **Old Lion Inn** (1830) was an ancient inn overlooking Old Lion Colliery, but it was gone by 1912.

On the approaches to Old Hill, **Cooksey's Hotel** was originally the town's court house and police station before becoming a pub in 1850. It was named after the Cooksey family who owned and ran it until 1878, and was popular with colliery workers and pigeon fanciers. It was later bought by Hanson's (Dudley), but was demolished in 2007. In the 1930s, it was kept by Benjamin Timmington, father of local footballer, David, who played for Halesowen Town and West Bromwich Albion in the 1960s. Nearby, at the **Castle** (1871), landlord John Ashcroft was known to lift cast iron tables with his teeth in the 1950s, but it was replaced by housing in 2001. The Pig & Whistle (1841) became the **Victoria Hotel** (or Vic) in 1901, and was a popular venue for boxing matches, with its own gym, before being demolished in 2004.

On the southern side of town in Halesowen Road, the **Rose & Crown** existed before 1833. In 1903, it was kept by Thomas Edge, whose son helped to design the first Austin 7 motorcar. It was rebuilt in the 1920s and was converted into housing in 2015. In 1869, the **Haden Cross** also had a butcher's shop, slaughterhouse and malthouse. It features as Billy Mucklow's HQ in Thomas Dearn's recent 1950s based gangster novel, *Once Upon a Time in the Black Country*, and survives as a popular real ale pub after a successful campaign to save it in 2015.

Along Reddal Hill Road, Jeremiah Laister had his Fox Oak Brewery at the **Waggon & Horses** in the 1840s. In 2018, it became an Ostler's Ale House, based on the micro-brewery at Harborne, and is now a popular weekend music venue. Other historic pubs included the **Why Not** (1865-1990), **Rose & Crown** (1841-1965) and **Bridge** (1870-1959). In Powke Lane, Charles Price brewed beer at the **Neptune** (1861-2006), whilst the **White Lion** (1850-1990) was home to brewers Thomas and Emily Cole; both pubs are now café/takeaways.

So, although Old Hill has lost most of its most historic pubs, a few remain to serve a wide range of excellent beers.

OLDSWINFORD

Oldswinford was originally an ancient parish and manor covering most of Stourbridge. Its name derives from *swine ford*, a crossing point of the nearby Swin brook. It's now a largely residential suburb of Stourbridge, but has several historic buildings, including Old Swinford Hospital, founded in 1667, as well as a few old pubs.

One of the focal points of Oldswinford is the crossroads of Hagley Road, Heath Lane and Glasshouse Hill. Prominent on the corner is the **Cross**, first licensed in 1828. Before it was taken over by Mitchells & Butlers, it was a home-brew pub, where Philip, George and Isabel Perrins and James Jeffries brewed their own beer until 1942. Other long-serving licensees included Kenneth and Beatrice Fowler (1958-1979). Just to the north of the crossroads was the **Waterloo**, first licensed in 1828, with a bowling green, but closed in the 1940s.

Just to the south lies the **Bird in Hand**, which stands on the site of an old building dating back to 1699, when Edward White, a baker, leased a cottage, shop and stable from the Blue Coat Hospital School. In 1832, Job Coley bought the property for £340 and opened a beerhouse called the Lion Inn, which he kept with his son, Richard, until 1871. In 1861, it was renamed the Old House at Home and was sold to Charles Hill for £525 in 1886. He also owned a shoe warehouse and was an enthusiastic pigeon flier. The pub was rebuilt as the Bird in Hand in 1896, with a small brewery at the rear, which operated until 1926, along with a bowling green and tiled pigeon house. In April 1926, it was bought by Batham's (Brierley Hill) for £2,000 and kept by Daniel Batham until 1932. Thomas and Mary Southall kept the pub until 1960, during which time it was sold to Wolverhampton & Dudley Breweries. By an ironic twist of fate, it was bought back by Batham's in 2019, saving it from replacement by a supermarket. The pub retains several historic interior and exterior features, and remains one of the iconic Batham's pubs.

Returning to Glasshouse Hill, on the corner of Redhill Road was the **Labour in Vain** (1845), remembered for its inn sign. Once a Hanson's (Dudley) pub, it was popular with railway workers, but closed in 2012. Opposite the entrance to Stourbridge Junction station is the **Seven Stars**, originally dating from 1845, but rebuilt as a flagship Edwardian pub for Mitchells & Butlers in 1907. It retains its etched windows, ornate glazed tiles, bar counter and mirrored bar back, fully justifying its Grade II listing. At one time, it was known locally as the Rat Hole, frequented by "loose women" and "men of a fast turn of mind". More recently, its Blues Club hosted the early career of rock legend, Robert Plant, and it's now a popular Black Country Ales' pub (see below).

Along Heath Lane is the **Shrubbery Cottage** (1881), acquired by William Butler (Wolverhampton) in 1930 and by Holden's (Dudley) in 1986. Known locally as The Shrub, popular landlord Leonard Bristow (1965-1978) brought it to life as a music venue for local groups, and it remains a popular community pub (see below). Further along Heath Lane was the **Village Tavern** (1903), a Dare's (Birmingham) pub, which closed in 1940.

Not far from the entrance of Mary Stevens Park is the **Plough & Harrow**, opened in the 1840s as a home-brew pub for a century where Henrietta Moorcroft brewed her own beer. It passed to Holt's (Birmingham) in 1940 and eventually to Ansell's, before becoming a Holt, Plant & Deakin pub in 1988. It retains some features of this brewery. It's now one of Dave Craddock's (Stourbridge) Brewery pubs.

On the corner of South Road is the **Old White Horse**, originally dating from 1829 and kept by the Parkes family until 1921. It was later rebuilt and is now a "Sizzling" pub. Near the corner of Hagley Road was the **Star & Garter**, another historic pub dating from 1829 and previously the home of surgeon Dr Downing. In 1990, it became a wine bar, offices and convenience store.

In Cherry Street, the **New Inn** (1881) is a popular traditional two-room local, which was another Holt, Plant & Deakin pub in the 1980s. On the corner of South Road and The Broadway, is the **Gigmill,** originally dated from 1860, it was rebuilt in 1963 and refurbished in 2002 at a cost of £260,000. Incidentally, its name refers to a type of textile machine used to produce the nap on cloth and flannelette.

Travelling south along Hagley Road, we'd soon come to the **Swan,** a Davenport's (Birmingham) pub dating from 1860. In the early years, it was used for meetings of nailmakers, but became The Retreat restaurant in 1997. On the corner of Rectory Road is the **Crabmill,** once one of Flower's (Stratford-on-Avon) pubs. It was originally built in 1828, but in 1970, the pub moved across the road to Thornleigh, the late 19th century home of W. Boulton (glassmaker) and Ernest Lunt (coal merchant). In 1990, it was renamed Oldswinford Lodge, but returned as the Crabmill after being refurbished in 2008. Its name refers to the machinery used for pressing crab apples (there was a cider mill nearby in Farlands Road). But it's also known to be haunted by an elderly gentleman, dressed in a black suit and top hat, believed to be Doctor Kirkpatrick, who used to live here and was in charge of the military hospital at Wordsley during the First World War.

Further along Hagley Road is the **Crown,** dating from 1862. It was once owned by Thomas Plant's Brewery (Netherton) and passed to Ansell's in 1956. Often remembered for licensees Dorothy and William Homes (1956-1969), it regularly raises funds for Mary Stevens Hospice, just opposite. In Pedmore, the **Foley Arms** originally dated from 1835, but was later rebuilt. In 1864 and 1867, landlord Jacob Burford was fined 16s 6d and £1 4s for having his pub open on a Sunday when it only had a six-day licence.

So, Oldswinford retains several interesting historic pubs, which are well worth visiting to sample a great range of beers. Long may they prosper!

Rock stars in Oldswinford

Some might find it difficult to believe that Oldswinford was the cradle of rock culture in Stourbridge. Several pubs were the hot-bed and venue for the early careers of many local rock bands and, in some cases, rock superstars! The **Seven Stars** is remembered for its popular Blues Club, where in 1963, a young Robert Plant, then aged 15 years old, made his first public performances, playing harmonica and singing with the Delta Blues Band and later with the Crawling King Snakes and Jess Roden's Shakedown Sound. This club was also the launching place for many West Midlands groups, including Sounds of Blue, which became Chicken Shack, with Stan Webb, Christine Perfect and Andy Sylvester. At the nearby **Shrubbery Cottage,** popular landlord, Leonard Bristow, made the pub home for many local rock bands, including Ned's Atomic Dustbin, Pop Will Eat Itself and the Wonder Stuff. Even Judas Priest played at Old Swinford Hospital School in 1970 and 1971!

PELSALL

I doubt whether many would say that **Pelsall** is in the Black Country, but with its collieries, ironworks, brickworks and other industries, it shares many similarities with Black Country towns. As a small village to the north of Walsall, it was first mentioned as Peolshalh in a charter of 994, on land given by the Heantune Monastery at Wolverhampton.

As the Industrial Revolution arrived, Pelsall became a mining village, with rich reserves of coal and fireclay, including the notorious Pelsall Hall Colliery, where 22 miners were left stranded underground when it flooded in 1872. Further growth came with the opening of the Wyrley and Essington Canal in 1797 and railway in 1849, when several ironworks and brickworks were established, including Pelsall Iron Works and Yorks Foundry. Over the years, around 20 pubs served the local community and a handful remain open today.

The centre of Pelsall is focused around the crossroads on Pelsall Common, which still provides a rural setting for the village. The **Queen's Hotel** dates from before 1869 and was often used for inquests. In 2003, it was briefly renamed the Block & Chopper, before returning as the Queen's (its original name) in 2007. Overlooking the common in Victoria Road is the **Railway**, dating back to 1855. In 1893, James Moore, stationmaster at Pelsall station was awarded a purse of gold at a supper given in honour of his retirement. The pub was kept by Austin and Eva Aspinall from 1904-1940 and by Thomas Tom Osbourne from 2007-2012.

Opposite the former Pelsall railway station in Station Road was the **Station,** built in 1860 as the Travellers Rest. In 1872, it was used for the inquest into the Pelsall Hall Colliery disaster, as well as for receiving the bodies and storing coffins; it closed in 1939. On the other side of the common, opposite St Michael and All Angels Church, was the **Old Kings Arms,** dating back to 1849, but closed in 1911. Nearby, Hall Lane is known to be haunted by ghostly miners from the colliery disaster.

At the southern end of Pelsall Common is Heath End, where the **Old Bush Inn** dated back to the 14th century as the Holly Bush, but it was rebuilt in 1890 when it was taken over by Showell's (Langley) Brewery. It was also used for miners' meetings and more recently it had a popular golfing society, before closing in 2015. At the end of Allens Lane, the **Red Cow** (1861) was known locally as the Letters, but was converted into housing by 2015.

At the northern end of the common was the **New Inn,** built in 1861, but closed by 1927. In 1917, landlord John Francis Peabody was awarded the Distinguished Conduct Medal (DCM) after displaying the greatest gallantry at the Battle of Hill 60, near Ypres. Close by, on the main road, the **Old House at Home** was originally built on the site of an abattoir in 1890. In the 1950s, it was rebuilt nearby and it still serves the local community.

Further along Norton Road, the Wyrley and Essington Canal provides a canalside setting for the **Royal Oak** (1849). Unfortunately, landlord Michael Hughes was found battered to death in the pub in April 2003, and it has since been renamed the Fingerpost, recalling the signpost at the junction with Wolverhampton Road. Opposite Moat Farm was the **White Lion Inn,** dating from before 1818 and later acquired by William Roberts' Station Brewery (Brownhills), but closed in 1943. Early landlords John Harrison and Alfred Cooper were farmers and, in 1939, licensee D. Nicholls had a miniature zoo here, with wild cats, monkeys, racoons, owls, wallabies and wombats.

Further towards Brownhills, the **Railway Colliery Hotel** (1857) was also alongside the canal, as was the **Jolly Collier,** dating from before 1818. This pub was popular with colliers and canal workers and was kept by Chatty Chapman, George Yates and by Bill and Olive Hopley for 20 years until it closed in 1982.

In Pelsall Wood, the **Forge Inn** (1861) was kept by home-brewer Richard Sherrett until 1881, but closed in 1911. Not far away, the **Free Trade Inn** dated from 1858, but was closed by 2007. Kept by James Fox and his family until 1912, it was well known for its New Concert Hall, which opened in 1865. Along Wolverhampton Road, farmer John Snape kept the **Swan Inn** (1818-2007) (see below).

In the 1890s, several pubs were granted an hour extension to their licences during the Pelsall Wakes. Highlights of the day featured wheelbarrow races, donkey and pony racing, "Swarming the Pole for a Leg of Mutton", running for geese, "two young women grinning through a collar to win a new gown", "two old women in a bag race", brass and string bands, dancing and other English sports. Sad to lose such merriment today!

The adventures of the King of Pelsall

In the 1850s, local farmer, John Snape, styled himself as the King of Pelsall. With his family, he kept the **Swan Inn** on Wolverhampton Road, opposite Pelsall Colliery, until 1871. This was an ancient inn, reputedly dating back to the 16th century, but rebuilt in the late 1930s and converted into a restaurant in 2007. When dealing with a dispute about access rights to a well in 1858, John Snape said he had *"often curbed the strong emotions of his breast when under the influence of nut-brown ale, but it was merely a question of time before he would strike a blow which would shake Pelsall to its very centre, and show his neighbours that he had more power than even lay in the breath of kings".* After he and his son had destroyed fences and gates around the well and assaulted the alleged owner, Joseph Cooper, he was accosted by a policeman. He replied, *"I don't care for any policeman, I have plenty of money and care for no man. I am the King of Pelsall and don't care for you or your masters"*. In order to show that a *"King cannot swagger or get drunk like a beggar"*, the magistrates fined him 5s with costs.

Later that year, the King of Pelsall was in trouble again. He sallied from the Swan Inn in his cart and drove to Norton Canes without reins on the horse. He was accosted by a policeman and eventually fined 10s. He was also fined 10s for serving three short measures in his pub. In 1862, the "King" was trying to claim the fishing rights to a nearby canal. When the owner objected, the monarch of Pelsall came to grief when he was ignominiously precipitated into the water, costing him 5s in damages.

In 1863, he was accused of being drunk and disorderly at a housewarming party in the Railway Tavern. After the police threw him out, he was fined 40s with costs and £3 with costs for assaulting the policeman. A year later, he assaulted his son-in-law Eli Ball and James Fox, and was fined 5s with costs. He assaulted James Fox again in 1865 after an acrimonious dispute about a harmonium at the opening of Mr Fox's New Music Hall at the Free Trade Inn, and was fined 20s with costs. He even assaulted James' 12-year-old daughter, Hannah, and her aunt, Mary Boyden, and was fined 10s with costs for each case.

PENSNETT

Pensnett was once at the heart of an extensive area of common land known as Pensnett Chase, mainly owned by the Earl of Dudley and used for grazing and hunting. During the 19th century, the Industrial Revolution began to change the face of Pensnett, with coal and fireclay mines, brickworks, iron and steel factories, canals and mineral railways. All this heavy industry was thirsty work and, over the years, around 40 pubs served the area.

Surrounded by collieries, canals and mineral railways, the settlement pattern of Pensnett falls into several distinct areas. The village first started to develop on the southern side of High Street, opposite St Mark's Church – the iconic "Cathedral of the Black Country" – on the slopes of Barrow Hill and consecrated in 1849. On the corner of Bell Street was the **Lion Hotel,** originally licensed before 1856 and rebuilt nearby in 1965. Formerly a home-brew pub, it became a Hanson's (Dudley) house in 1934, when William and Eliza Bagott kept it for almost 20 years. Renamed Poets Corner in 2003, it closed in 2011 and was replaced by a supermarket.

On the corner of Church Street, the **Fox & Grapes** originally dated from 1834, but was rebuilt in 1932. Another former home-brew inn, it passed to Ansell's (Birmingham), became a Holt, Plant & Deakin pub in 1984 and was acquired by Batham's (Brierley Hill) in 1999.

In the back streets was the **Rifle Inn** in Church Street, dating from before 1871 and recalling the nearby rifle range on Barrow Hill, but it closed in 1939. Nearby in Bell Street was the **Bell** (1871-1976), kept by Lily Woodfield for over 25 years until 1966 and popular with pigeon fanciers. A few doors away, the **Holly Bush** (1870) was originally owned by the Earl of Dudley and acquired by Batham's in 1965, but it was closed and demolished in 1999.

In Chapel Street, the **Reindeer** (1854) was a popular home-brew pub until it closed in 1909. On the corner of Queen Street, the **Old Swan** (1854) was converted into flats in 1997, opposite the **Samson & Lion,** a former Simpkiss (Brierley Hill) pub dating from 1845, rebuilt in 1936 and converted into flats by 1995.

Continuing along High Street, on the corner of Swan Street was the **Swan,** a historic pub dating back to 1854. It was used for meetings of freeholders to implement the provisions of the Pensnett Chase Enclosure Act in 1857. But in 1870, landlord Samuel Page committed suicide by hanging himself from the bedpost after he became bankrupt. It was later rebuilt and kept by landlady Muriel Middleton for over 20 years until 1977, before becoming the local Liberal Club.

At the junction with Commonside is the distinctive **High Oak,** originally a home-brew pub dating from 1835 and rebuilt in 1933. It was briefly renamed Roost in 2008, but returned as the High Oak in 2011.

Further along High Street, on the corner of Tansey Green Road, was the **Four Furnaces** (1834), where Heber and Sarah Hubbold brewed their own beer until 1899. It is now a popular fish and chip shop. Next door is a new micro-bar, **Pens Ale,** opened in 2021. At the far end of High Street is the **Talbot,** dating from 1845 and renamed the **Lenches Bridge** in 2012, recalling the original licensees and the adjoining canal bridge.

Tansey Green was a small colliers' hamlet with its own pubs, shops and brickworks, including the aptly named **Brickmakers Arms** (1861-1997). In 1912, a chapel behind the pub became one of the first cinemas in the Black Country, which was later used as a sewing factory at the outbreak of war. Nearer the brickworks was the **Tansey Green Arms,** a home-brew pub dating from 1822, but gone by 1891.

Returning to Commonside, on the corner of Bradley Street was the **Fountain** (1865), which became a Working Men's Club in 1925. On the corner of Broad Street, Ernest and Annie Ward kept the **Albion** (1856) for over 25 years until 1958, but it was converted into housing in 1998.

Popular with local miners, on Sunday nights local women hired a room here and sang hymns enthusiastically!

Further along Broad Street was the **Royal Oak** (1870), a former Showell's Brewery (Langley) pub, but closed by 1940. The **Queen's Head** (1845), a Banks's pub, was well-placed on the corner of Queen Street, but was demolished in 2010. In 1939, local brewer, Tommy Booth, built the Corbyns Hall Brewery nearby in Tiled House Lane, with a tied estate of 10 pubs. It was sold when he died in 1954 and later demolished.

On the corner of Bromley, the **King's Head Inn** (1834) was kept by James Parfitt and his son from 1883-1935, but it was damaged by fire in 2003 and later replaced by a supermarket. Along the lane to Bromley, the **Elephant & Castle** (1835) was originally a home-brew pub, but was rebuilt in 1939 and bought by Holden's (Dudley) in 1983 for £7,566. It closed in 2002 and is now a day nursery. Across the road, the **Rose & Crown,** a Hanson's pub dating from 1845, was the meeting place of the Cork Club and Dreadnought FC, but was demolished in 1988. In the heart of Bromley Village, the **Commercial Inn** and **Jolly Collier** both dated from 1864, but were closed or demolished by 2007.

Continuing along Commonside, the **Crown Inn** (1862) was a former home-brew pub, later acquired by Hanson's. It was known locally as the Crown in the 'ole, or Sammy's after long-serving landlords, Samuel Porter (1870s) and Sammy Brooks (1950s). Bromley Ironworks FC changed here and it had a popular pigeon fanciers club, but was converted into flats in 1997. A few doors away was the **Fish Inn** (1845), another Hanson's pub, popular with pigeon fanciers and Bromley FC's headquarters before being demolished in 2010.

There were several old pubs around Brockmoor Bridge, where the road crosses an arm of the Stourbridge Canal leading to Grove Pool and Fens Pool. The **Bull's Head** was probably the oldest pub around here, originally dating back to before 1818. It was once owned by the local canal company, had stables, and its early landlords were boaters at Brockmoor Wharf. It was later rebuilt, briefly renamed Brewsters (1985), but resumed as the Bull's Head in 1993, before being converted into flats in 2012. Opposite Hay Wharf was the **Shinglers Arms** (1845-1907), a home-brew pub kept for many years by John and Thomas Holloway. Incidentally, its name recalled a shingler, who worked with wrought iron. The **Cross** dated from 1829, but its licence was not renewed in 1921 because there were too many pubs in the area!

Much of old Pensnett was wiped away when new housing and industrial estates were built between 1920-1980. Out of the 40 or so pubs in the area, most have been demolished or converted into other uses, and nowadays just three survive. Long may they prosper!

QUARRY BANK

It's difficult to believe that **Quarry Bank** was once a very rural place, surrounded by farmland, with smallholdings and a few nailmakers. It grew up around the crossroads close to the Blue Ball pub, where the bank is crossed by the old Dudley-Worcester Saltway turnpike, and extended down the High Street in the 19th century. The Industrial Revolution began here in 1610, when Dud Dudley established his wrought iron foundry at Cradley Forge, and Quarry Bank began to grow as nailmakers and colliers settled here. It later became associated with hollow-ware, including fabricating, welding, galvanising and enamelling, making bins, buckets, teapots and bread bins, along with spades, shovels, chains and anchors. Others worked in the local collieries, claypits and brickworks.

Quarry Bank always enjoyed its independence as a separate urban district from 1894, before being amalgamated with Brierley Hill in 1934 and later with Dudley Borough Council in 1966 and 1974. The workers' thirsts were catered for by many local breweries, pubs and beerhouses. Over the years, around 40 pubs served Quarry Bank, although barely a handful remain today.

Starting at the crossroads, the **Blue Ball** was one of the oldest pubs in Quarry Bank, first licensed in 1829, but rebuilt in 1960 and converted into a restaurant in 2003. It was first owned by Jesse Billingham, but was kept for some years by Thomas Wood, a glass engraver who often displayed his collection of insects, birds, paintings and curiosities in the pub. He also brewed his own beer here, until it passed to Netherton Brewery, Atkinson's (Birmingham), Hanson's (Dudley) and Whitbread, before being bought by Jeff Billingham in 1986. He also collected ties, but was he related to the original owner?

Turning into Old High Street, we'd soon come to the **Sun Inn,** a former home-brew and North Worcestershire Brewery pub. It was first known as the Happy Return in 1868, but was rebuilt in the 1930s and demolished in 2008. Jesse Billingham also owned the **Royal Oak,** on the corner of Oak Street, dating from 1834, and kept it with Edward, Joseph and Elizabeth Paskin until it became an Atkinson's pub in 1897. It's remembered for its long bar and sweet smelling sawdust on the floor, along with the bread, cheese and snuff on the counter. It was sold at auction in 1929 for £2,500, but was replaced by modern buildings in the 1980s.

We'd soon come to Christ Church, constructed of distinctive local refractory bricks in 1847. Opposite is the **Church Tavern,** first licensed in 1854, when local builder, Daniel Williams, was in charge. In 1866, landlord Nebo Cartwright was not only an innkeeper, but also a cordwainer (shoemaker), but he became bankrupt. In 1884, the pub passed to William Showell's Crosswells Brewery (Langley), and later to Ansell's (Birmingham). In the 1890s, landlord Levi Willetts kept the pub when it was a popular tap for Bloomers chainmakers. Despite its proximity to the church, it was frequently used for gambling, and in 1919, landlord David Eli Brooks was charged for holding an illegal lottery and fined £10. In 1984, it became one of Holt, Plant & Deakin's branded pubs, based on their small brewery at Langley. Variously known as the Long Pull, Three Shovels and Nailmaker, it has now reverted to its original name. Incidentally, the long-pull refers to the practice in pubs of serving more than the requested measure of beer. In some cases, landlords were giving double measures of beer, which led to an agreement to restrict the long-pull to just 25% over-measure. Eventually, this practice was banned.

On the corner of Victoria Road was the **Vine,** first owned by the Astley family in 1857 and then becoming a local Home Brewery pub. Popular with pigeon fanciers, it was also the headquarters of Quarry Bank Celtic FC until the 1930s. The pub closed by 1940, but the distinctive red-brick building remains as a beauty salon.

In Victoria Road, we'd find the **Fountain Inn,** dating from 1864, sold at auction in 1933 for £2,500 and briefly owned by Batham's (Brierley Hill). It closed in 2009 and was converted into flats. In 1906, a notorious murder took place in the cottage behind this pub, when Joseph Jones hit his son-in-law, Edmund Clarke, with a poker and then cut his throat (see below).

Around the corner was the **Sheffield Inn,** a popular local home-brew pub dating from 1872, and kept by the Mobberley and Dunn families until it closed in 1956. Not far away was the **Birch Coppice,** a modern pub which closed in 2010. Back on High Street, another famous murder took place on the street outside the **New Inn** (1845). In 1856, David Taylor, a local horse-nailmaker, was killed by Joseph Chivers after a fight. The inquest was held at the Royal Oak, just up the road, and he was later found guilty of manslaughter and given 15 years transportation. The pub closed in 2011 and was converted into housing. Walking down the steep hill past the school, we'd come to the **Queen's Head,** a former home-brew pub dating from 1845, but closed and demolished in the late 1970s. Local boxer, Tommy Cartwright, was born here in 1924, when Arthur and Rose Bucknall kept the pub.

New Street was once a busy commercial street, where the first Daniel Batham, then a nailmaker, lived from 1825. On the corner of Queen Street was the **True Briton**, dating from 1868, but closed by 1913. A few doors away is the **White Horse,** built in 1851, with its popular bowling green. It was threatened with closure after a fire in 2005, but thankfully the pub was reopened and became a popular real ale hostelry.

Returning to High Street, on the corner of Rose Hill was the **Elephant & Castle,** another former Home Brewery pub dating from 1856. From 1919, it was owned by Daniel Batham's brother, Roland, who brewed here until Batham's bought the pub in 1940. It closed in 1962 and became a motorcycle shop. Almost opposite was the **Three Horseshoes** (1858), home to Quarry Bank Rangers FC in the 1940s, but replaced by houses in 1998.

Continuing down the road, we'd come to Cradley Forge, where the **Waggon & Horses,** originally dating from 1849, remains as a popular local pub. In the early days, dog fights were popular here, but it was rebuilt in the 1890s and sold by auction in 1929 for £2,900. Nearby was the **Pilgrim's Cottage,** another former Home Brewery pub, dating from 1872, but closed by 1927.

In the crowded back streets of Quarry Bank there were two breweries. Brewing at Evers Street was first mentioned in Matthew Batham's will of 1857, when the **Swan Brewery** was established here. It was once part-owned by Joel Batham, but from 1903 was run by Joseph Paskin Simpkiss, a member of another local brewing family. He established the **Home Brewery** here and, at its height, it brewed over 300 barrels of beer a week, owned over 30 pubs and had three dray horses named Sammy, Prince and Darky. In 1916, J.P. Simpkiss lost control of the brewery after a lawsuit, but it continued under William Clewes until 1921 and was demolished in 1959. In East Street, George Nock established **Nock's Brewery** in the 1920s, but it was taken over with its four pubs by Mitchells & Butlers in 1942 and closed by 1950.

From 1878-1883, George Nock kept the **Red Lion** (Maughan Street) dating from 1871, where in the early 1900s, blind Henry Griffiths would often lend a hand behind the bar. He not only served beer and spirits, but also changed the barrels quicker than the landlord. He even played darts, when he was placed on the mark and advised to go up or down a bit, like in the Golden Shot! He was also a formidable draughts player, using a specially made draughts board with holes to fit the pegs of the draughts. He often paraded the streets as Quarry Bank's town crier, clanging his bell, along with his dog who collected money in his panniers. Henry was something of a comedian, when tuning a piano he would ask for a candle to be lit so that he could inspect an intricate part of the mechanism (even though he was totally blind!). He died in 1930 after lighting many a dark corner, but never seeing the light of day himself!

After 1883, George Nock kept the **Cottage in the Bower,** dating from 1854, where he issued tokens, but he left in 1891 to take on the **Hope & Anchor** (1854) down the hill in Bower Lane, and his former pub was closed by 1987. Interestingly, Roland Batham kept the Cottage in the Bower after he married Matilda Nock in 1912, before he took on the Elephant Castle in High Street. The Hope & Anchor was briefly renamed Pot o' Beer before closing in the early 1990s.

On the western side of Quarry Bank in Mount Pleasant is the **Brickmaker's Arms,** dating from 1849 and known locally as the Brick. Early landlords, Alfred Dunn and Joseph Hollis brewed their own beer here from 1899-1947. On the corner of Amblecote Road is the modern **Corn Exchange,** built by Tony Whittaker on the site of an old malthouse. It was opened by Bill Maynard in 1983 as the Nine Locks & Chainmaker and renamed in 1992. Further along Amblecote Road is the **Roebuck,** another former Holt, Plant & Deakin pub, originally dating from 1871, but rebuilt in 1930.

Along Thorns Road is the **Thorns** (now Koyla Kitchen), whilst the new **Round Oak** in Pedmore Road opened in 1999. Further along Pedmore Road was the **Robin Hood,** dating from 1857 and originally known as the Little John, with its pleasure gardens, bowling green and theatre.

In the mid 1950s, a concert hall was built here, which became the Citizens Theatre in 1970, famous for its Black Country Night Outs and Mike Hamblett's Robin R'n'B club. The pub was closed in June 2003, damaged by fire in 2004, demolished a year later and is now incorporated into the Merry Hill complex.

So, of the 40 or so pubs originally serving Quarry Bank, just seven survive, but they include a handful of popular local pubs serving a great variety of ales for everyone to enjoy!

A murder most foul in Quarry Bank

Edmund Clarke, a bachelor of the parish, was married at Christ Church, Quarry Bank in 1900 to his sweetheart, a local girl, Ethel Jones.

Edmund was born into a family of chainmakers, he grew up in the Quarry Bank area. But Edmund did not want to follow in his father's footsteps as a chainmaker; he had ambitions for greater things and a work ethic to match, and so he sought another career path to fulfil his ambitions.

In the same year that he married Ethel, Edmund made two other momentous decisions. The first was to purchase, in partnership with his brother, a horse and a heavy cart and they began a business as hauliers. The second decision was to move into the house of Joseph Jones, his father-in-law, who lived at 18 Victoria Road, Quarry Bank.

Joseph Jones was reported to be a hard-working man, but unlike Edmund, he also "played hard", involving himself in heavy drinking sessions and gambling. He had lost his wife some years earlier, and had resorted to the bottle for solace at his loss. Then, in 1902, he lost his job and dived deeper into the bottle. Out of work and with limited finances, it wasn't long before he ran out of beer money.

However, being a somewhat prudent man and dreading ending up in the workhouse, he had realised it was important to have some security for a rainy day. That is why, as a younger man, he had worked hard and scrimped and saved to buy the house he now lived in and shared with his daughter Ethel and son-in-law Edmund.

Out of cash and with no work prospects, Joseph decided that he would have to sell his house to keep himself from the workhouse and he agreed to sell to Edmund. It appears that, for a few years at least, Joseph was able to manage his life style.

But 1906 must have been a particularly bad year, money-wise, as Joseph was soon in financial trouble again. He was forced to ask his son-in-law for beer money, much to his own displeasure, and it became a continual source of rows between the two men. Neighbours were said to have had great sympathy for the young Edmund and told of Joseph's ongoing complaints about Edmund and being heard saying, "I'd sooner swing than die in the work house".

On 1st December 1906, Edmund had ferried local football supporters in his horse and cart to a match and had returned home to relax. Ethel had gone out shopping with the children and when they returned later, they were greeted with a scene of great horror as Edmund lay dead on the sofa, covered in blood and with his throat cut from ear to ear. Joseph had hit his son-in-law, Edmund Clarke, with a poker and then cut his throat.

He surrendered himself to the local police and admitted to the murder of Edmund. He was charged with "wilful murder" and remanded in Winson Green Prison, before being sent for trial in Stafford. The verdict was of no surprise and, in March 1906, Joseph was condemned to death by hanging. He was hanged a few months later after an appeal by his defence lawyers was refused. And all this happened in a cottage behind the **Fountain Inn** in Victoria Road!

SEDGLEY & WOODSETTON

Sedgley dates back to Anglo-Saxon times as *Secgesleage,* referring to Secges' woodland estate, and is one of nine villages making up the ancient Manor of Sedgley, which also covers Coseley, Gornal and Woodsetton. It lies on the old turnpike road from Dudley-Wolverhampton along an elevated ridge line, with Sedgley Beacon (777ft) offering an excellent vantage point over the Black Country. Originally a farming settlement, the centre of the town focused on the Bull Ring, with its courthouse, bull-baiting and dancing bear.

The Industrial Revolution brought coal and limestone mining, brickworks, claypits and iron and steelmaking, adding to the local nailmaking trade. In fact, Eliza Tinsley, owner of the well-known nail and chainmaking factory in Old Hill, was born here in 1839 and lived at The Limes. All this heavy industry was thirsty work, and by 1901, there were over 200 pubs serving the local workers and expanding population of over 38,000 in the wider Sedgley Manor area. Of the 30 or so pubs in and around Sedgley town centre, barely a handful remain today.

Many of Sedgley's oldest inns were grouped around the Bull Ring. The **Court House** had its roots in a medieval building originally named the Dudley Arms and owned by the Earl of Dudley. First licensed as a public house in 1803, and kept by Michael Ebery and his family, it was the venue for the manorial court until 1925 and was used for meetings and dinners. It's a listed building (Grade II), with tunnels leading to nearby All Saints' Church and the Red Lion, which housed the town jail. It was subject to major refurbishment in 2000, but is now an Indian restaurant.

On the opposite side of the Bull Ring is the **Red Lion,** dating from 1818. It was originally a coaching inn, where stagecoaches (with names like Criterion, Bang up and Everlasting) pulled into its yard on their way to Dudley, Wolverhampton and Worcester. Until 1913, the Court Leet met here, as did nailmakers and local farmers, and Sedgley Rovers FC changed here for football matches. Originally a home-brew pub where John, George and Sarah Jenkins brewed, the ladies toilet was reputedly haunted.

On the opposite side of the roundabout, Sedgley's first super cinema, the **Clifton,** was opened in 1937, named after Captain Sidney Clift, the man who brought cinemas to the Black Country. It later became a bingo hall and was converted into a Wetherspoon's pub in 1998, and the cinema projectors are still believed to exist in the booth upstairs. It's even haunted by a little girl who runs around the kitchen!

At the top end of the Bull Ring was the **Pig & Whistle,** dating from 1828. In 1921, it was the HQ of the National Federation of Discharged and Demobilised Sailors and Soldiers. Popular with nailmakers, it was haunted by Old Short, the Moneyman, but was converted into houses in 1933.

In Dudley Street, the **White Horse** (1859) was originally a home-brew house owned by Benjamin Stanley and Joseph York, and remains a popular, lively pub. At the junction of High Holborn and Tipton Street, the **Grand Junction** dated from the 1840s. Built of Gornal stone, some say it was named after George Stephenson's Grand Junction Railway, but this is several miles away. In the early days, it was used for inquests, was kept by Robert and Elise Turley from 1927-1941, and was a popular drop-off point for the trams and buses. However, it was converted into a dental surgery in 2006.

Along High Street, the **Crown** was first licensed in 1845 and was the HQ of Sedgley Cycling Club from 1899-1903. It was rebuilt on the opposite side of the road in 1946 and remains today, complete with the ghost of Bob Foster, a previous landlord. Further along High Street is the **Mount Pleasant** (1851), with its mock Tudor-style frontage. Known locally as The Stump, it stood on the drover's road from Wales to the Black Country, where sheep were driven past the door and shepherds paused for refreshment. It became a Holt, Plant & Deakin pub in 1984 and, in 2005, was taken over by Philip Bellfield who used to brew at the Britannia in Upper Gornal.

Opposite the church at the top of Gospel End Street, the **Swan** was first licensed in 1818 and is another listed building (Grade II). It was popular for meetings and dinners and was remembered for the robbery of Hadley Greaves, a female impersonator, in 1928. Early landlord, Thomas Sheldon, helped to invent the first hand-made steel pen nib, whilst a later landlord, George Mills (1912-1952) was an Alderman, JP and member of Sedgley Urban District Council for 28 years, including its chairman in the 1930s. Close to the junction with Vicar Street, the **Old Bush** (1828) was demolished in 1925.

Opposite was the **Seven Stars,** a home-brew house dating from 1841, also in the hands of the Sheldon family until 1898, but it was converted into a house in 1962. A new pub with the same name was built further down Gospel End Road on the site of Hanson's malthouse. In 2015, it survived the threat of closure and replacement with a supermarket. In Gospel End Village, the **Summer House** dates from 1845, was kept by Horace Hancox from 1948-1977, and is well known for its Christmas decorations.

In Bilston Street, the **Bull's Head** is another venerable home-brew pub dating from 1794 (listed Grade II), and acquired by Holden's (Dudley) in 1984. Further along Bilston Street, the **White Lion** was first licensed in 1818, and may date back to the Civil War. It was not only popular for bagatelle, but also the HQ of Sedgley White Lions FC. It was kept by the Baker family until 1858, but unfortunately, landlord Alfred Caswell was found to be hanged in the smoke room in 1900. It is also said to be haunted by a Royalist Cavalier in full uniform and Anne, the wife of a former landlord, who often enjoys a shot of gin. Current owners, Keith and Lyn Garbett, moved here in 2013 from the Jolly Crispin in Upper Gornal. Just opposite, we leave Sedgley's best for last – the **Beacon Hotel,** a famous local home-brew pub (see below).

Woodsetton lies between Sedgley and Dudley town centre on the main routes from Sedgley to Tipton. In the early days, it was mainly farmland, including the 70-acre High Arcal Farm, but there were also collieries and limestone pits nearby. A dozen or more pubs once served this area, but less than a handful now remain.

Along Tipton Road, the **Prince of Wales** dated from 1851 and was popular with pigeon fanciers. Landlord Steve James previously played for Manchester United FC, but the pub was demolished in 2014. On the corner with Park Road is the **Bramford Arms,** a modern pub opened in 1956 and previously named Garfield's and Fast Eddie's. There was another modern pub in Parkes Hall Road, the **Hillyfields,** but it closed in 2008. Not far away was the **British Queen** (1873), also once owned by the Earl of Dudley, but converted into housing in 2010.

In Brook Street, the **Cottage Spring** dates from 1871 and became a Black Country Ales' real ale pub in 2012. I can well remember calling there one Sunday afternoon and sitting on a stool at the bar. The landlady kindly asked me to move since "That's George's sayt and if he finds sumwun on it, he ain't half gonna be angry"!

Further along Brook Street, in Bourne Street, is the **Brook** (1835), kept by the Turley family until 1929. It used to be frequented by "pitmen, moulders, millmen and skilled artisans – a clay pipe smoking, hard-working, tough crowd, conversing jovially as they thirsted for Charley Turley's home-brewed ales". On Fridays, Charley would only allow the miners one pint before they went home and handed over their pay packets. Apparently, the beer was so strong that no-one ever drank more than three pints!

In Swan Village, the **Park Inn** in George Street is home to Holden's Hopden Brewery. The pub dates back to at least 1831 and has always been a popular home-brew pub. By the time Edwin, Lucy and Teddy Holden acquired it in 1920, the brewer was Harry Ossie Round, who brewed a strong, very dark mild ale twice a week, along with a special strong ale at Christmas. The pub was well-known for its roaring log fire in the taproom, free cheese sandwiches on a Friday night and clay pipe smoking competitions. The bowling green was Lucy Holden's pride and joy and always maintained in impeccable condition for the pub's bowling team. A sign of the times, and progress, was when Coseley UDC helped towards the cost of converting the two privies behind the pub into flush water closets! The pub remains as a popular and welcoming taphouse for Holden's Brewery.

In Sedgley Road, the **Summer House** (1859) was once kept by Edwin and Lucy Holden and was a popular prize-fighting pub and headquarters of Woodsetton Villa FC. But it closed in 2017 and was replaced by a supermarket. Not far away, the **Swan** (1854) was once a Showell's (Langley) pub, but was converted into offices in 2014. In the back streets of Regent Street, the **New Inn** (1871) was gone by 1913.

Further along Sedgley Road, the **Foxyards** dated from 1845 and was originally owned by the Earl of Dudley. Known locally as the Rag & Mop, in 1916, landlord Albert Hughes was fined £5 for neglecting to treat his horse. Later, in 1921, he was fined 20s for being drunk in charge of his horse and trap. Georgina the Gypsy and Val the Pegman once lived in a wigwam behind the pub, next to their parent's caravan, but Val died in 1930 aged 103, after being well known for selling pegs all around the Black Country. In 1994, the pub was actually renamed the Rag & Mop House, but was demolished in 2017.

So, although Sedgley and Woodsetton have lost some of their most historic inns and taverns, some of the old buildings survive and there are still plenty of beers to sample in the remaining pubs, with two local breweries supplying the beer.

A Beacon in Sedgley

The **Beacon Hotel** is a home-brew pub, first licensed in 1852, and is listed as a historic building (Grade II) and included in CAMRA's national inventory of historic pubs. It's an unspoilt four-room pub with an unusual glazed bar servery with hatches, and a mid-Victorian tower brewery at the rear. The pub was originally established by Abraham Carter and kept by him and his wife, Nancy Ann, until she died in 1890. It was later owned by John and Ellen Baker until 1910, when James Fellows was brewing beer here. In 1920, the pub and brewery were put up for auction and bought by Sarah Hughes in 1921. At that time, James Fellows was the brewer until 1924, followed by Alfred Hughes.

Sarah Hughes died in 1951, but brewing continued with Sarah's grandson, John Hughes until 1958. In 1984 John decided to restart brewing using the original brewing equipment, assisted by Andy Brough and later Martyn Powell. In 1987, he launched the famous Sarah Hughes' Dark Ruby Mild, along with Pale Amber, Sedgley Surprise and the seasonal Snowflake. He spent £80,000 restoring the brewery's taproom, which now wins CAMRA awards for both the pub and its beers. And some believe the pub is still haunted by Sarah Hughes herself!

SARAH HUGHES BREWERY
ORIGINAL HOME BREWED ALES 1921

Drink DARK RUBY MILD (OG 1058) and SEDGLEY SURPRISE (OG 1048) at THE BEACON HOTEL *(Free House)* 500yards from the Sedgley Bull Ring.

✶ Open Days commencing shortly

✶ Watch beer being brewed in an original Black Country Victorian Tower Brewery

Telephone: Sedgley (0902) 883380

SMETHWICK

In the early part of the 19th century, **Smethwick** was a small village with a population of barely 1,000. The Industrial Revolution first came to the area when James Brindley's Birmingham Canal opened in 1769. Foundries were established, including James Watt's Soho Foundry in 1796 and, by 1851, its population had grown to over 8,000. Chance's Glassworks had been established, supplying glass for the Crystal Palace Great Exhibition and many lighthouses, along with other notable firms including Avery's scales, Tangye's pumps and Nettlefold's screw works. All this heavy industry was thirsty work and, over the years, more than 150 pubs served the area, supplied by several local breweries, the largest being Mitchells & Butler's (M&B) Cape Hill Brewery.

Probably the oldest pub in Smethwick is the **Red Cow** in High Street, originally dating from 1706, where the country's last bull-baiting competition was held in 1845. It was taken over by Ansell's (Birmingham) in 1927 and replaced by one of their Fewer & Better pubs in 1937. Nearby was the **Sow & Pigs,** a home-brew pub dating back to 1818, before being taken over by M&B in 1893 and replaced by the **Park** (1893-2011), purpose-built by local architects, Wood & Kendrick.

At the other end of High Street, the **Blue Gates** dates from 1781 and was rebuilt on the other side of the road in 1932. It was at the heart of the local community, holding functions for local clubs, firemen, policemen, postmen and Cape Hill Brewery draymen. Nearby, the **North Western** (1871-1970) was known for its regular boxing matches, whilst the **George** (1864-1981) was demolished to make way for the bypass.

Henry Mitchell, founder of M&B, kept the **Crown** (1851-1981) from 1854-1871 and built his original Crown Brewery here in 1866 before moving to Cape Hill in 1878. Joseph Whitehouse brewed his Golden Sunbeam Crystal Shilling Ale at the **Old Talbot** (1841) until it was acquired by Cheshire's Brewery in 1898, whilst the **New Talbot** (1855-1965) was once an Atkinson's (Birmingham) pub. The **Golden Cross** (1835) was known locally after the Stuffed Donkey, kept in the passageway, but was replaced by a bank in 1936. In Queen Street, Frederick Webb kept the **Queen's Head** (1855-1965) between 1948-1963.

Oldbury Road was home to almost 20 pubs, including the **Swan Hotel,** a home-brew pub originally dating from 1733. It was rebuilt on the opposite side of the road in 1829 and again in 1934, but closed in 2003. Landlord Samuel Downing was a maltster at the **Plough** (1834-1935), who let Howson Taylor use his kiln to produce pottery for the famous Ruskin Pottery. At the **Britannia** (1839-1968), landlord John Lucas was fined 40s in 1888, when three men were found drinking after hours, hidden under a bed!

Galton Bridge was built by Thomas Telford in 1829, named after Samuel Tertius Galton, Quaker industrialist and economist, and was once the longest canal bridge in the world, next to the **Galton Bridge Inn** (1861). The **Waggon & Horses** (1851), once a Showell's Brewery (Langley) pub, was rebuilt in 1970 and later renamed Desi 2. The **Grapes** (1861-1923), **Five Ways** (1864-1931) and **Duck** (1870-1939) became cafés, whilst the **Railway Tavern** (1871) closed in 1960. The Shenton family kept the **Spon Croft** (1870-1999) from 1910-1931, but it was rebuilt on the other side of the road in 1938 and kept by William and Edna Tonkinson until 1963. At the **Glasshouse Tavern** in George Street (1861-1939), landlord William Powell set the cellar on fire when he was boring a hole in a rum cask and killed his son.

The oldest pub in Rolfe Street was the **Boot & Slipper** (1850), which became a printers in 1932, not far from the **Staffordshire Knot** (1871-1982). The Local Health Board held their first meeting at the **Star** (1851-1997), known locally as the Wrexham (after Peter Walker's Wrexham Ales). In 1870, Edward Cheshire started his brewing career at the **Cock** (1851-1903), before moving on to the **New Church** in Windmill Lane (1870-1969) and establishing Cheshire's Windmill Brewery in 1886. Nearby in Suffrage Street, the **Robin** (1870) was originally the Robinson Crusoe until it was renamed in 1994. On the corner of Cross Street, the **Crown & Anchor** (1851-1975) was rebuilt in 1893. The **Railway** (1871-1903) was another Showell's pub, whilst the **Station** (1870-1970) was once a Cheshire's Brewery pub.

On the corner of Crocketts Lane/Union Street, the **New Inns** (1845-1970) was originally a home-brew pub where John Morris brewed his own beer until it was acquired by M&B. In Lewisham Road, the **New Navigation** (1818-2007) was originally known as the Old Navigation, but changed its name when the new line of Thomas Telford's Birmingham Canal opened in 1829. In Halfords Lane, the **Old House at Home** (1861-1997) was originally coal-dealer Daniel Holloway's house, built in the 1840s. In Great Arthur Street, the **Boatman** (1834-1971) was home to J.W. Kingstone's Summit Brewery.

In Soho Street, the **Old Corner House** (1861) on the corner of Rabone Lane was originally the White Horse, renamed in 1990. The **London Stores** (1883-1966) was known locally as the Plug Dodger, whilst the **Old Crystal Palace** (1861-1964) was known locally as the Coppertop, due to its large dome. At Six Ways, the **Victoria** was originally the Crystal Palace, before being renamed and rebuilt in 1893 and closing in 1960. In Baldwin Street, George Hudson kept the **Falcon** (1861-2011) from 1928-1961.

In Cranford Street, the **Moilliet Arms** (1850-2013) was named after local landowner and financier, John Lewis Moilliet. At the **Castle** (1861-1931), landlord Walter Hamer was fined £9 5s in 1908 for allowing customers to fire air guns for pints of beer! William Butler, one of the founders of M&B, began his brewing career in 1866 at the **London Works Tavern** in London Street (1851-2011). The **Soho Foundry Tavern** (1861) in Foundry Lane recalls James Watt's nearby foundry. In Grove Lane, the **Globe** (1882-1910) was once a Holder's Brewery (Birmingham) pub, whilst the **George** (1860) became Maan's Bar before closing.

In Cape Hill, the **Cape of Good Hope** originally dated back to 1814, but was rebuilt in 1925 and replaced by a McDonalds in 1994. It was once kept by James Mason, the father of Titus Mason, founder of the well-known mineral water company. Titus Mason also kept the **Windmill** (1855-2001) in Windmill Lane and the **Waterloo Stores** off-licence in Shireland Road. This was rebuilt in 1908 as the **Waterloo,** a flagship pub for M&B by Wood & Kendrick. The **Seven Stars** was rebuilt for Cheshire's Brewery in 1890, whilst the **Dudley Arms** (1916) became a shop in 2011.

Another venerable tavern is the **Old Chapel** at The Uplands, dating from before 1737. Originally the Hand of Providence, it was renamed in 1889 and acquired by Cheshire's Brewery in 1898. Nearby, the **Holly Bush** dated from 1861, but was rebuilt in 1903.

The oldest pub in Bearwood is undoubtedly the **Bear,** originally dating from 1718, when it was a farmhouse and inn. Rebuilt in 1906 for Holt's Brewery (Birmingham), it once held popular dances. Several nearby Fewer & Better M&B pubs include the **Barleycorn** (1939) and **Shireland** (1924), purpose-built by George Webb, along with the **Abbey** (1931) and **Thimblemill** (1928), built by Wood & Kendrick. Newer pubs in Bearwood include the **Midland,** formerly a bank and converted into a pub by Black Country Ales in 2014, and the **Craft Inn,** a new micro-pub near Hagley Road.

Although Smethwick has lost much of its heavy industry and many historic pubs, around 20 remain to bring back memories.

SPON LANE

In 1694, **Spon Lane** was recorded as one of West Bromwich's main industrial areas, and reflected many elements in the industrial development of the Black Country. Its name probably refers to *William atte Sponne,* a local landowner in 1344. Starting in Smethwick, it soon crosses both the Old and New lines of the Birmingham Canal (1769/1829) and Spon Lane station on the main Birmingham-Wolverhampton Stour Valley railway line (1849). Nearby were collieries, iron foundries, railway works, hollow-ware factories and Chance's glassworks (1824). At its northern end, it crosses the former Birmingham-Wolverhampton Great Western railway line (1854), now the Midland Metro route, to reach West Bromwich town centre.

In the 1940s-1950s, there were once 22 pubs along Spon Lane, virtually a pub on every street corner, and there are many stories about those who attempted to have a drink in all of them in a single session! There was even a brewery to slake your thirst. Unfortunately, much of its grimy history has disappeared through road improvements and redevelopment, with little of its former character remaining.

Starting at its southern end, our first port-of-call would be the **Spon Croft,** dating from 1870, where Alfred Shenton was landlord from 1910-1931. Originally apprenticed in the jewellery trade, he ran away to join the Staffordshire Regiment and served in Egypt, India, Burma and South Africa. A popular licensee who suffered from gout, he also converted the pub's loft into a "shilling" dining room. In 1938, the old pub was demolished and rebuilt on the opposite side of Spon Lane by Mitchells & Butlers as a large roadhouse-style pub, but this was demolished in 1999.

Crossing Spon Lane station and the canal bridge, a group of pubs clustered around the entrance to Chance's Glassworks. The **Britannia, Spon Lane Tavern** and **Royal Oak** were all swallowed up in the expansion of the factory in the early 1900s. Just beyond Spon Lane canal bridge was another group of pubs, including the **Cape Hotel** (1818), where glassworkers would slake their thirst with a 4d beer. Some of the early landlords also operated boats on the canal, and next door was a mortuary for people who drowned! The pub was replaced by a much larger building in 1894, which was used for meetings and other functions, but was closed by 1966.

On the left-hand side was the **North Western** (1868-1895), opposite the **George,** kept by Charles Darby (of Darby's Brewery fame) from 1860-1871, but closed in 1912. Earlier, it had been kept by William Perry, England's champion bareknuckle fighter (the Tipton Slasher), who briefly named it the **Champion of England** in the 1850s. On the corner of Grice Street, the **Stour Valley** (1868) was known locally as Crees's after long-serving landlords William and Harry Crees (1876-1949), but was demolished for road improvements in 1972. Opposite was the **White Swan** (1841), known locally as the Manchester House and popular for its free-and-easy nights, before it closed in 1965. On the corner of Union Street was the **Greyhound** (1871), acquired by Holder's Brewery (Birmingham) in 1905, but closed in 1956.

Continuing along Spon Lane, we'd soon come to the **Shoulder of Mutton** (1845-1954) and **Waggon & Horses** (1868-1927). By 1901, the **Highland Laddie** (1871-1956) had the reputation of being something of a disorderly house, when customers were reported for using obscene language and assaulting the landlord, who was also fined £2 for permitting drunkenness. Nowadays, Kendrick/Kelvin Way cross Spon Lane at this point, with a new pub, the **Island Inn,** on the corner of the roundabout.

Further along Spon Lane is the only original surviving pub, the **Flower Pot.** Originally a home-brew pub, it was bought by Hanson's in 1938 and rebuilt in 1948, and today's pub dates from 1973. In 1852, its first licensee, Edward Woodward, would sit on the doorstep waiting for customers to come in for a drink or have a bed at the adjoining men's lodging house (8d per night), but his wife, Mary Ann, thought this was very unprofessional. On the corner of Sams Lane was Thomas Bates' **Sponwell Brewery,** established in 1865 (see below). One of its tied houses was on the opposite street corner, the **Anchor,** dating from 1871, but closed in the mid 1960s. The **Brewer's Arms** (1870), next to the brewery, had closed by 1896.

Just before the bridge over the GWR railway line were the Old and New Bell. The **Old Bell** was one of the oldest pubs in West Bromwich, first licensed in 1801 and boasting a bowling green. John Brinton, the first licensee, was also a butcher and home-brewer, and Arnold & Bates' Ales were advertised here in 1904. The **New Bell** was only a few years younger, dating from 1818, but was left as a brewhouse in 1850 when Samuel Mason moved the business a few doors away. Just beyond the railway bridge was the **Bridge** (1881), home to Dai William Davies, a well-known boxing promoter who managed local boxer Dick Mann, who took part in 55 professional contests between 1932-1937. Opposite the **Steam Packet** (1871) was the **Cottage Spring** (1868), originally a home-brew pub, but bought by Mitchells & Butlers in 1930. All these pubs were lost as part of road improvements and redevelopment in the 1960s.

At the top of Spon Lane, Sandwell College now dominates the scene. It's hard to believe there was once a farmhouse on the corner of Paradise Street, originally named The Boot (after nearby Boot Meadow) and first licensed in the 1750s. It was renamed the **Bull's Head** in 1802 and rebuilt on the opposite side of the road in 1825. Known as the Top Wrexham (after Peter Walker's Wrexham Brewery), in 1901 it advertised comfortable public smoke rooms with all the football results, but closed in 1959.

The original Bull's Head was replaced by the **Dartmouth Arms** in 1834 which, as the Dartmouth Hotel, became the town's premier commercial hotel and coaching inn and centre for official business and social meetings. Dinners were held here to commemorate Crimean and Waterloo war heroes in 1885, for Chance's football team in 1900, and for local cricket, cycling, bowling and athletic clubs. Between 1906-1920, it was kept by William Isaiah Billy Bassett, a famous footballer who played for West Bromwich Albion (1886-1889), gained 16 caps for England and later became chairman of the football club. The next landlord, Harry Clements (1920-1939), also played for the Albion. The pub closed in 1977 and was demolished soon afterwards.

So, of the 22 pubs originally along Spon Lane, just one survives within an area that has been transformed out of all recognition by modern development.

A brewery on Spon Lane – The Sponwell Brewery

The Sponwell Brewery was on the corner of Sams Lane, and was established by Thomas Henry Bates in 1865 and later run by his son, Henry. By 1924, it had merged with George Arnold's Dartmouth Brewery behind the New Inn in New Street, West Bromwich. He'd built that brewery in 1903 and by 1913 it was a modern, well equipped brewery brewing "pure palatable and nourishing beverages". One of the directors of the Dartmouth Brewery was Charles Perry, a well-known local figure who'd played for West Bromwich Albion, whilst George Arnold's son, Edward, was a past Mayor, JP and Alderman. After the merger, the Sponwell Brewery became Arnold & Bates Ltd, but in 1928, it was taken over by Darby's Dunkirk Brewery, along with its nine tied houses, and closed shortly afterwards.

STOURBRIDGE

It's time to take a walk in and around **Stourbridge** town centre ... a century ago in 1921. The country was still recovering from the loss of 888,000 soldiers in the First World War, and in November, the British Legion had held their first poppy day. In Stourbridge, the first Council houses had been built, costing £800 each, and the new library, cinema and police station had opened. The first public bus services had started, and with an average annual wage of £178, a pint of beer cost around 6d. But what of the town's pubs?

We'll start our journey in Lower High Street, home to many of the town's oldest inns and taverns. At the bottom of Lower High Street, Edward Bennett kept the **Woolpack,** originally dating from 1820. Nearby, Julian Barlow was in charge of the **Saracen's Head** (1820), then a Jackson's Diamond Brewery (Dudley) pub. The **Vine** was an old coaching inn dating from 1573, with a library and newsroom, but would be demolished when the grammar school was extended in 1925. At the junction with Enville Street, Ethel Harris kept the original **Mitre,** then a commercial hotel with stabling, dating from 1741. It would be rebuilt in 1934 in Brewer's Tudor style, designed by Percy Clark, with original features that still exist today. Opposite was the **Board Inn,** another venerable hostelry dating from before 1797, which would later become Nickolls & Perks' wine shop.

Coventry Street was originally called Pig Lane, due to the number of abattoirs. There used to be several pubs along this street, but most had closed by the end of the 19th century. Henry Harry Moore kept the **Angel Inn,** dating back to 1614 and home to Rowland Hill's Angel Brewery. Previous landlord, Henry Kelly, used to keep bowls on the bar to accept coins when foul language was used. The money was later used to erect a memorial drinking fountain in Promenade Gardens. Mary Higgs kept the **Britannia** (1829), but pride of place had to be given to the relatively new **Duke William,** rebuilt in 1903 as the taphouse for the nearby North Worcestershire Brewery, which had been taken over by Wolverhampton & Dudley Breweries (W&D) in 1909.

Other old inns clustered around Ryemarket and in and around Market Street and New Street. Florence Jordan was landlady at the **Exchange** (1861), recently acquired by W&D, whilst Frank Greatwick was in charge of the **Market Hall Vaults** (1865), then a Holt's Brewery (Birmingham) pub. The **Cross Keys** dated from before 1861, and was a former home-brew pub now owned by W&D and kept by Horace Oliver. The **Nags Head** (1820) was kept by Mr Skelding, but both pubs would close a few years later. The **Woodman** (1841) was a Dare's (Birmingham) pub, kept by Joseph Brookes, whilst Elizabeth Correll kept the **Bell** (1820), an old coaching inn which once had the "finest and best-kept bowling green in the Midlands".

In Upper High Street, the **Talbot Hotel** is probably the oldest licensed premises surviving in the town centre (see below). Other historic inns included the **Eagle Vaults** (1835), another Holt's Brewery pub kept by William Phillips, and **Horse & Groom** (1845), kept by Mary Scriven. In the 1920s, former boxer, strongman and acrobat, Harold Leo Phillips, was landlord of the **Star** (1820) and offered a substantial cash prize to anyone who could carry a 4 cwt sack from the front door to the bar, but it was never paid out! The **Coach & Horses** (1820) was an old coaching inn with stables, kept by Albert Breese, whilst George Henry Downs was behind the bar at the **Royal Turf** (1841) until it became a restaurant in 1928. Opposite, the **Royal Exchange** (1870) was another former home-brew pub now owned by W&D, and kept by John Preece. We know it now as the Cock 'n Bull.

On the corner of Foster Street was Bordeaux House, the office and wine and spirits merchant's outlet of local brewer, Edward Rutland, whose name would later be recalled by a nearby pub of the same name. These premises occupied the former site of the **George Inn,** dating from 1549, which became a Temperance Hotel in 1865. At the top end of High Street, the **Chequers** was originally a coaching inn first licensed in 1820. In 1921, it was owned by Bent's Brewery (Stone, Staffordshire) and kept by Alphonse Smets from the Handel Hotel (Blackheath). It would later become a Wetherspoon's pub.

The railway had arrived at Stourbridge Town from Stourbridge Junction in 1879. Close to the station was the **Vauxhall Inn** (1854), then owned by Thomas Plant's Brewery (Netherton) and kept by Enoch Wharton. Just around the corner in Church Street we'd find the **Old Crispin** (1862), with its music hall, kept by landlord Francis Frank Matthews until 1946. At the top end of Hagley Road was the **Swan** (1850), then owned by John Rolinson's Five Ways Brewery (Netherton), with Joseph Barnes in charge. Across the road, the **Fountain** (1862) was an Atkinson's (Birmingham) pub, then kept by Harry Wakefield.

Enville Street was home to several old inns, including the **Cottage** (1871), **New Inn** (1820), **Foley Arms** (1850), **Malt Shovel** (1861), **Noah's Ark** (1841) and the reputedly haunted **Somerset House** (1835). **The Royal Exchange** (1855) was originally a butcher's shop, then kept by Issac Digger, but would later become a Batham's (Brierley Hill) pub, whilst the **Queen's Head** (1862) was home to Edward Rutland's brewery. Further along Enville Street, the **Golden Lion** was Mary Faulkner's one-roomed home-brew beerhouse dating from 1844, which we now know as **Katie Fitzgerald's.**

In Worcester Street, Smith & Williams (Town Brewery, Brierley Hill) owned the **Waggon & Horses** (1835), kept by John Pearsall, which was reputedly haunted by spectres from nearby Gibbet Gullet footpath. Near the roundabout where Mary Stevens Park would be opened a few years later, Henrietta Moorcroft was the long-serving landlady who kept the **Plough & Harrow** (1840) until 1940. This was a home-brew pub, where she'd been fined £2 in 1902 for supplying liquor to a police constable while on duty. Across the roundabout, the **Old White Horse** dated from 1782 and was kept by farmer, Thomas Parkes. Nearby, the **Longlands Tavern** (1864) was kept by Elizabeth Gray, whilst the **Garibaldi** (1851) was owned by Edward Rutland and kept by Thomas Richards.

So, that's a run-down of all the pubs we could visit on our pub crawl around Stourbridge a century ago. Several of the town's historic inns and taverns still survive to offer a wide range of beers. Long may they prosper!

The oldest hotel in town

The **Talbot Hotel** is probably the oldest surviving hotel in Stourbridge town centre. Originally the home of Richard Foley in 1627, it had become a hotel by 1685. The first landlord, Jonathan Pyrke, was not only the town's postmaster, but also set up cockfighting pits behind the hotel. It was the centre of the town's social and commercial life, used for meetings, dinners, dances, inquests and property auctions, including parish meetings, local Freemasons, Rotary Club, turnpike trustees and the local Excise Office. Its assembly room became the New Theatre, and it had a gentleman's club in the Windsor Room. It was also the town's principal coaching inn, where horse-drawn stagecoaches and omnibuses, with the distinctive names of Bang-up, Everlasting, Invincible & Victory called to pick up passengers and mail. Even a spare set of keys for the fire station in Market Street was kept here! It's also haunted by the ghost of a lady in white who's searching for her lost baby.

STOURBRIDGE – PUBS AND THE LOCAL MUSIC SCENE

In the late 1970s, I remember going to the **Stewponey** in Stourton to see my office colleague, Terry Green and his band performing their version of *Get Your Kicks on the A456*. Terry lived in the same street in Halesowen where Robert Plant, former frontman of Led Zeppelin, grew up. The **Stewponey** was one of Stan Webb's local pubs and Chicken Shack regularly performed and rehearsed here. Hearing from friends that they'd seen bands at other local pubs got me thinking more about the Stourbridge music scene over the years, particularly its links with local pubs.

Stourbridge Town Hall hosted many events and performances over the years, but many especially remember the Big Beat sessions in the 1960s, promoted by Freddie Bannister. The list of bands who performed here is almost endless and includes The Who, The Spencer Davis Group, Cream, The Moody Blues, The Hollies, The Animals, The Nashville Teens, The Kinks, The Zombies, The Yardbirds, Pretty Things, The Move and Small Faces. Some of those early groups, like The Banned, included musicians who would become iconic, such as Robert Plant. **Stourbridge Art College** was also a seedbed for the local music scene, and many groups started off performing in the local pubs and drinking in the nearby **Swan.** When he became famous, Robert Plant turned up in a Rolls Royce outside King Edward Grammar School to disprove his headmaster's view that he would never make anything of himself! And talking about schools, who would believe that Judas Priest played at **Old Swinford Hospital School** in 1970 and 1971!

The **Seven Stars** in Oldswinford is well remembered for its Blues Club in the 1960s. In fact, Robert Plant first performed here in 1963 when, at 15 years old, he played harmonica and regularly sung with the Delta Blues Band. He later performed with The Crawling King Snakes and Jess Roden's Shakedown Sound. The club was the launching pad for many West Midlands groups, including Sounds of Blue, who became Chicken Shack with Stan Webb, Christine Perfect (later Christine McVie, who was voted Melody Maker Girl Singer of the Year in 1969) and Chris Wood (later in Traffic).

In the late 1980s and early 1990s, an idiosyncratic music scene arose in Stourbridge, named "Grebo" after a slang word for a scruffy layabout, combining punk rock guitars with electronic beats and hip-hop influenced sampling. The **Mitre** pub in the centre of Stourbridge became the launching point for many of these local bands. Landlord John Knight was an accomplished singer and guitarist who kept the pub from 1975, and helped to put it on the musical map in the late 1980s and early 1990s. It became a hotbed of musical talent, where members of The Wonder Stuff, Pop Will Eat Itself and Ned's Atomic Dustbin regularly performed before exploding on to the music scene and enjoying chart success.

At that time, Stourbridge had a huge amount of musical talent and John ensured that musicians always had a place to play, finding space for any type of music to entertain his diverse bunch of customers. After leaving the pub in 2001, John continued to play gigs and hosted folk, acoustic and open mic nights at pubs across Stourbridge, including the **Garibaldi** and **Britannia.** Sadly, John passed away in 2016, but the Mitre keeps his memory alive by holding regular nights where up-and-coming bands and comedians can perform and entertain the loyal customers.

Diamond Head were formed in 1976 by schoolmates, Brian Tatler and Duncan Scott, and their first gig was at **High Park School.** In 1981, they also played at Stourbridge Town Hall. They were a major influence on Los Angeles based Metallica, when Lars Ulrich said they produced "some of the greatest Heavy Metal songs of all time". In fact, Lars thought that their iconic album, *Lightning to the Nations* was "one of THE classic pieces of vinyl"; he also fell in love with Batham's Bitter when he visited the Royal Exchange!

Witchfinder General were formed in Stourbridge in 1979 by Zeeb Parkes and Phil Cope. They took their name from a 1968 British-made horror film and were strongly influenced by Birmingham-based band, Black Sabbath. **Pop Will Eat Itself** were formed in 1981, and were later joined by Fuzz Townshend on drums and keyboards. Their first album, *Poppies say Grrr* was sold in a brown paper bag at Martin's Newsagents in Stourbridge. Fuzz later went on to star in Channel 4's *Car SOS!*

The **Wonder Stuff** were formed in 1986 and based in Stourbridge, with frontman, Miles Hunt, whose uncle was the keyboard player with Wizzard and ELO. In 1991, they scored a No.1 hit single with Vic Reeves' *Dizzy*. **Ned's Atomic Dustbin** were formed at Halesowen College of Education in 1987, with frontman, Jonn Penney. They took their name from an episode of *The Goon Show* and also performed their first gig at the Mitre.

It's said that there isn't a pub in Wollaston that hasn't been visited by Roy Wood, frontman of The Move and Wizzard, when he lived at Gothersley Hall, near Stourton. In fact, he wrote *I Wish it would be Christmas Every Day* in the kitchen there in 1973. The **Plough** had regular music and folk nights, where Robert Plant was often seen. On the crest of the ridge on the edge of Stourbridge, the **Forester's Arms** was also the venue for many groups and bands over the years. It's said that Stan Webb named his band Chicken Shack after the tiny tin-shed rock venue behind the pub. The pub was also a venue for planning a book recording the life of JB's, a famous music club in Dudley.

Katie Fitzgerald's (formerly the Golden Lion) has been at the heart of Stourbridge's music scene for 20 years and is still a great music venue where up-and-coming and established bands, such as Steve Gibbons, Ricky Cool and Danni G, have performed. The **River Rooms** are a popular music venue too, where Pop Will Eat Itself and Diamond Head performed.

Stourbridge-based Witchfinder General were regular performers at the **Rose & Crown** in the 1980s. The **Shrubbery Cottage** in Oldswinford was also a popular venue for local groups, including Ned's Atomic Dustbin, Pop Will Eat Itself and The Wonder Stuff. In the town centre, the **Bell** was a venue for up-and-coming bands, whilst the **Rock Café** (formerly Vauxhall Inn) was well known for its indie/rock and tribute bands, including Diamond Head. Local acoustic singers, such as Esther Turner, often appear at the **Red House Boutique** (formerly Hogshead) in Foster Street.

Not far away at Merry Hill was the **Robin Hood.** This was the venue for Mike Hamblett's Robin R'n'B club, which opened in April 1992, where top groups and bands performed, along with up-and-coming artists. The opening night featured The Journeymen, with Trevor Burton and the Red Lemons, and in later weeks Soul Survivors, Steve Gibbons Band, Chicken Shack, The Groundhogs and The Trevor Burton Band often performed. The Citizens Theatre not only hosted the R'n'B club, but also Chris Tarrant's "OTT" and Black Country Night Out. With a capacity of 350, it had just one gent's toilet and a dressing room in a portacabin! It lasted until 2003, when the club moved to Bilston.

Stourbridge's music scene is still vibrant, with plenty of pubs and other venues available for both up-and-coming and successful bands. Long may it continue!

SWAN VILLAGE & GREETS GREEN

Swan Village lies along the road to Great Bridge, to the west of West Bromwich town centre. It's remembered for the largest gasworks in the country, Ryders Green Tar Works, the automatic glassblowing works, John Spencer's Phoenix Ironworks and the Victoria Blue Brick Tile Works. At night, the sky would be lit by the glare of the furnaces at these factories. Just to the south is **Greets Green,** once an area of common land, which some say is the spiritual birthplace of West Bromwich Albion, since many of the original players lived at nearby Albion. Over the years, around 50 pubs served these communities, but few survive today.

The oldest pub in **Swan Village** was undoubtedly the **Swan Inn,** originally dating from 1550 and owned by Richard Sperry in 1638. It was once a coaching inn where coalmasters met and Lord Dartmouth held courts. Rebuilt in 1860, it was bought by Joules (Stone) in 1926, kept by Samuel and Ann Butler from 1949-1968, but demolished in 1993.

Around the corner in Phoenix Street was the **Bird in Hand** (1875), kept by William Caggy Roberts from 1915-1922, but converted into a pizza shop in 1999. A few doors away was the **George** (1871), kept by Frank Fearns from 1949-1964, when it was a popular music venue until it was converted into housing in 2012.

There were several pubs along Great Bridge Street, including the **White Lion** (1868-1924), **Three Crowns** (1868-1969) and **Golden Cup** (1858-1978). Closer to Great Bridge were the **Kings Arms** (1868), **King William** (1849-1930) and **Black Horse** (1870-1927), originally the Miners Arms. Around the corner in Ryder Street were the **Wellington** (1868-1983), popular with pigeon fanciers, and **Boilermakers Arms** (1868-1955), known locally as Worrall's after long-serving landlord Joseph Worrall (1906-1930). In William Street, the **Plough & Harrow** (1871-1973) was kept by Thomas Withington from 1914-1942.

Ryders Green is probably best remembered for the aptly-named **Eight Locks** pub (1845), next to Ryders Green canal bridge. The pub was originally owned by boatman Joseph Gwilt, who later sold it to a coalman for £380. Boat-people quenched their thirst here and Jack Judge (of Tipperary fame) performed here regularly. A few doors away, the **Coach & Horses** (1845) was closed by 1920.

Whitehall Road was also home to several old pubs. Near St Peter's Church were the **Royal Oak** (1854-2012), which provided accommodation for artists performing at Dudley Hippodrome, **Britannia** (1845-1987), where landlord Fred Leeson was Mayor of West Bromwich in 1957, and **Whitehall Tavern** (1870-1960).

There were a few pubs in the crowded back streets next to Farley Park, including the **Bulls Head** (1861-1954) in Grout Street, kept by home-brewer Benjamin Dunn for nearly 40 years until 1940. The **New Inn** (1881) was closed in 1913. In Cape Street, Samuel Dudley and his family kept the **Royal Exchange** (1861-1914) throughout its life, with Dudley's Home-Brewed Ales etched on the windows. A few doors away was the venerable **Olde Rose & Crown,** dating from the 1850s and kept by John Hadley from 1953-1979. It had a bowling club, shooting club and jazz band, but was closed by 2008.

In Dunkirk Street, Dunkirk Hall, originally dated from 1660, was converted into the **Dunkirk Inn** in 1860 and kept by George Yates from 1914-1944 before closing in 1977. In 1894, Charles Darby established Darby's Dunkirk Brewery here and built a new brewery next to the pub in 1902, which was taken over by Mitchells & Butlers in 1951 with over 100 tied houses.

The centre of **Greets Green** is the junction of Whitehall Road and Greets Green Road, where the **Union Cross** (1827-1984) stood guard. Daniel Williams brewed ale and porter at the Union Cross Inn Brewery from 1845. It passed to William Bowen in 1883, and was taken over by

William Butler (Wolverhampton) with eight tied houses in 1945. A few doors away is the **Fox & Goose** (1872), rebuilt in 1935, where Thomas Harris brewed 600 gallons of beer a week until the 1914-1918 war. Next door was the **Eagle Tavern** (1864), renamed Manchester House in 1891, but converted into a shop in 1915.

Further along Greets Green Road we'd find **Greets Green House** (1858-1911) and the **Boat** (1870-1963), kept by Henry Jones for over 30 years until 1961. At the junction of Claypit Lane was the **Bush** (1835), where George Darby first started brewing with his son, Charles, in 1872. Rebuilt in 1937, with the architect's hallmark green-tiled roof, it was renamed Darby's in 1984. In 2002, it became a community centre, with its history recalled on a blue plaque. Not far away was the **Oliver Cromwell** (1861-2007), once a Woodall's (West Bromwich) pub kept by Mark Copson from 1903-1925 and Frank Yank and Mary Hadley until 1951.

Around the corner in Bull Lane was the **Albion Tavern** (1868), known locally as Duffield's after long-serving licensees David, William and George Duffield. They kept the pub until 1947, before it became a Royal Naval Association club in 1972. A few doors away was the **Bulls Head** (1870), rebuilt in 1957 and converted into flats in 1997.

Oldbury Road was once home to much industry, with several pubs serving the thirsty workers. The **Vulcan** (1860) was close to the Vulcan Foundry, and was later rebuilt due to mining subsidence and converted into flats in 1930. A few doors away, the **Albion** (1861-1982) was a Darby's Brewery pub where landlords John Jack Reece issued tokens and Jim Hope was formerly a boxer in the 1950s.

Around the corner in Vernon Street was the **White Swan** (1874), another pub kept by William Caggy Roberts, with its own marching jazz band. In 1962, it was replaced nearby with the **Jolly Sailor**, a modern pub named after Able Seaman Joseph Weston, who was lost with his ship in 1944. On the corner of Stour Street was the **Red Lion** (1870-1927), opposite the **Cottage Spring** (1881-1979), kept by William Read for over 30 years until 1965.

Not far from the Albion canal bridge and railway station was the **Roway** (1851), recalling the name given to the local tributary of the River Tame. It's also close to Roway Ironworks, one of the first factories producing nail rod, Philip Williams' Albion Ironworks and the Albion Blue Brick & Tile Works. In 1901, landlord William Barratt was fined £5 for watering down the spirits, and from 1933-1956, the pub was kept by Albert and Edith Brookes before closing in 1966.

Finally, along Albion Road at Ireland Green we'd find the **Yew Tree Inn.** James Downing bought this pub in 1850 for £63 12s and brewed his own beer with his father, Samuel, and son, James, until 1941. Apparently, a famous racehorse, Golden Fleece, was buried under the bowling green in the 1950s, but the pub was rebuilt nearby in 1971 and renamed Poacher's Pocket in 2008. However, it returned as the Yew Tree in 2014 and is now an Indian grill.

So, although the area around Swan Village and Greets Green has changed dramatically and has lost most of its heavy industry, a handful of interesting and historic pubs remain. Long may they prosper!

TETTENHALL & PENN

Tettenhall and **Penn** are historic settlements to the west of Wolverhampton. The history of Tettenhall goes back to the Battle of Tettenhall in 910, when Saxon King, Edward, inflicted a crushing defeat on the Danish Vikings. The parish church of St Michael and All Angels dates from the 14th century and it's one of the few villages with two village greens.

It also has several historic pubs, the oldest of which was the **Angel,** dating from 1754, but now long gone. One of the oldest remaining pubs is the **Rock Villa** in Old Hill, dating from before 1814 and previously known as the Old Rose & Crown. The Rock Villa Pleasure Gardens opened in 1843, with a bowling green and bandstand, and attracted 1,000 visitors each week in the summer. In 1858, landlord George Spink was cautioned about allowing a band to play music in the gardens on a Sunday. After becoming a training centre for Ansell's in 1988, it reopened in 2011 as the Rock, and is now known as Two Greens.

Other venerable taverns included the **Rose & Crown** (1818-1955) in Upper Street. During the Michaelmas Wake celebrations in the 1890s, it had the custom of tying a cord from the upper windows of the pub to the opposite side of the hill, on which would be suspended ducks, geese, turkeys and other poultry. Local men and youths would then be blindfolded, placed on donkeys and ponies and sent down the hill. Anything they could drag off the line as they rode underneath would be theirs!

In Lower Green, the **Mitre** was first licensed in 1818, but closed in 2012. In Wergs Road, the **Crown** was originally a farmhouse, first licensed in 1834, advertising Russell's Fine Ales. It was rebuilt in 1906 and later became a Harvester inn. In School Road, the **Royal Oak** (1847) was originally known as the Spotted Cow until the 1920s and kept by brewers, Catherine and Jacob Cartwright from 1891-1916. It had a fine bowling green and orchard, with an air raid shelter for 55 people! In Wood Road, the **Shoulder of Mutton** (1843) was originally a butcher's shop, but was rebuilt in 1981 and replaced by housing in 2010 after an unsuccessful campaign to save it.

In Swan Street, the **New Inn** dated from 1849, but was closed by 1940. **The Swan** (1854) in Lower Street was originally a coaching inn, which became a Holt, Plant & Deakin pub in 1992 and was extensively refurbished in 2007. In Wrottesley Road, the **Dog & Gun** dates from 1871 and is popular with ramblers.

Tettenhall once boasted two pubs named the **Bird in Hand.** One was in School Road, Tettenhall Wood, dating from before 1871, but later rebuilt and converted into shops in 2014. The other was in Mount Road, dating from 1901, but closed in 1940.

In Mount Road, the **Mount Hotel** was originally built for the Mander family in 1865, before they moved to Wightwick Manor. In 1952, it was sold by Sir Charles Mander and is now a Grade II listed luxury hotel. In Perton Road, the **Fieldhouse** originally dates from 1770 and was first licensed in 1802. Nearby in Wightwick, the **Mermaid** in Bridgnorth Road dates from 1834. It was originally owned by Theodore Mander, former Mayor of Wolverhampton, who once rented it to the People's Refreshment House Association as a temperance house.

Newer licensed premises include the **Kingswood** (1969) in Regis Road, which became a restaurant in 2009, and the **Claregate** (1970) in Codsall Road, built on the site of the Old Fieldhouse Inn. Nearby is the CAMRA award-winning **Hail to the Ale** micro-pub (2013).

Penn is another historic settlement, with Anglo-Saxon roots and a parish church dating back to the 11th century. It occupies a key position on the main route between Wolverhampton, Stourbridge and Kidderminster, and its main feature is Penn Common, now occupied by farmland and a golf course.

There's also a handful of historic pubs, the oldest of which is the **Barley Mow** at Penn Common. Originally built in 1630, it was first licensed in 1851 and has won several local CAMRA awards for its real ales. Also in Penn Common, the **Turf Tavern** (1851-1921) had a fine bowling green and was popular with punters visiting the nearby racecourse. At the top of Church Hill, the **Old Stags Head** (1818-2014) originally dated from 1635 and held a commanding view over the common. In the late 19th century, the handbells of St Bartholomew's Church were pawned for ale here. The pub was also haunted by the vicar's wife, who used to chase the vicar into the pub through a tunnel and turn off the beer taps!

In Penn Road, several pubs were first licensed in 1818, including the **Rose & Crown,** originally the terminus of Sampson Tharme's horse-drawn omnibus to Wolverhampton town centre. In 1936, it was rebuilt to the designs of James Swann, and rebuilt again in 1980 due to subsidence. The **Fox & Goose** became a Holt, Plant & Deakin pub in 1989, and is now a restaurant, whilst the **Roebuck** was rebuilt in the 1950s to the designs of local architects, A & T Butler. The **Holly Bush** (1834) was originally a home-brew pub, also rebuilt for Wolverhampton & Dudley Breweries by Bertram Butler in 1937, whilst the **Mount Tavern** was built in 1938 for Frank Myatt's (Wolverhampton) Brewery. In Lower Penn, the **Greyhound** in Market Lane is a village pub dating from 1830, popular with ramblers and canal users.

More recent pubs include the **Springhill** in Warstones Lane, built for William Butler in 1936 by local architects, Lavender & Twentyman. Nearby, the **Flying Dutchman** (1978-2011) was probably named after a ghostly ship which haunts the seas around the Cape of Good Hope and gave its name to a winning horse in the 1849 Derby. In Birchwood Road, the **Battle of Britain** was built for William Butler in 1959, but replaced by housing in 2008. In Bruford Road, the **Bruford Arms** (1967) may recall William and Mary Bruford who lived at Compton Hill Lodge, and helped to establish the Steam Brewery in Market Place, Wolverhampton in 1864. The **Starting Gate** (2018) is a new real ale micro-pub in a former bank at Penn Fields, whilst the **Penn Cottage** is now a Miller & Carter steakhouse at Penn Common.

The western suburbs of Tettenhall and Penn have now been absorbed into Wolverhampton and have been subject to much development and expansion. But they still retain important remnants of their past, including several historic pubs. Long may they prosper!

A brewery on Penn Common

Penn Common was also home to the **Penn Wood Common Brewery,** established by John Millard in 1860. It had its own source of pure well water and used locally grown barley. From 1872, it was run by Thomas Allin and became Hall & Haden's Penn Brewery in 1888, supplying around a dozen pubs, as far away as Halesowen and West Bromwich. But by the 1890s, it was suffering serious competition from the larger commercial breweries and had problems transporting the beer, since the brewery drays had to climb steep hills in all directions. In 1897, it was acquired by the Burton Brewery, who sold it to Wolverhampton District Brewery in 1899; it later passed to Ansell's (Birmingham). The brewery buildings were later converted into a family home.

TIPTON

Nowhere is more typical of the Black Country than **Tipton.** Originally a farming area recorded in the Domesday Book *(Tibintone),* the Industrial Revolution saw the town exploited for its rich mineral resources of coal and iron. The opening of the canals in 1769 and railways in 1850 saw a massive growth in the town. From a population of 4,300 in 1801, it grew to over 30,000 a century later. The most concentrated areas of heavy industry included engineering forges, iron and steel foundries, tube works and brickworks, along with factories making chains and anchors, machine tools, and bedsteads. And in 1890, Palethorpe's converted George and Elisha Whitehouse's old brewery into a model sausage and pork pie factory.

In Tipton's industrial heyday, the main source of leisure was the public house. Like many Black Country towns, most pubs brewed their own beer, some having their own brewery. Over the years, around 120 pubs served Tipton (excluding Princes End, Great Bridge and Dudley Port), but fewer than a dozen survive today.

The centre of Tipton is focussed on High Street and Owen Street, once a thriving shopping centre with around a dozen pubs. One of the most memorable is the **Fountain,** a favourite for canal boatmen, first recorded in 1828 and now a Grade II listed building. It became the headquarters of William Perry (the Tipton Slasher), England's champion prizefighter from 1850-1857, celebrated by a plaque on the wall and a statue in Coronation Gardens. He once trained in the attic, and some believe he still haunts the pub! Once owned by Holt's (Birmingham) and Showell's (Langley) Breweries, it reopened as the first Holt, Plant & Deakin pub in 1984 and is the only surviving pub in Owen Street.

Opposite St Paul's Church was the **Britannia** (1818), once a commercial hotel, but closed in 1978. On the corner of Albion Street was the **Albion** (1828-1978), where landlord James Whitehouse helped to back William Perry. The **Black Cock** (1828-1978) had etched windows depicting fighting cocks and was kept by William and Florence Brown from 1946-1964. The **Miners Arms** dated from 1859 as the Round of Beef, known locally as The Widders after landlady Marjorie Buxton (1929-1950), but closed in 1977. Two shorter-lived pubs included the **Cow & Calf** (1881-1924) and **Grapes** (1848-1937).

Another of Tipton's oldest pubs is the **Noah's Ark** in Wood Street, dating from 1841. Landlord Isaac Chater brewed his own beer here and kept pigs in the yard. But it's probably best remembered for the Cartwrights, a local boxing family who kept the pub from 1933-1970 and trained local boxers in their gym. Some say it's still haunted by Tom Cartwright's wife, Milda! The Black Country Society held their first meeting here in 1967, which is marked with another plaque. On the corner of Furnace Parade was the **Three Furnaces** (1828), which closed in 1938 after frequent flooding.

On the corner of Elliotts Road, the **Beehive** (1849-1978) had its own brewery and was kept by featherweight boxer, Hal Cartwright from 1958-1964. In Union Street were the **Hop & Barleycorn** (1851-1925), **Globe** (1859-1928) and **Union** (1851-2002). Tipton Harriers were founded at the **Waterloo** (1870-1972) and nearby were the **Rose & Crown** (1851-2008) and **Barrel** (1903), which closed in the 1970s.

At the end of High Street, the **Castle Hotel** (1837) was a prominent landmark, kept by Joseph Whitehouse until 1876. William Perry sparred in the boxing gym here, but it was demolished in 1957 for road improvements. Walter Woodhall brewed his own beer at the **Two Furnaces** (1870-1939), opposite the chainworks. In the back streets were the **British Oak** (1861-1901), **Bell** (1818-1926) and **Queen's Head** (1861-1956). **The Barrel** (1881-2006) had "Good Stabling and Well-Aired Beds", whilst the **Cape** (1851) was rebuilt around 1939, but converted into flats in 1990.

Around Lower Green were the **True Briton** (1834-1908) and **Crown & Anchor** (1864-1931), where John Purnell brewed his own beer. Alongside the canal were the **Navigation** (1818-1926), home to Tipton Volunteer Rifle Corps, and the **Boat** (1818-1925) in Boat Row.

At the top of Park Lane West is the **Red Lion,** Tipton's oldest surviving pub, dating from the late 18th century, first licensed in 1818 and now a Grade II listed building. In the 1830s, landlord Richard Nicklin was a popular bare-knuckle fighter, and Thomas Round brewed his Celebrated Lion Old Ales, Stout & Porter here until 1872. Between 1919-1958, it was kept by long-serving landlords Sydney Smith and Frederick Cherrington.

Other historic pubs in Park Lane West included the **Cross** (1847-1929), used for miners' meetings, whilst landlord Harry Scriven worked in the ironworks as a puddler, giving his name to the **Puddlers Arms** (1861-1928). The **Bridge** (1871) was known locally as Annie's after landlady Annie Harvey, who introduced live music and table service. The **Black Horse** (1844) was demolished by 1970, whilst the **Bush Inn** (1845) was badly damaged during a Zeppelin raid in 1916, then rebuilt after the war and converted into a shop in 1995. Near Victoria Park, two pubs were named the **Boscobel,** one in Boscobel Street dating from 1861. It closed in 1978 when a replacement pub opened in Park Lane West, which was converted into a nursery in 2008.

In Park Lane East, the **Park Inn** was built as a hotel in 1900 to replace the old Seven Stars Inn. It was reputedly haunted by the ghost of Lady May, a little girl who died when she was accidentally trapped in the attic, but the pub was converted into flats in 1996. Further along were the **Park Lane Tavern** (1858-1920), originally known as the Poor Man's Friend, and the **Wellington Inn** (1848-1999), a former home-brew pub next to Thomas Morris' ironworks. Tipton's only roadhouse was the **Tipton Arms** along Birmingham New Road, which was designed by local architects, Scott & Clark; it opened in 1939, but closed in 1994.

Dudley Road was the main route between Dudley and Princes End, with the tramway and several pubs. The oldest was probably the **Old King's Head,** first licensed in 1818, but closed in the mid 1970s. On the corner of High Street, the **Waggon & Horses** (1840) was home to licensees Benjamin and Annie Meller, who were not only brewers, but also saddle-makers. Vera Langford was a popular landlady who kept the pub from 1949-1960. The **Victoria** (1851) was originally the Bird in Hand, known locally as the Bird, but converted into a takeaway in 2012.

At the crossroads with Sedgley Road West is the popular **Pie Factory,** originally built as the Five Ways Inn in 1857. It was rebuilt in 1923 by Showell's (Langley) and renamed the Doughty Arms after William Doughty, chairman of Tipton UDC between 1917-1924. Landlord Tom Whitehouse (1929-1943) was a professional boxer (Tipton Tornado), but in 1987, it became one of Mad O'Rourke's Little pubs as the Pie Factory, which it remains to this day. It's allegedly haunted by three ghosts, Nobby, a former landlord dressed in a black cloak, a little girl who sings and laughs, and a cavalier.

Further along Hurst Lane was the **Factory** (1848-1965), opposite the former Bean Motor Works. At Factory Bridge, the **Old Bush** (1818) was rebuilt in the 1920s and kept by James and Betsy Morgan from 1923-1964, but survives as a bar and grill.

So, although many of Tipton's historic pubs have gone, there are still a handful serving up happy memories and good pints!

WALSALL – PUBS RECALLING FAMOUS NAMES & LOCAL TRADES

From the late Middle Ages, pubs (or ale-houses, taverns and inns) needed to identify themselves in some way at a time when most people were illiterate. So simple signs evolved, ranging from a crooked piece of wood, holly bush, tradesman's sign, or a type of heraldic sign borrowed from religion or aristocratic coats of arms. There are probably upwards of 17,000 different signs for pubs, the most popular of which are the Red Lion, Crown and Royal Oak.

Walsall was no different, with 20 pubs called the Crown (or Crown & Anchor, Rose & Crown or Three Crowns), 10 pubs named the Royal Oak and five pubs called the Red Lion. But there were also 11 pubs named the New Inn and 10 pubs called the Miners Arms, Colliers Arms or Jolly Collier.

There were half-a-dozen pubs with the generic name of Kings Head, Kings Arms or Old Kings Arms. **King Edward VII** was remembered at pubs in Ablewell Street (1872-1963) and High Street (1861-1939). Several pubs recall King George, including the **George Hotel** in Digbeth (1781-1978), one of the town's main commercial hotels, along with the **King George V** at Pleck (1937). His name was also recalled at the **George** in Bloxwich (1830-2012) and **Royal George** in Wolverhampton Street (1846-1882) and Rushall Street (1822). The **Black Boy** in New Street (1818-1923) and West Bromwich Road (1888) referred to King Charles I, known for his jet-black hair and swarthy skin. **King William** was remembered at a pub in Little Bloxwich (1849-1906), whilst the legendary **King Arthur** is recalled at the pub in Park Hall (1968).

Apart from six pubs named the Queens, Queens Head or Queens Hotel, the **Victoria** in Lower Rushall Street (1840) and **Victoria Stores** in Bloxwich (1871-1928) recall the long-reigning monarch. In the Butts, **Queen Caroline** (1835) recalled the wife of King George IV, who was originally from Brunswick in Germany.

Princes are not forgotten, with the **Prince of Wales** in Portland Street (1857-1908), Queen Street (1865-1966) and Bloxwich (1861). There was even a pub named after **Lady Diana** in Bloxwich (2011-2017). In Caldmore, the **Cambridge Arms** (1930) probably recalls the title given to Prince Aldophus, one of King George III's sons, also reflected in the **Duke of Cambridge** at Short Heath. Less well known was **Prince Blucher,** a famous Prussian field-marshal who defeated Napoleon at Laon in 1814 and commanded the Prussian army at Waterloo, aged 73. He was remembered at a long-standing pub in Stafford Street (1818-2017).

Several of Walsall's pubs were named after military figures. The **Lord Nelson** in Stafford Street (1834) and Birchills (1908-1912), **Old Peal & Nelson** in Peal Street (1813-1894) and **Nelson** at Bloxwich (1866-1914) all recalled the famous admiral who fought at the Battle of Trafalgar on *HMS Victory* in 1805. But less is probably known about **Lord Raglan,** who fought with the Duke of Wellington at the Battle of Waterloo in 1815 and in the Crimean War in 1853. His name was recalled at a pub in Rushall (1858-2006), rebuilt in 1938, but replaced by housing.

The Crimean War was remembered at the **Crimea Tavern** in Bloxwich (1859-1928), whilst the **Alma** in Paddock Lane (1857-1933), which was later rebuilt in Bentley Lane, recalled the site of another Allied victory over the Russians in the Crimean War. The **Saracen's Head** in Stafford Street (1862-1909) recalled the battles in the Crusades.

In Birmingham Street, the **Duke of Wellington** (1853-2006) recalled the national hero who defeated Napoleon at Waterloo in 1815 and later became Prime Minister. The **Duke of York** in Blue Lane (1841-1845), Dudley Street (1831-1937) and at Chuckery (1937) recall probably the best remembered holder of that title who commanded the English army in Flanders in 1794-1827. However, the popular song misrepresents the facts, since this Duke was only 31, had 30,000 men, and there were no hills in the area where he was fighting!

Admiral Rodney is best remembered for his victory over the French in 1782 at the Battle of the Saintes in the West Indies. His name was recalled at a pub at Pelsall Common (1849-1865) and at the **Old Rodney** in Park Street (1818-1876). Sir **Charles Napier** was a distinguished officer who fought in the Peninsula War against Napoleon and in the American War of Independence, before later serving as Major General and Governor in India. A pub in Palfrey (1856) was named after him.

The Marquis of Anglesey was an English General who commanded the British cavalry at Waterloo, losing a leg during the battle. He was also a local landowner in the Brownhills area, who was recalled at the **Anglesey Arms** (1861-1961), a first-class beerhouse in Upper Forster Street. The **Lord Hill** in Bloxwich (1841) and the **General Hill** in Blue Lane (1834) recalled Viscount Rowland Hill who served in the Battle of Waterloo and became Commander-in-Chief of the British Army in 1828.

The landed gentry are not forgotten in Walsall. The **Bradford Arms** in Lower Rushall Street (1831-1932), Palfrey (1932) and Pleck Road (1858) recall the Earl of Bradford, who supported King Charles I in the Civil War and was also a leading local landowner. At Little Bloxwich, the **Bridgewater** (1964-2006) was probably named after the Duke of Bridgewater, the father of modern canals, whilst the **Scott Arms** (1858-1929) probably recalled the local family, first recorded in 1332, who owned Great Barr Hall until 1909. In Darlaston, the **Dartmouth Arms** (1841-1967) recalled the local Legge family, who became the Earls of Dartmouth, and were local landowners, playing an active part in the life of Walsall and West Bromwich.

Baron Hatherton (Edward Littleton) owned substantial estates in Staffordshire, including mines, quarries, brickyards and canals around Bloxwich, whilst his son was Liberal MP for Walsall and South Staffordshire from 1847-1857. He's remembered at the **Hatherton Arms** in Bloxwich (1880), which displays the family crest, and Rushall (1849-2012). Lady Hatherton opened Walsall Arboretum in 1874, which was extended in 1922 on land given by Mr Featherstone-Dilke, who's remembered at the **Dilke Arms** in Aldridge Road (1939). The **Gough Arms** in Willenhall (1845-1946) recalled another local landowner, whilst the **Romping Cat** in Bloxwich (1849) recalls the emblem of Sir Gilbert de Wakeringe, a 16th century local dignitary.

Famous politicians are also remembered in Walsall. The **Sir Robert Peel** in Burrowes Street (1858-1924) and Bloxwich (1849) recall the founder of the modern police force who was British Prime Minister in 1834 and 1841. In Stafford Street, the **President Lincoln** (1858-2006) recalled the US president who was assassinated in 1865.

Famous local people are also remembered in Walsall. In Bloxwich, the Old Electric Palace Cinema opened in 1912 and seated 400 people, but closed in 1922 to make way for the Grosvenor Cinema, built by Pat Collins. He was a local amusements and fairground owner who established the Showman's Guild. When Wetherspoon's refurbished the building at a cost of £1.9m in 2014, it was named the **Bloxwich Showman** after him.

As in most towns, homage is often paid to writer William Shakespeare. In Walsall, he was recalled at the **Shakespeare** in High Street (1801-1889). In Church Street, the **Paul Pry** (1834-1926) referred to an 1825 play by John Poole, whose main character meddles in other people's affairs because he has nothing to do himself!

The Industrial Revolution changed Walsall from a village of 2,000 people in the 16th century to a town of over 86,000 two centuries later. Coal mining and limestone working began during the 18th century and later, the town manufactured a wide range of products, including saddles and other leather goods, chains, buckles and plated ware, along with iron and brass foundries.

The town's leather industry is remembered at several local pubs, particularly saddle-making, including the **Saddlers Arms** in Station Road (1871-1912) and Bloxwich (1962). More specialised leather trades were recalled at the **Tanners Arms** in Hatherton Street (1858-1909) and Day Street (1862-1966), **Tannery** in Burrowes Street (1983-1914) and **Leathercutters Arms** in Duncalfe Street (1840), which closed in 1925. A currier was a horse groom who helped to dress, colour and finish tanned hides, a trade recalled at the **Curriers Arms** in Day Street (1858-1923).

Many of the town's saddles were destined for horses, so it's not surprising that associated trades were reflected at the **Farriers Arms** in Dudley Street (1855-1860) and **Bridlecutters Arms** in Burrowes Street (1858-1958). "Hames" are curved pieces of wood or metal put around a horse's neck or collar, and were made locally. The trade was recalled at the **Hamemakers Arms** in Blue Lane West (1851), which was rebuilt in 1937 but demolished in 2004.

Coal mining was reflected at three long-gone pubs called the **Jolly Collier** and the **Colliers Arms** in Pelsall (1861). Seven pubs were called the **Miners Arms,** including those at Bloxwich (1858-1907), Pelsall (1858-1895) and Rushall (1845-1945). Pubs named the **Engine,** such as that in Wolverhampton Street (1834-1966), usually referred to colliery pumping engines.

Iron and steel foundries began to be established in the 19th century, and are recalled by the **Forge** at Pelsall (1861-1908), **Forge Hammer** in Rolling Mill Street (1861-1966) and **Forge & Fettle** in Pleck Road (1858-1999). More specialised trades were recalled at the **Grinders Arms** in Pleck (1851), along with the **Shinglers Arms** (1857-1910) and **Puddlers Arms** in Birchills (1869). The **Chainmakers Arms** in Green Lane (1841-1966) and **Spurmakers Arms** in Tantarra Street (1862-1966) reflected other specialised trades in the town.

There were several brickworks around the town, recalled at the **Brickmakers Arms** at Walsall Wood (1939). Associated trades were recalled at the **Bricklayers Arms** in Lower Rushall Street (1871-1882), at Pleck (1834-1866) and Pelsall (1843-1876), along with the **Builders Arms** in Wisemore (1837-1966), **Plasterers Arms** in Upper Rushall Street (1851) and **Slaters Arms** at Pleck (1858).

There were many other industries and trades in Walsall that were reflected in the names of its pubs. They included the **Brushmakers Arms** in Bloxwich (1868-1904), **Clockmakers Arms** in Rolling Mill Street (1871-1896) and **Coachmakers Arms** in Bridgeman Street (1871-1966). There was also a **Fitters Arms** in Hatherton Street (1856-2009) and **Gas Fitters Arms** in Stafford Street (1869). The **Plumbers Arms** in Littleton Street (1852-1939) was originally a home-brew pub known as the Slaters Arms, whilst the **Bakers Arms** in Caldmore was first licensed in 1834, but converted into shops in 2007.

Local breweries are remembered at the **Butlers Arms** in Bloxwich (1865-2007), rebuilt in 1925 for William Butler's (Wolverhampton) Brewery. The local Highgate Brewery was recalled at the **Brewery Stores** in High Street, which was allegedly haunted and, after being renamed the Market Tavern, closed in 2009.

Canals and railways were important in the growth of the town. The **Canal Tavern** at Bloxwich originally dated from 1853 as the Lamp, but was replaced by the **Bridgewater** pub in 1964. There's also a **Boat** in Birchills (1857-1923), a **Boathouse** in Rushall (2017), and a **Boatman's Rest** in Walsall Wood (1849).

The **Railway** in Station Street (1851-1937) was once a commercial hotel with an American bowling saloon, whilst the pub in Bloxwich (1851) was rebuilt in 1923 and the one in Pelsall (1855) remains open today. In Duncalfe Street, the **North Western** (1857-1909) was once owned by the London & North-Western railway company, who also owned the **Refreshment**

Room at Walsall railway station until 1933, originally built by the South Staffordshire Railway in 1855. In Park Street, the **New Station** (1872) became the New Station Hotel before it closed in 1929. Other railway stations were recalled at the **Station** in Pelsall (1860-1939) and Walsall Wood (1891), and **Station Hotel** in Bloxwich (1859-2012). **George Stephenson,** the famous railway engineer, is recalled at a pub in Stephenson Avenue (1998).

The days of the old coaching inns were recalled at the **Coach & Horses** in Ablewell Street (1828-1906), originally built in 1750 on the site of John Hare's garden. Other similarly named pubs were in King Street (1822) and Walsall Wood (1861-1932). Carriers of goods were recalled at the **Carriers Arms** in Bloxwich (1874-1928).

In the early days, Walsall prospered from the surrounding agricultural areas, with local pubs recalling some of those trades. They included the **Haymakers Arms** in Bloxwich (1881) and **Wheatsheaf** in Birmingham Road, originally dating from 1801 as the Greyhound, and haunted by a soldier in RAF uniform. The **Wheatsheaf** in Bloxwich (1834) originally dated from Tudor times, but was later rebuilt, whilst its namesake at Leamore (1872) was closed by 1949. The **Old Wheatsheaf** in Birmingham Street was originally a home-brew pub dating from 1858, but was closed by 1904. The **Barley Mow** in Bloxwich originally dated from 1827, but was demolished in 2012, whilst its namesake in Hill Street (1818) lasted until 1898. There was also the **Plough** in Bloxwich (1846-1913) and **Plough & Harrow** in Ablewell Street (1818).

Three pubs were named the **Bull's Head,** at Bloxwich (1812-2010), Birchills (1842-1909) and Stubbers Green (1858-1915). In Sutton Road, the **Longhorn** originally dated from 1856 as the Red House, but was rebuilt in 1933 for the Lichfield Brewery and now recalls a breed of cattle. The **Durham Ox** in Park Street (1861) recalls a heavyweight beast that toured the country in the early 1800s, whilst the **Dun Cow** in Wolverhampton Street (1839-1961) referred to a similarly monstrous beast that went on a murderous rampage until it was slayed by Guy, the Earl of Warwick. There's also a **Spotted Cow** in Bloxwich (1849) and a **Red Cow** in Goscote (1861-2015).

Farm animals were recalled at the **Lamb** in Caldmore (1869-1967) and **Hen & Chickens** in Lower Rushall Street (1811-1881). The woollen trade was remembered at the **Woolpack** in Digbeth (1796-1966), a late Medieval timber-framed pub, which was once the centre of cockfighting in Staffordshire. In Wolverhampton Street, the **Flitch of Bacon** (1861-1922) recalled the name for a salted and cured side of pork.

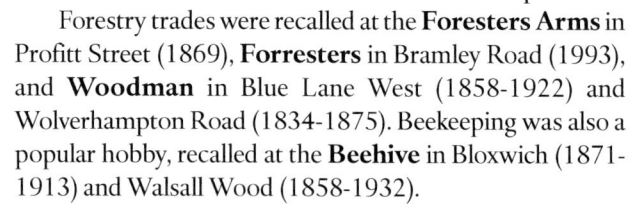

Forestry trades were recalled at the **Foresters Arms** in Profitt Street (1869), **Forresters** in Bramley Road (1993), and **Woodman** in Blue Lane West (1858-1922) and Wolverhampton Road (1834-1875). Beekeeping was also a popular hobby, recalled at the **Beehive** in Bloxwich (1871-1913) and Walsall Wood (1858-1932).

Racing was also remembered in Walsall, in Upper Rushall Street, at the **Greyhound** (1801-1901) and **Hare & Hounds** (1801-1905). There were also three pubs called the **Horse & Jockey**, in Bloxwich Road (1841), Green Lane (1856-1911), and Walsall Wood (1824-1940).

Walsall had many pubs named after a fascinating range of famous people and recalling its local industries and trades. Few survive today, but those that remain retain many memories.

WALSALL – OLD PUBS

Walsall was first settled by the Celtic tribes between 600BC-43AD (as *Wal's Valley*), and until the 18th century was a largely rural area. The 19th century was a period of tremendous social and economic change, as the urban population grew due to industrial growth. During this time, the number of pubs increased dramatically, becoming the social and commercial centres of the town, as well as providing venues for meetings and social events and catering for thirsty workers. Since the early 18th century, around 600 pubs have served Walsall's local community.

Walsall's oldest pubs dated from the 16th century, but all are long-gone. In Digbeth, the **Woolpack** was a late-Medieval timber-framed pub, known as one of the premier cockfighting venues in Staffordshire. In 1651, Col. John Lane mustered Royalist troops here to fight against Charles II at Worcester, but the pub was rebuilt in 1899 and demolished in 1966. The **Old Still** originally dated from Tudor times and was first licensed in 1818, but was demolished in 1959. It had Dr Johnson's Corner, who rested here on his visits from Lichfield. Other historic pubs included the **Talbot** (1801-1963) in Digbeth, **Three Swans & Peal** (House that Jack Built) (1811-1891) in Peal Street, **Three Tuns** (1801-1902) in Lower Rushall Street and **Angel** (1841-1861) in Park Street.

In Rushall Street, there were 11 inns and four beerhouses, where legends told of tunnels leading to places like Rushall Hall. Other historic pubs clustered along Church Hill, opposite St Matthew's Church, included the **Barley Mow** (1783-1898), **Leathern Bottle** (1818-1939) and **Old Queen's Head** (1845-1903). At the foot of Church Hill, the **Shakespeare Inn** (1801) was a Georgian building, which became a lodging house in 1889, with much older cellars leading to limestone caverns. Nearby, Bull's Head Yard recalls the existence of the **Bull's Head,** once an important coaching inn, but demolished in 1892.

Walsall's oldest remaining building that was a pub is the **White Hart** in Caldmore Green. Originally built as a residence by George Hawe in 1560, it became an inn in 1801. During reconstruction work in 1870, workmen discovered a mummified human arm and sword dating from the Civil War. Tradition said that this was the hand of a hanged man torn from the body as it swung on the gibbet – the "Hand of Glory", but it was more probably the hand of a child, surgically removed for use in a medical school or hospital. The building is no longer licensed (but listed Grade II) and the hand was donated to Walsall Museum.

Another famous inn was the **Green Dragon,** where Emphraim Deykin was recorded as the first licensee in 1707. But the pub and adjoining Guildhall were rebuilt in 1773, after which it was kept by Thomas Fletcher. Its assembly rooms were used as a theatre from 1787-1803, where actress Sarah Siddons is reputed to have performed before it became a Catholic chapel. However, the pub's licence was not renewed after 1909, when it was used by magistrates' clerks. In 1976, it was modified, refurbished and relicensed as a pub, and its historical significance was recognised in its Grade II listing. It's also reputedly haunted by Mary Hemming, a lady in a blue dress who stands at the second floor window. After closing in 2008, it reopened as the **Black Country Arms** and is a regular winner of CAMRA's local Pub-of-the-Year Award.

The **George Hotel** was another venerable tavern, also established by Thomas Fletcher in 1781 on The Bridge. After obtaining an Act of Parliament to build a new road to Stafford, it became Walsall's premier commercial hotel and principal coaching inn, with stagecoaches running to London, Bristol, Manchester, Sheffield and Liverpool. It was rebuilt as a modern hotel in 1935, but replaced by shops in 1979.

In 1750, Mr Siddons ran the **London Apprentice** in Rushall Street. He wanted his son, William, to become a barber, but he preferred the stage, became an actor and married Sarah

Kemble (Siddons), one of England's greatest actresses. In 1774, the **New Inn** opened in Park Street, taking advantage of the new turnpike road to Wolverhampton, and was well known for its cockfights during Walsall Races. In 1777, John Jacam was the first licensee of the **Brewery Stores** in High Street. It later became the stores for Highgate Brewery and, after being renamed the Market Tavern, closed in 2009. It was reputedly haunted by a disembodied monk's head and an old lady.

In 1796, John Mountford first kept the **Dog & Partridge** in Sandwell Street, but it was rebuilt by 1934 and closed in 2017. For over 80 years, William Brown's family kept the **Blue Pig** in New Street, dating from 1813, but it closed in 1932. In High Street, the **Bear & Ragged Staff** was originally built in 1815 as the residence of the master of Walsall's pig market. When it was owned by Walsall Council, it was known as the Corporation Arms where, in 1906, licensee Josiah Burgess paid an annual rent of £70; the pub was demolished in 1966. The **Black Boy** (1818) in New Street was used by "Cobdenites", campaigning to repeal the Corn Laws, but closed in 1923.

Facing across Bath Street were the **White Swan** and **Seven Stars.** In 1783, Thomas Carless was the first licensee of the **White Swan,** but by 1851, it was kept by John Osbourne, who also collected the poor rate, but it closed in 1938. The **Seven Stars** (1834) was originally a Georgian beerhouse and was a rival to the nearby **Jolly Bacchus** (1834-1906), but lost its licence in 1901. In Stafford Street, the **Criterion** was first licensed in 1818 as the Duke of Wellington and later renamed the Earl Grey, but was demolished in 1980. It had a music hall and was known locally as the "Madhouse" or "Blood Bath", due to the heated political arguments which took place.

In Lichfield Street, **St. Matthew's Hall** was originally built in 1831 in Greek Doric style as the town's first permanent library, becoming the County Court in 1847. Now a listed building (Grade II), it was converted into licensed premises in 1998 and became a Wetherspoon's pub in 2011. In Leicester Square, the **Black Swan** dated from 1837 and was variously known as the Stork Hotel and Dirty Duck before closing in 2007.

On the corner of Ablewell Street, the **Borough Arms** is one of the town's finest examples of a Victorian pub, purpose-built for Mitchells & Butlers in 1903. It still displays Walsall's coat of arms on the frontage, retains some original features and became Flan O'Briens, an Irish-themed pub. On the edge of the town centre, the **Pretty Bricks** started life as the New Inn in 1838, but was rebuilt in 1871. It gained its current name in 2008 and retains many original features, including the attractive glazed-brick frontage and interior stained glass screens.

Pubs were regularly used for meetings of Friendly Societies, workers' groups and religious organisations. Live entertainment was also popular, with plays, comedies and variety shows being performed in the larger pubs. In the 19th century, cockfighting, bull-baiting and bare-knuckle prize fighting also took place clandestinely in pubs – you could also win a pig in the skittle alley! Sadly, this merriment is not available nowadays, but we can still enjoy an excellent pint of beer in the remaining hostelries.

WEDNESBURY

Wednesbury can trace its origins back to Saxon times, as one of the few settlements (including Wednesfield) named after the Saxon God, Woden. In 1898, a Daily Mail reporter visited the town to investigate a spate of underground fires in disused mine workings. He observed that *"the good folk of Wednesbury go on their sooty way happy in the knowledge that nothing more dreadful than life in their own town is likely to occur"*. By the time of the Industrial Revolution, Wednesbury's well-known metal-bashing industries had developed from its early nailmaking trade, with gun barrels, tool and tube manufacture earning it the name of "Tube Town". Workers' thirsts needed quenching by more than 230 pubs and beerhouses, of which barely 25 remain today.

High Bullen was the medieval centre of the village, although most of the historic buildings were replaced by Crown Tube Works in 1902 and a new road in 1969. Several old pubs grouped around the junction with High Street, the oldest being the **Horse & Jockey**, a "most ancient and venerable hostelry" dating from the early 1700s. It was rebuilt in 1913 when the roof collapsed, and was demolished in 1968. Nearby, the **King's Arms** (1822) was a home-brew pub, where landlords Thomas Jones and John Jackson brewed their own beer. It was later home to Hickman & Pullen's High Bullen Brewery, before closing in 1932. Thomas German was the bandmaster of the Crown Tube Works Band and kept the **Elephant & Castle** (1818), which later became a nightclub, but was demolished in 2010. The **Bull's Head** (1822) was a popular Showell's Brewery (Langley) pub, which was demolished in 1968.

Amongst the cluster of pubs around the Crown Tube Works, the **Rising Sun** (1818) was a Highgate Brewery (Walsall) pub, rebuilt in 1939 and later converted into an old people's home. In Meeting Street, the **Old Royal Oak** was a Hanson's (Dudley) pub dating from 1818, with its own music hall. Along Trouse Lane, gunlock maker Samuel Samson and his family kept the **Fortune of War** (1834) until 1881, followed by Harry Pitcock from 1929 until it closed in 1945.

In Hall End, the **Old Blue Ball** dates back to 1786 and is Grade II listed, with some original features. Known locally as Spittle's after landlord Jonah Spittle who organised cockfights, it had a concert hall, and the adjoining Vauxhall Gardens were used for al-fresco dances as "the resort of the giddy youth of the town". It features in the local ballad entitled *Wedgebury Cocking*, recalling cockfights between colliers and nailers, and it is reputedly haunted by an old man with a dazzling white beard who could be landlord Spittle! It survives today, as does the **Woden** (1904) in Church Street. The **Rose Hill Tavern** in Church Hill (1841) once dispensed Henry Jerrams' "Noted Ales and Porter" from the Golden Ball Brewery, Oldbury.

Near the Theatre Royal in Upper High Street was the **Lamp** (1818), later to become the Midland Vaults and converted into a restaurant in 2013. Next door was the **Malt Shovel** (1841-1892), also kept by the Spittle family. They also kept the **Blue Ball** (1864-1921) in Earps Lane, which was also the home of Charles Exley's Wednesbury Brewery. In Walsall Street, the **Bell Inn** was first licensed in 1818, but was later rebuilt. After closing in 1984, it was extended and relaunched as the **Bellwether** in 2008, now a popular Wetherspoon's pub.

The Market Place was another focus for old inns and pubs, the oldest being the **Golden Cross,** where John Wesley preached on the steps outside in 1743. It was rebuilt in 1901, and later renamed the Pig & Trumpet, but more recently it returned as the Golden Cross. **The George** occupied a focal point on the corner of High Street/Union Street, originally dating from 1818 as the King's Head. Known locally as the Top Wrexham, serving Peter Walker's Wrexham Ales, it was replaced by a new pub in 1959 and is now named after former Sandwell mayor, **William Archer.**

The **Talbot** was originally a half-timbered Elizabethan inn, which featured in miners' and colliers' strikes in 1824. It was rebuilt in fine style for wine and spirit merchant John Taylor Duce in 1879, and was where Sidney Webb started his undertakers business in the cellar! The building became a furniture store and survives today. **The Royal Exchange** (1839-1955) was an Atkinson's (Birmingham) pub, whilst the **Green Dragon** (1818-1963) was an old coaching inn, where the Tally-Ho stopped on its way to Birmingham. The **George & Dragon** dated from 1777 and was popular for its daily lunches (with free second helpings), but it was demolished in 1965.

In Lower High Street, historic pubs included the **Turk's Head** (1818), an old coaching inn, which was rebuilt in 1903, and later extended and renamed the Tavern in 2014. Nearby was the **Nag's Head** (1834-1980), while on the corner of Holyhead Road was the **White Horse Hotel** (1818-1996). It was a former home-brew pub where William Beebee and the Millward family brewed their own beer, and was the terminus for the local trams.

In 1826, the old town centre was effectively bypassed by Thomas Telford's new Holyhead Road and other hostelries took the place of the old coaching inns. The **Red Lion** in Bridge Street became the town's premier coaching inn, with coaches leaving for Birmingham, Bridgnorth, Shrewsbury and Holyhead. It featured in the Wednesbury Riots when John Wesley preached here in 1743, and in the early 1800s, when English aeronaut, James Sadler made an unsuccessful balloon flight from here, but it was demolished in 1983. On the corner of Mount Street, the **Coachmaker's Arms** (1834) was converted into housing in 2015.

In Holyhead Road, the **Anchor Hotel** (1870) was a commercial hotel and meeting place for many of the town's societies who used its popular function room (Ski Room), including the local bicycle, swimming and cricket clubs, striking tube workers, Freemasons and Ratepayers Association. Apparently, the pub was haunted, with doors opening and closing and the dumb waiter working by itself! It closed in 1985 and was later converted into a fitness centre, but the ghosts still play their tricks by smashing photographs.

Around the busy junction with Dudley Street were the **Dartmouth Arms** (1834-1963), known locally as the Bottom Wrexham, the **Stores** (1871-1966) and **Queen's Arms** (1849), which was converted into a restaurant in 2004. The **Three Swans** (1818) was also known as The House that Jack Built, but was demolished in 1986. Nearby in Dudley Street, the **Pack Horse** (1818) was rebuilt in 1837, but closed in 1960.

However, the oldest pub around Wednesbury is undoubtedly the **Olde Leathern Bottel** in Vicarage Road, formerly the main road to Walsall. Established in 1510 in old nailmakers' cottages, it was once a coaching inn reputedly patronised by Dick Turpin, but was rebuilt in 1913. The snug was originally part of a vicarage and is said to be haunted by an old man in grey who seems to resent the presence of ladies in that room, along with a former regular customer of the pub who was a victim of a Zeppelin raid in 1916!

So, although Wednesbury has lost many of its old pubs, several interesting historic pubs remain to serve some excellent beers.

WEDNESFIELD

Wednesfield is one of the oldest townships in the Black Country, and is one of the few places to be named after the Saxon God of War, Woden. Referred to as *Wodensfelde* in the Domesday Book, its historic claim to fame is its location for the Battle of Tettenhall between the Saxon Mercians, led by Edward the Elder (son of Alfred the Great), against the Vikings in August 910. But it was also famous for making all types of locks, keys and traps, including rat-traps and man-traps. In 1703, the town's first recorded locksmith was Richard Tomkys, whose family later kept several of the town's pubs, and many landlords were also lock and trap-makers.

Like many Black Country towns, the township's population increased dramatically from 1,100 in 1801 to over 14,500 a century later, with many of its workers employed in metal-based industries. But even with the coming of the canals and railways, in 1868 writer J.C. Tildesley thought the town still retained its *"quaint mixture of town and country, garden and workshop, toil and ease ... with a tortoise pace of progress"*. Wednesfield jealously guarded its independence as a separate urban district, but the 20th century saw much urbanisation and industrial development as it began to be swept up in the Black Country's expansion. Several major factories were established in and around the town, from paint-making to confectionery, tube works and factories making radiators and axle boxes. All this heavy industry was thirsty work, with more than 100 pubs serving the town.

The town's oldest pub is undoubtedly the **Dog & Partridge,** the oldest building in the High Street, dating from before 1782 and now a Grade II listed building. Samuel and Edward Marston were the first landlords, and from 1879 it was kept by John and Ernest Gregory and their family for nearly 80 years. As a result, the pub was known locally as Gregory's, and they brewed their own beer here until 1953. In October 1923, it was the loading point for the first trolley bus to Wolverhampton and it was also the headquarters of Wednesfield Bowling Club. The **Royal Tiger** originally dated back to 1818, as the Tiger or Old Tiger. Until 1842, it was kept by cabinet key-maker Joseph Tomkys and his wife Ann, but was rebuilt in 1875 as the Royal Tiger. In 1998, the bakery next door was rebuilt as the new Royal Tiger at a cost of over £870,000 and it's now a modern Wetherspoon's pub.

Nearby, the **Angel** was originally a 16th century coaching inn, first licensed in 1830 and rebuilt in 1936. Rat-trap makers, Luke Nicholls and Thomas and James Howe sold their "fine home-brewed ales" here until 1958, using water from their own well, hops from Herefordshire and yeast from Walsall's Highgate Brewery. The **Rose & Crown** (1830) was popularly known as Vinny Ostin's after landlord Vincent Austin (1932), but was demolished by 1940. Backing on to the canal opposite St Thomas' Church is the **Boat** (1861), another Grade II listed building. It was once noted for its cock and dog fights, whippet racing and rat catching, and it remains a popular and attractive village hostelry.

In the back streets, Rookery Street was home to several old pubs, including the **Pyle Cock** (1867). Originally a beer shop before being taken by Banks's (Wolverhampton) in 1881, it had a popular bowling green, nicknamed The Old Umbrella due to its shape. It was kept by George and Bertie Hargreaves from 1932-1970 and by Ada Loftus until 1986, but it closed in 2015 and is now a day nursery. The **Royal Oak** (1830) was a popular home-brew house and grocer's shop ran by the Corkindale and Corbett families until 1862, and kept by Sybil Ansell from 1929-1940, but it was demolished in 1982 for road improvements.

The **New Inn** was kept by rat trap-maker John Tomkys and his wife and daughter, Frances and Fanny, between 1833-1872, before becoming an Atkinson's (Birmingham) house. It was known locally as Sammy Frankie's, but was demolished by 1940. The **Old Crown** (1833) was a popular home-brew pub where John Marshall brewed his own beer, but it was gone by 1922.

The Hickman Estate lay between Rookery Bridge and Graiseley Lane and was home to a few old pubs and beerhouses. They included the **Black Horse** (1851-1867), **Star** (1881-1940) and **Talbot** (1834-1940), but the area was cleared for redevelopment in the 1960s.

Over the canal bridge in Lichfield Road is the **Vine,** originally built in 1881 (see below). A few doors away was the **Cross Guns** (1841), which was rebuilt in the 1930s and remembered for its weekly horticultural show. It became a Holt, Plant & Deakin pub in 1984, and is now a restaurant. Further along Lichfield Road is the **Lancaster,** a relative newcomer of 1940 and originally known as the Albion. It recalls the time a Lancaster bomber crashed nearby in May 1945, and is now a Harvester pub/restaurant.

Once in the countryside at Wood End, the **Pheasant** originally dated back to 1637, but was rebuilt in the 1930s. It was a rambling coaching inn, where early landlords were also farmers. The sons of landlord Frank Mason would often ride horses on burglarious missions to isolated churches in the Shropshire countryside, stealing silver plates. But eventually they were caught red-handed and their criminal careers were ended by the hangman's noose. Originally a home-brew house where Elizabeth Lane and William Taylor brewed their own beer, it became another Holt, Plant & Deakin pub in 1993 and is now known as the New Pheasant.

Also in Wood End is the **Castle Inn,** originally dating from 1853 and popular with pigeon fanciers, but rebuilt in 1961 and still serving the local community. The **Noah's Ark** dated from 1869, was rebuilt in 1964, but converted into a shop in 2016. In Amos Lane, the **Red Lion** is another relative newcomer, dating from 1938, designed by local architect Richard Twentyman. Landlord Harry Davenport (1938-1957) hosted his annual rose show here, whilst later landlord, Harry Hulse (1975-1987) was a Burma war veteran. In March End, the **Falcon** (1851) with its popular bowling green, was demolished in 1997, whilst the **Greyhound,** built in 1885 by Charles Lewsey, was closed in 1983 and acquired for road widening which never happened.

So although Wednesfield has lost some of its old pubs, several interesting historic pubs remain to serve a wide range of excellent beers.

"Young and Old" in Wednesfield

The **Vine** near the canal bridge in Lichfield Road originally dated from 1881, but was rebuilt in 1938 for brewers Truman, Hanbury & Buxton to a design by Burslem architects, Watkin & Maddox. It stands out as an exceptionally complete and largely unaltered example of a small inter-war pub, retaining many features from this time, including its original bar and counter, separate public bar, smoke room and lounge, terrazzo and parquet tiled floors, glazed tile fireplaces, wooden seats, stained glass panels, bell pushes and largely unaltered toilets. Known locally as the Young & Old, it's listed as a historic building (Grade II) and included in CAMRA's National Inventory of Historic Pubs. Florence Lathe was a popular landlady who was not only born in the pub in 1928, but also kept it from 1957-1992. It's now a CAMRA local award-winning Black Country Ales' real ale pub.

WEST BROMWICH – PUBS RECALLING FAMOUS PEOPLE & LOCAL TRADES

From the late Middle Ages, pubs (or ale-houses, taverns and inns) needed to identify themselves in some way at a time when most people were illiterate. So simple signs evolved, ranging from a crooked piece of wood, holly bush, tradesman's sign, or a type of heraldic sign borrowed from religion or aristocratic coats of arms. There are probably upwards of 17,000 different signs for pubs, the most popular being the Red Lion, Crown and Royal Oak.

West Bromwich was no different, with 13 pubs called the **Crown** (or Crown & Anchor, Crown Cushion, Rose & Crown or Three Crowns), six pubs called the **Red Lion** and five pubs named the **Royal Oak**. But there were also eight pubs called the **Royal Exchange,** referring to the trade and exchanges that took place in pubs. Seven pubs were called the **White Swan,** six pubs were named after **Britannia,** with five referring to **Albion,** and six pubs were called the **Roebuck.**

There were half-a-dozen pubs with the generic name of **Kings Head** or **Kings Arms.** In Loveday Street, the **King & Constitution** (1834-1957) recalled the time when King John was forced to accept the Magna Carta in 1215. **King Edward VII** was remembered at a pub in Old Meeting Street (1871-2006), whilst **King William** was recalled at a pub in Swan Village (1849-1930). Six pubs recalled King George, including the **George** in Carter's Green (1861-1914), Phoenix Street (1871-2012) and Spon Lane (1880-1912). His saintly relation was recalled at the **George & Dragon** in Barton Street (1881-1920), originally called the Wellington.

The **Star & Garter** in High Street (1841) recalls the Order of the Garter, first instituted by King Edward III in 1348. The **Black Boy** in Lyndon Street (1818-1932) usually referred to King Charles II, known for his jet-black hair and swarthy skin. Pubs named after the **Royal Oak** generally refer to the Boscobel Oak near Shifnal, where Charles II hid to escape from the Roundheads after the Battle of Worcester in 1651. The **Rising Sun** in Barton Street (1879-2012) referred to a common heraldic symbol related to King Edward III and Richard III. At Greets Green, the **Union Cross** home-brew pub (1834-1984) probably refers to the Act of Union in 1707 between England and Scotland.

Apart from four pubs named the **Queens Head,** the **Victoria** in Lyng Lane (1845) recalls the long-reigning monarch. Her consort, **Prince Albert,** is recalled at pubs in Moor Street (1871-2012) and Sams Lane (1857), whilst her son, the **Prince of Wales,** is recalled at pubs in High Street (1868), John Street (1861) and Paradise Street (1879-1912). The Royal Family's home at **Windsor Castle** was recalled at a pub in Sams Lane (1853-2001).

In Church Lane, the **Duke of Wellington** (1871-1910) recalled the national hero who defeated Napoleon at Waterloo in 1815 and later became Prime Minister and introduced the Beerhouse Act in 1830. He's also remembered at the **Wellington** in Great Bridge Street (1868-1983) and Newhall Street (1871-1957). The **Duke of York** in High Street (1870-1878) recalled probably the best remembered holder of that title who commanded the English army in Flanders in 1794-1827. However, the popular song misrepresents the facts, since the Duke was only 31 years old, had 30,000 men, and there were no hills in the area where he was fighting!

Other military figures included the **Nelson** in New Street (1861-2008), recalling the famous admiral who fought at the Battle of Trafalgar on *HMS Victory* in 1805. The battles in the Crusades were recalled at the **Saracen's Head** in Greets Green (1849-1870) and **Turk's Head** in Great Bridge Street (1869-1957), Moor Street (1818-1842) and Sams Lane (1845-1948).

At Carter's Green, the **Inkerman Cottage** (1864-1958) recalled the location in Ukraine of important battles during the Crimean War in 1854. The **Dunkirk Inn** at Greets Green (1860-1977), home to Darby's Brewery, probably recalled the time when Cromwell captured the French port of Dunkirk from the Spanish in 1658. In Wood Lane, the **Oliver Cromwell** (1881-2007) recalled the leader during the English Civil War of 1642-1651.

References to the landed gentry include the **Dartmouth Arms** at Dartmouth Square (1841-1977), one of the town's leading hotels. It recalls the local Legge family, who became the Earls of Dartmouth and played an active part in the life of West Bromwich, endowing schools and engaging in other philanthropic activities. The 4th Earl of Dartmouth was the last to live in Sandwell Hall (demolished in 1928, although the gatehouse survives), before the family moved to Patshull Hall, near Wolverhampton. The **Lewisham Arms** in Hill Top (1881-1920) and High Street (1858-2001), home to Arthur Price's Lewisham Brewery, recalls Viscount Lewisham, the alternative title used by this family.

Famous local people are remembered at the **Asbury Tavern** in Grove Vale (1929), recalling Francis Asbury, who lived at Great Barr in the house now known as Bishop Asbury Cottage. He took to religion and toured the USA on horseback spreading his evangelical message of the Methodists and became a Bishop in 1784. The **Gough's Arms** at Hateley Heath (1849) recalls another local landowner, whilst the **Champion of England** referred to William (Tipton Slasher) Perry, who kept this pub on Spon Lane in the 1850s.

Religious references include the **Samson & Lion,** at pubs in Cooper Street (1864-1915) and Hill Top (1872-1994), referring to the exploits of this popular biblical figure. **Jenny Lind** was a popular singer in the 1880s, known as the "Swedish Nightingale", recalled at a pub in Hateley Heath (1871-1903). In High Street, the **Mazeppa** (1868-1910) recalled a poem by Lord Byron in 1819 about Polish nobleman, Ivan Stepanovitch Mazeppa, who was discovered in embarrassing circumstances with the young wife of a local magnate and later became leader of Ukraine.

Rail and canal transport was important to the development of West Bromwich during the Industrial Revolution. Several pubs named the **Boat** are located close to canals, including those at Brades Bridge, Golds Hill (1871-1937) and Greets Green Road (1870-1963). At Ryders Green, the **Eight Locks** (1845) refers to a flight of locks on the Walsall Canal, whilst the **Navigation** at Golds Green (1869-1911) and Tame Bridge (1869-1998) also referred to local canals. In Spon Lane, the **Steam Packet** (1871-1966) recalled the canal boats which plied between Birmingham and Wolverhampton, whilst pubs in High Street (1840-2007) and Spon Lane (1871-1965) recalled the **Anchor.**

Railways are recalled at pubs named the **Railway** in Harwood Street (1874), St Michael's Street (1878-1933) and Hill Top (1871-1922). The Great Western Railway was recalled at the **Great Western** in Chapel Street (1872-1960) and **Great Western Hotel** in High Street (1858-2006). The London & North Western Railway was recalled at the **North Western** in Spon Lane (1868-1895). Also in Spon Lane, the **Stour Valley** (1868-1972), known locally as Cree's after the long-serving family of licensees, referred to the railway line between Birmingham and Wolverhampton.

Other forms of transport are recalled at the **Coach & Horses** in Hateley Heath (1959), Lyng Lane (1861-1958) and Greets Green (1845-1919), along with more basic travel at the **Waggon & Horses** in High Street (1830-2003) and Spon Lane (1868-1927). On Birmingham Road, the **Three Mile Oak** was a historic coaching inn dating back to 1800, next to the turnpike toll house and close to West Bromwich Albion's football ground. It was rebuilt in 1900, but demolished in 1990. Pubs named the **Junction,** such as those at Carter's Green (1841-1871) and Hill Top (1953-2011), usually referred to road, railway or canal junctions, and there were also two pubs named the **Bridge,** at Bromford Lane (1845) and Spon Lane (1881-1957).

West Bromwich came of age at the time of Victorian industrial and commercial growth, increasing its population from 5,687 in 1801 to over 65,100 a century later. The town was then producing axle boxes and hollow shafts, fenders and fire-irons, locks, bolts and hinges, saddle-wear and coach furniture, scales and spring balances, coffee mills, cutlery and utensils, chains, spades, steel toys and ornamental ironware, saucepans and hollow-ware, steam gauges, gas tubes and water pipes, with smelting furnaces, foundries and slitting mills, boat yards, lime kilns and brickyards. There were also several maltings supplying the local breweries who provided beer to the many pubs serving the thirsty workers.

The town's coal mining industry was recalled at the **Jolly Collier** in Seagar Street (1861) and **Miner's Arms** in Bagnall Street (1875) and Hill Top (1868-1907). Pubs named the **Engine,** such as those in High Street (1861) and Swan Village (1828), usually referred to colliery pumping engines.

Manufacturing was at the heart of West Bromwich and is recalled at the **Furnace** in Hill Top (1870), **Three Furnaces** at Golds Green (1834-1913), **Forge Hammer** in Spon Lane (1864-1938) and **Old Forge** in Great Bridge Street (1868-1910). The **Vulcan** at Greets Green (1860-1930) was close to the Vulcan Iron Foundry. More specialised local trades were recalled at the **Boilermaker's Arms** in Ryder Street (1868-1955), **Box Iron** at Hill Top (1801-1911), **Jolly Nailor** in Lyndon Street (1818-2014), **Smith's Arms** in Pleasant Street (1868-1957) and **Springmaker's Arms** at Hill Top (1868-1958). The construction industry was recalled at the **Bricklayer's Arms** in Spon Lane (1855) and **Plumber's Arms** in Hargate Lane (1818-1977) and Tyndal Street (1868-1959).

Engineering, particularly on the railways, was remembered at the **Engineer** in Cophall Street (1870), **Locomotive Engine** in Spon Lane (1920), **Steam Gauge** in Sams Lane (1920) and **Wheel** in Elwell Street (1887-1909). An older form of transport was recalled at the **Horseshoe** in High Street (1871-1976) and **Three Horseshoes** in High Street (1872) and Hill Top (1864). Farriers were recalled at the **Farrier** in the Sandwell Centre (1971-1986) and **Farriers Arms** in Queen Street (1858-1948).

Recalling West Bromwich's brewing industry were the **Brewers Arms** (1870-1896), close to Spon Lane Brewery, and **Malt Shovel** in Dove Street (1858-1959), Grove Vale (1935) and Sandwell Park (1878-1881). Some of the ingredients for making beer were recalled at the **Hop & Barleycorn** at Carter's Green (1876-1887) and Dartmouth Street (1861-2004), **Hop Pole** at Hill Top (1872-1955), and **Old Hop Pole** (1867) and **New Hop Pole** (1858) at Carter's Green.

The town once relied on its agricultural surroundings, recalled at the **Wheatsheaf** in Carter's Green (1868). Agricultural equipment was recalled at the **Plough & Harrow** in Mares Green (1818-1915) and Swan Village (1871-1963), along with the **Mill** at the Charlemont Farm Estate (1967-2012). Forestry was recalled at the **Foresters Arms** in Ault Street (1871-2012), whilst beekeeping was also a popular hobby, recalled at the **Beehive** at Hill Top (1868) and Great Bridge Street (1852-1988).

Farm animals were not forgotten, at the **Hen & Chickens** in Messenger Lane (1835-1969) and Hill Top (1818), along with the **Sow & Pigs** at Hill Top (1799), one of the oldest pubs in the area. Butchers were recalled with the **Shoulder of Mutton,** a popular joint of meat, in Spon Lane (1845-1954), Hill Top (1887-1930) and Greets Green (1835-1870). The **Dun Cow** was a particularly savage beast with an inexhaustible supply of milk, which roamed the countryside until it was slain by Guy, Earl of Warwick. It was recalled at the pub of that name at Cronehills (1871-1968).

There were four pubs named the **Bull's Head** in West Bromwich, including those in Bull Lane (1870-1997), Greets Green (1861-1954), Hill Top (1853-1955) and High Street (1790). This was one of the town's oldest pubs, rebuilt on the opposite side of the road in 1825, but closed in 1959.

There was also a **Red Cow** at Golds Green (1871-1911) and a **Loving Lamb** in Dartmouth Street (1868-1986), although this latter name tends to have more religious connotations.

We mustn't forget horses, such as the **Nag's Head** in Church Lane (1828-2014), Dudley Street (1871-1957) and Hall End (1851). Several pubs were also named the **White Horse,** including those in Paradise Street (1845-1889) and Phoenix Street (1872-1913), along with the **Black Horse** in Great Bridge Street (1870-1927) and **Black Pony** in Reform Street (1870-1908). The **Hare & Hounds** were recalled at a pub in Seagar Street (1828), along with the **Fox & Dogs** in High Street (1818), **Fox & Goose** in Greets Green Road (1872) and **Dog & Duck** in Braybrook Street (1864-1960), the first pub to be kept by brewer, George Darby.

References to the lion usually relate to heraldic images. In West Bromwich, they include the **Lion** in High Street (1864-1911), with its music hall, **White Lion** in Great Bridge Street (1868-1924) and Woodward Street (1861-1924), **Brown Lion** at Hill Top (1872-1921) and **Golden Lion** in Hall Green Road (1938-2007) and Hill Top (1835-1938). There were also six pubs named the **Red Lion,** including those in All Saints' Way (1818), Greets Green (1870-1927) and Union Street (1858-1969), along with a **Leopard** in Church Vale (1870-1965) and Moor Street (1871-1999).

Birds were recalled at the **Peacock** in Dartmouth Street (1864-1938), **Pheasant** in Albert Street (1861-1960) and Oldbury Road (1891-1913), and **Golden Pheasant** at Hill Top (1861-1932). Not forgetting the **Bird in Hand** in Phoenix Street (1875-1999) and Hill Top (1864-1966), and **Phoenix** at Swan Village (1868-1872). There were also five pubs named the **Swan,** including the oldest pub in Swan Village, originally built in 1550, rebuilt in 1860 and closed in 1992, and Hill Top (1868-1915). Seven pubs were named the **White Swan,** including those in Bromford Lane (1868), High Street (1870-1903), Hill Top (1881-1923) and Spon Lane (1841-1965).

Sports are not forgotten in West Bromwich, remembered at the **Cricketers Arms** in Lower Trinity Street (1858) and the **Horse & Jockey** in Hall Street (1864) and Stoney Lane (1818). The **Billiard Hall** in St Michael's Ringway was originally built by local architect, Albert Bye and opened in 1913, but became a Wetherspoon's pub in 2000.

Although West Bromwich is many miles from the coast, a life on the ocean wave is not forgotten, with pubs like the **Jolly Sailor** in Greets Green (1962-2007), named after Able Seaman Joseph Weston, who was lost with his ship, *HMT Pine*, in 1944.

West Bromwich had many pubs named after a fascinating range of famous people and recalling its local industries and trades. Few survive today, but those that remain retain many memories.

WEST BROMWICH – THE GOLDEN MILE & BEYOND

West Bromwich came of age at the time of Victorian industrial and commercial growth, increasing its population from 5,687 in 1801 to over 65,100 a century later. The town centre was the commercial hub of the town, with the "Golden Mile" of the High Street at its heart. Focused on Dartmouth Square, it abounded with shops, public buildings, pubs and other entertainments. In fact, over the length of High Street, there were no fewer than 25 pubs!

One of the oldest pubs was the **Bull's Head** on the corner of Paradise Street. Once a farmhouse called The Boot (named after Boot Meadow), first licensed by Farmer Kempson in the 1790s, it was renamed the Bulls Head in 1802 and rebuilt on the opposite side of the road in 1825. Known locally as the Top Wrexham (after Peter Walker's Wrexham ales), it closed in 1959.

In 1834, the original Bull's Head was replaced by the **Dartmouth Arms,** which became the town's premier commercial hotel, coaching inn and centre for official business and social meetings, until it was demolished in 1977. Between 1906-1920, it was kept by William Isaiah "Billy" Bassett, a famous footballer who played for West Bromwich Albion (1886-1899), gained 16 caps for England and later became chairman of the football club. Later landlord, Harry Clements (1920-1939), also played for the Albion.

Carter's Green is well known for its clock tower, erected in 1897 as a memorial to local benefactor, Alderman Reuben Farley. From 1841, the **Junction Hotel** was near here, with its notorious concert hall, but was replaced by a Wesleyan chapel in 1875. A few doors away was the **Nags Head** (1871), where landlord "Bobby" McNeal also played for West Bromwich Albion, but it became a furniture shop in 1957. On the corner of Guns Lane is the **Old Hop Pole** (1867), which once had etched windows advertising Showell's (Langley) beers and became a Holt, Plant & Deakin pub in 1986 (see below).

On the opposite side of the road was the **Marksman,** originally dating from 1644 as the Cross Guns, where one of Cromwell's troops was court-martialled and shot for desertion. It was kept by the Darby family from 1818-1851 and by local entrepreneur, Thomas Brennand until 1929. It was rebuilt, renamed the Marksman in 1973, and became a restaurant in 2008. A few doors away was the **Oddfellows Arms** (1868), once a Holder's (Birmingham) pub. It was kept by the Turley family between 1925-1960 and by Vic and Mary Baldwyn in the 1960s, but was incorporated into the adjoining wallpaper shop in 2009. Nearby, the **Wheatsheaf** also dates from 1868, and became a popular Holden's (Dudley) pub in 1972.

At the junction with Dartmouth Street is the **New Hop Pole** (1858), originally owned by Thomas Brennand, whose relatives established the Malthouse Brewery in Bratt Street. Known locally as the Bottom Wrexham, it was renamed Strollers in 2011. Opposite was the **New Church Tavern** (1871), another Holder's pub, which closed around 1959. Amongst the civic buildings was the **Old Post Office,** dating from the 1850s, converted into a pub in 1994, but closed in 2005. Further along High Street was the **Anchor** (1840), another Holder's pub where landlord James Raybould was regularly fined for permitting gambling, but was also a director of West Bromwich Albion. It was later kept by Albion footballer Billy Bassett from the Dartmouth Arms and became a nightclub.

At the junction with New Street, the **Sandwell** dates from 1851 as Birmingham House. Rebuilt as the Sandwell Hotel in 1895, it became a key social and commercial centre of the town for holding meetings, dinners and property auctions. Kept by popular landlord Harry Dale from 1928-1952, it's been known as the Goose & Granite and Goose, but is now simply the Sandwell. Just along St Michael's Street, opposite the bus station, is the **Billiard Hall,** designed by local architect, Albert Bye, in 1913 and now a popular Wetherspoon's pub. On the corner of Price

Street is the **Golden Cross** (1868), now known as Woodman Corner, but the **Railway** (1878-1933) is long gone.

Continuing along High Street, now pedestrianised, was the **Star & Garter,** dating from 1841, but recently demolished. The **Great Western Hotel** (1858) also had a frontage onto Paradise Street, with its popular dining room and jazz club, and was used for inquests into railway accidents. Kept by Florence Nodder between 1969-1988, it became a Holt, Plant & Deakin pub in 1989 and is now a café. Nearby was the **Horseshoe** (1871-1976), kept by Albion player, Bob Roberts, where the FA cup was displayed in 1888. On the corner of Queen Street was the distinctive **Corner House** (1911-1959), once known as Bass' Corner.

Near Dartmouth Square, the **Grapes** (1835) also had a frontage onto Paradise Street and was popular with anglers and pigeon fanciers, but closed in the 1960s. In Paradise Street itself, the **Albion Hotel** (1872-1958) was kept by John Shilton in 1889. He was also a cricketer with Warwickshire CC and had the "leading football and cricket depot in the district". In 1901, complaints were made about landlord Richard Wells, who played gramophone records on a Sunday, causing "great nuisance to the neighbourhood".

Beyond Dartmouth Square, there were more pubs and inns, including the **Stores** (1891-1958), opposite George Salter's offices and originally known as the Coachmakers Arms. The **Waggon Horses** (1830-2003) was home to George Griffin's small brewery, whilst the **Fox & Dogs** (1818) was home to Samuel Woodhall's Borough Brewery and is now a nightclub. On the corner of George Street is the **Prince of Wales,** opposite the **Olde Wine Shoppe,** both dating from 1868. This was previously known as the Old Grapes and the George, where Emily Fletcher (1935-1950) and Jimmy Lee (1961-1985) were long-serving licensees. Nearby was the **Golden Cup** (1871-1915), a former Cheshire's Brewery (Smethwick) pub. Opposite Trinity Road, the **Lewisham Arms** dated from 1858 and was home to Arthur Price's Lewisham Brewery. It was taken over by Holder's in 1908 and regularly used for meetings, dinners and concerts. Although the distinctive building remains, with its cornice stone showing the initials AJP, it was renamed Desi Junction in 2001.

Just beyond the Golden Mile, Guns Village was so called because of its historic links to the production of gun components. Little remains of that industry, but some of the pubs survive. In Guns Lane, we'd find the **Black Cock,** (1864-2002), originally financed by a breed of fighting cocks – "Smacker's Black Uns", bred by its first landlord, William "Smacker's" Beddoes. Near the railway in Harwood Street is the eponymous **Railway,** opened before 1874 and once a Holder's (Birmingham) pub. For almost 60 years, from 1906-1962, it was kept by just two families, Charles and Mary Morris and Leonard Dodd.

On the corner of Dartmouth Street and Oak Lane, the **Peacock** (1864-1938) was once a Cheshire's (Smethwick) pub, described in 1899 as a "house of disorderly character". On the corner of Lambert Street, the **Vine** (1871) was originally a home-brew pub. On the corner of Brook Street, the **Loving Lamb** (1868-1986) was another home-brew pub where Edward Bailey brewed until 1899, and was kept for many years by Archibald and Violet Simcox. On the corner of Duke Street, the **Hop & Barleycorn** (1861) was also a home-brew pub, which passed to Joules (Stone) in 1929. It was kept by Stanley North from 1959-1986, but was demolished in 2007.

In the back streets between Oak Lane and Lyng Lane, in Barton Street we'd find the **George & Dragon** (1881-1920) and **Rising Sun** (1879-2005). In Richard Street, the **Oak Tavern** (1871-1956) was once a Rolinson's (Netherton) pub. In Moor Street, the **Leopard** (1871-1999) was believed to be haunted by landlord/brewer Peter Pearson. Nearby, Sarah Hale brewed her own beer at the **Prince Albert** (1871-2012), whilst Major George Cox brewed at the **Kings Arms** (1871-1913). There were two Showell's (Langley) pubs in Bromford Lane, the **Turks Head** (1845-1948), which featured as the Saracen's Head in the Victorian novel *Joseph's Coat*, and the **White Swan** (1868), which became a restaurant in 2014. Alfred and Sarah Freeman kept the **Bridge** (1845-1961) from 1906-1937, whilst Alfred and Martha Woodhall kept the **Royal Exchange** (1871-2014) from 1909-1944.

Along Lyng Lane were the **Coach & Horses** (1861), **Horse & Jockey** (1864) and **Victoria** (1845), renamed The Vic in 2003. In the back streets, we'd find the **Barrel** (1870), **Malt Shovel** (1858), **Smiths Arms** (1868) and **Golden Cup** (1855), where landlords Charles Perry and George Woodhall played for West Bromwich Albion. Most of these pubs disappeared during the redevelopment of this area from the late 1950s.

In Braybrook Street, the **Dog & Duck** (1864) was first kept by Charles Darby, who was later to establish Darby's Dunkirk Brewery. By 1901, it was described as another "house of disorderly character", but was later kept by James Stanton. He was one of the first footballers to play for West Bromwich Albion in 1878 (then called West Bromwich Strollers) and also played in their first FA cup match in 1883. By 1906, he was brewing Stanton's Pure Malt and Hop Ales at his small brewery here, and was "a gentleman held in high esteem by all who know him for his sterling business qualities". In 1926, he retired from brewing, but died in 1932 while on a Mediterranean cruise. The brewery and its associated pubs were then sold to Darby's Dunkirk Brewery.

In Sams Lane, the **Prince Albert** dates from 1857, whilst the **Windsor Castle** (1853-2001) was kept by the Chapple family between 1902-1932. In Newhall Street were the **Albion** (1873-1966) and **Wellington** (1871-1957), which was kept by Thomas Fleet for 37 years until 1950. George Street was home to the **Old Crown** (1868-1932), whilst in Trinity Road, the **Church Tavern** (1870) was once a Holder's (Birmingham) pub, but closed by the 1960s. In Roebuck Street, the **Vine** (1861) was kept for nearly 70 years by two families – John and Thomas Turley and Edith Burford.

On the other side of High Street, the **Windmill** (1872) in Temple Street was originally the Durham Cow, but closed in the 1960s. The **Royal Exchange** (1870-1978) was another home-brew pub where Reuben Blatchford brewed. For over a century, it had only 12 licensees, the longest-serving being William and Anne Tickle (1916-1937).

Sandwell Road leads to another **Old Crown** (1861), kept by Thomas and Emma Slim between 1934-1959. In The Cronehills, the **Boot & Slipper** (1858-1958) was once a Penn Brewery (Wolverhampton) pub. The **Crone Hills Tavern** (1871-1926) was another Holder's pub, and the **Dun Cow** (1871-1968) was a Darby's (West Bromwich) pub. In Bratt Street was the **Twelve Bells** (1871-1959), whilst in Loveday Street South we'd find the venerable **King & Constitution** (1834-1957).

In New Street, William Horton kept the **New Inn** (1868-1956) for almost 40 years until 1950, facing the **Nelson** (1861-2008) on the opposite corner of Pitt Street. The **Acorn** (1871-1958) was another Darby's pub, whilst the **Roebuck** (1870) was originally called the Stag and closed in the early 1960s. On the corner of Walsall Street was yet another **Old Crown** (1880-1957), which was kept by Thomas and Anne Agger from 1911-1950.

In Queen Street were the **Talbot** (1871-1938) and **Farriers Arms** (1858-1948), home to Thomas Oliver's first brewery. In Bull Street, the **Hope & Anchor** (1881) closed in the late 1950s, whilst the **Orange Tree** in Overend Street (1852) was gone by 1922. This must have been a rather dubious area, since in the 1880s, landlords at the **Plough** (1861-1957) were fined up to £10 for harbouring prostitutes.

Returning to Walsall Street, close to Thomas Oliver's Sandwell Brewery was the **Royal Exchange** (1851-1966). Charles Udall not only sold beer here at 1½d a pint, but also built a concert hall, which became the Theatre Royal in 1878, before it burnt down in 1895. On the corner of Herbert Street, the **White Hart** (1853-2005) was allegedly haunted and kept by Arthur and Mary Cartwright from 1909-1937, before being renamed the Drunken Duck in 2001.

In Reform Street, the **Globe** (1861) was once the headquarters of the local Homing Pigeon Society, and the **Black Pony** (1870-1908) was previously a Cheshire's pub. William Mason and his family kept the **Hen & Chickens** (1834-1969) for almost 70 years until 1934, whilst the **Samson & Lion** (1864-1915) in Cooper Street was another Showell's pub.

Near Mayers Green, the **Five Ways** in Seagar Street (1863) was kept for nearly 80 years by two families – Joseph and Elizabeth Powell and Ernest Willetts and his family. It was once known as the Fourpenny Shop (the price of a pint of beer!), but in 1994 it was incorporated into the adjoining **Hare & Hounds,** originally dating from 1797. On the corner of Lloyd Street, the **Crown & Cushion** (1871) was once kept by Stanley Davies (West Bromwich Albion's Mr Versatility).

In Taylors Lane, the **Plough & Harrow** was once a commercial hotel, first licensed in 1818, but became a bakery in 1915. It had an imposing frontage and extensive grounds at the rear. It also had a cage holding a thrush (throstle), the mascot of West Bromwich Albion when they played at Stoney Lane. Next to the football ground was the **Jolly Nailor**, originally the Red Lion dating from 1818, but converted into housing in 2014.

In Stoney Lane, the **Horse & Jockey** (1818) is another venerable hostelry, kept by horse-dealer Charles Cotterill and used in a Banks's TV advert in the 1990s. Nearby, the **Queens Head** (1839-2010) used to have etched windows advertising Bowen's Home-Brewed Ales.

Although the area in and around West Bromwich town centre has changed beyond recognition, a handful of interesting and historic pubs remain, serving some fine beers. Long may they prosper!

Ghostly happenings at the Old Hop Pole

The **Old Hop Pole** at Carters Green dates back to at least 1867, when it was granted a beerhouse licence under the regulations of the Duke of Wellington's 1830 Beerhouse Act. It's also known to be (very) haunted! One of the previous landlords experienced things going missing and getting moved around in the cellar. He also said that once he felt that he was being physically picked up and hurled against the cellar wall! The pub also has a small snug, where apparitions of a little boy talking to a little girl dressed in Victorian clothes have been seen, accompanied by icy chills. The snug is also inhabited by an old man in a cap, thought to be the ghost of a much earlier landlord who reputedly died in that room while counting his takings! Others say it could be the ghost of another landlord, Alfred Kendrick, who not only brewed his own beer, but was also a lime merchant. He met with a sudden and unexplained death in 1885 in one of the pub's outhouses and is often known to stare intently into the snug. Something to look out for when you're having a pint in the Old Hop Pole!

WILLENHALL

In 1843, **Willenhall** was described as "La Ville des Serruriers" (the town of locksmiths) by French politician and social reformer, Léon Faucher, who recorded some 280 lock-makers and 90 key-makers in the town. The town's famous lock-making industry was originally based in small family businesses working in tiny workshops, before expanding into larger factories. In the 19th century, many pubs opened to serve the thirsty lock-makers, miners and foundry workers. By 1851, 38 pubs and 23 beerhouses served a population of 11,930, which by 1911 had grown to over 19,300, when there was one pub for every 196 people.

The Market Place was the commercial centre of Willenhall, with many inns and taverns. The **Bell** dates from 1660, is a Grade II listed building and is probably the oldest building in the town. This former coaching inn has its original cellars, with a reputed tunnel to St Giles' Church and, for many years, was kept by Thomas Wakelam's family. The local building society was founded here in 1839, but it closed in 2006 and was bought by the Willenhall Heritage Trust in 2010. Nearby, the **Angel,** dating from before 1818, was demolished in 1934 to make way for the gas company's new offices, whilst the **Talbot** (1818) closed soon after 1946.

Another of Willenhall's oldest pubs was the **Bull's Head** in Wolverhampton Street, first licensed in the 1730s. It was an important coaching inn where mail was dropped off to the post office in the yard. For more than 150 years, it was kept by Jeffery Tildesley and his family, and in 1825, novelist George Borrow stayed here and immortalised the inn and its landlord in his novels *Lavengro* and *Romany Rye*. But it lost trade when it was bypassed by the railway and New Road, and was demolished in 1927.

Another important coaching inn was the **Neptune** in Walsall Street, opposite St Giles' Church. In the 1830s, the Quicksilver horse-drawn stagecoach called here on its way between Wolverhampton and Lichfield. Local magistrates and manorial officials regularly used a room at the inn, and many public announcements and election speeches were made from its balcony. Unfortunately, it closed in 1937 and was later demolished. Other historic coaching inns included the **Kings Head** (Stafford Street) and **Lion** (or Red Lion) in Upper Lichfield Street, which have been converted into shops.

Walsall Street was home to several old pubs. From 1901-1916, lock-maker, local councillor and later mayor, Randle Hobley, kept the **Prince of Wales** (1864), which was rebuilt in 1939. It's also haunted by a jilted bride, with two men in morning suits, and an old lady dressed in an old-fashioned, high-necked dress. Nearby are the **Three Tuns** (1855) and **Old Oak** (1877), originally home to Henry Mills' brewery. On the corner of Gipsy Lane was the **New Inn** (1818), rebuilt in the 1920s and now named the **County.**

Revd William Moreton (notorious "Owd Mowton", who was often drunk) used to call in to the **Royal George** (1818) opposite Bilston Street before preaching his sermons at St Giles, but it was rebuilt in 1847 and is now an Irish-themed pub. In Bilston Street, the **Waterglade** (1833) had a gym for training boxers, but was rebuilt in the 1930s and demolished in 2007. Prisoners bound for Stafford Jail would have their final drink at the **Plough** (1818) in Stafford Street, which was converted into a shop in the 1980s.

Other surviving old pubs include the **Crown** in Cheapside (1833), **Three Crowns** in Stafford Street (1822) and **Ring O' Bells** in John Street (1841). The **Royal Artillery** in Lower Lichfield Street was a home-brew pub dating from 1818, but closed in 1932. The newest pub is the **Malthouse,** built on the site of an old maltings before becoming the Coliseum Cinema in 1914. Rebuilt in 1932 as the Dale Cinema, it became a bingo hall in 1968 and was converted into a Wetherspoon's pub in 1999.

In Gomer Street West, the **Falcon** was originally built before 1891 on the site of an old chapel, but the current building dates from 1936. It retains many original 1930s fittings, including terrazzo tiling, wooden bar back, benches and embossed wallpaper, and is included in CAMRA's inventory of historic pubs. It's been kept by the Taylor family for over 30 years and is advertised as Willenhall's flagship real ale pub. Not far away in New Road, the **Castle** (1841) also still serves a good pint.

In St Anne's Road, the **Rushbrooke Farthing** dated from the early 18th century, when it was called the Springvale Tavern. It was rebuilt around 1830 and from 1861-1896 was kept by Silas Lucy Tonks, whose son, Joseph became a renowned local surgeon (the "poor man's doctor"). However, he died young after a balloon accident in 1891, and is commemorated by the clock and fountain in the town's marketplace. When Emily Tonks married Jesse Lashford in the 1920s, they expanded the brewery business and acquired a few more pubs, before diversifying into the leisure industry, converting an old football ground into a greyhound track. In 1932, the brewery, pub, seven tied houses and dog track were sold to Truman's Brewery for £34,500. In 1976, the pub was renamed after a local grocer who issued farthing tokens, Joshua Rushbrooke, but unfortunately it closed in 2008. Silas Tonks, then a master locksmith, later kept the **Forge Tavern** (1908) across the road.

In the 18th and 19th centuries, not only did Willenhall develop and expand, but outlying communities like Short Heath and New Invention also established mining and metal industries. New pubs opened to serve these growing communities, like the **Duke of Cambridge** in Coltham Road. Originally a 300-year-old farmhouse, it was converted into a pub by a foresighted farmer in the early years of the Industrial Revolution and first licensed in 1868. Unfortunately, its first landlord, George Henworth, was killed in a gas explosion at the nearby Short Heath colliery in 1879. It's now a popular real ale pub, owned by Black Country Ales. Nearby, the **Swan** (1860) was originally called the Nanny Goat Inn and is popular with anglers, whilst the **Lame Dog** (1886-1940) recalled a poem where friends are encouraged to help a lame dog over the stile. Other pubs serving Short Heath include the **Whimsey** (1833), rebuilt in 1947, **Bridge Tavern** (1859), a historic canalside pub, **Cross Keys** (1871), which had a boxing club, and **United Kingdom** (1841).

In New Invention, the **Gate** (1833-2007) recalled another poem where "This Gate Hangs Well and Hinders None; Refresh and Pay and Travel On". The **First & Last Inn** (1871-1908) was so named because it was the first pub after crossing the border from Wednesfield and obviously the last when travelling the other way. And while in New Invention, some may ask "why the name?" There are several stories, but one of the best is about the owner of an old property that had a smoking chimney. He modified an upturned milk churn and put it on the chimney, curing the smoking and calling it his... "new invention"!

So although Willenhall has lost many of its most celebrated inns, several historic pubs remain to serve a wide range of excellent beers.

WOLLASTON

Wollaston is barely a mile from the centre of Stourbridge, yet remains on the edge of the Staffordshire countryside. The first known reference to Wullaston was as early as 1241, but it probably dates back to Roman times. It's now largely a residential suburb of Stourbridge, but in the past, local industries included spade and shovel works, Ashford's Creameries and BSR's factory at the former Wollaston Mill. Around 15 pubs have played a part in Wollaston's community life since the 19th century and many still survive.

Wollaston Village is focused along High Street and Bridgnorth Road, where there's still a variety of small-scale shops. At the roundabout, near the Kinver Light Railway tram stop, the **Waterloo Inn** was first shown on the parish map of 1827, but later moved to the opposite side of the road. It was acquired by Simpkiss (Brierley Hill) in 1923, and had a bowling green, but it became a restaurant in 2009.

There were several pubs along High Street, including the **Riflemans Arms,** first recorded in 1856. This was once a Darby's (West Bromwich) pub, fostering local football, but it served its last pint in 1978. Early landlord Timothy Brooks also made spades, whilst later landlord Harry Taylor (1952-1972) was a footballer with West Bromwich Albion. The **Bulls Head** (1852) was once owned by Davenport's (Birmingham), but became a restaurant in 2008.

George, James and Kezia Thomason kept the **Britannia** (1839) for over 40 years until 1952, and it's still a popular sports pub. In 1856, the Old Gooseberry Wake was celebrated here, including "Swarming the Pole", "Diving for Oranges" and "Roll & Treacle Matches". It was once a home-brew pub and, in 2007, landlord Dave Russell was runner-up in the World's Biggest Liar competition. The **Barley Mow** was built on the site of an ancient family residence, first licensed in 1827 and rebuilt in 1965, but converted into a shop in 2013. From 1862, landlords Richard and William Matty held an annual wake here, and for some time, it was the HQ of Furnace Sports FC.

Several pubs are interspersed amongst the shops along Bridgnorth Road. The **Princess** (1861) started life as the Alexandra (a Bent's Brewery pub), but was renamed in 1997. It was kept by William and Louisa Harris from 1909-1930, Daniel Bagnall until 1962 and Fred and Edna Jacobs from 1976-1990.

The **Unicorn** was first established in 1850 by Joseph Lakin, who was a bareknuckle fighter. In April 1904, Buffalo Bill's Wild West Show took place on the fields opposite the pub. In 1912, the pub was sold for £800 to James Billingham, whose family kept it for 80 years and advertised "Ales All Brewed On The Premises", including Mild, Bitter and Old Ale, until 1963. When Eric Billingham died in 1992, it was bought by distant relatives, Batham's (Brierley Hill), and was kept for the next two years by Matthew Batham, and remains one of their iconic pubs. However, watch out for the ghost of an old landlord who sometimes spills beer into customers laps!

The **Gate Hangs Well** is believed to date from 1806 and was first licensed in 1835. Originally a home-brew pub, it was bought by Atkinson's (Birmingham) in 1897 for £1,200 and passed to William Butler & Co. (Wolverhampton) for £5,000 in 1929. Kept by Clifford and Ivy Wood from 1939-1956, it has the smallest pub bench in Stourbridge and remains a popular community pub.

Towards Stourbridge, there was a cluster of pubs along Withy Bank. At the corner of King Street is a new micro-pub, the **Kingsbridge,** which opened in 2020, whilst opposite St James' Church is **Webster's Brewhouse.** This started life as the Cottage Spring (1864) home-brew pub, with its own pleasure grounds and bowling green. Kept by Claude Sargent and his family from 1968-1985, Graham Webster renamed it Graham's Place in 2010, and established his micro-brewery here in 2014, but it's currently closed. Nearby, the **Albion** (1841) was another Home Brewery pub, which became a house in 1921 and was demolished in 1975.

In Lower King Street, the **Eagle Tavern** (1852) was a friendly local, with a bowling green, but also closed in 1921, whilst the **Swan** (1841) in Mamble Road was a pub until 1968. Not far from the cemetery in Dunsley Road was the **New Inn,** a Mitchells & Butlers pub built in the 1930s, but replaced by new housing in 1991.

On the corner of Mamble Road, just over the parish boundary, is **Katie Fitzgerald's.** Starting life in 1844 as the Golden Lion, this old beerhouse was well placed to attract trade along the Stourbridge-Bridgnorth turnpike road, opened in 1816. In 1892, it was renamed the N.W.B Entire when it was leased to North Worcestershire Breweries. However, for many years, it was a home-brew pub where Thomas Homer, John Auden and Francis Matthews brewed their own beer until it was sold to Ansell's (Birmingham) in 1947. In 1989, it reopened as the Stourbridge Lion, named after the famous steam locomotive built locally at the New Foundry in 1829 by Foster, Rastrick & Co. In June 2000, it was renamed Katie Fitzgerald's after landlady Trina Kean's grandmother and has been a popular music venue ever since. Opposite was the **Bridge Inn,** dating from 1855, which became Cross' shop in 1916.

Travelling towards Bridgnorth, there are two memorable pubs. The **Plough** was formerly a home-brew pub dating from 1851 and rebuilt in 1905. John and Horace Pearson advertised their Pearson's Entire here, shown on the etched windows, and it later became an M&B pub, kept by George Foden between 1923-1952. Inside, there's an amazing collection of pub memorabilia, old wirelesses, cameras and other mechanical artefacts. Rock legends, Robert Plant and Roy Wood, occasionally attended the folk club established here in the late 1980s by licensee Margaret Hayward, and it still serves a good range of real ales.

At the brow of the hill, Kinver farmer, John Yardley, sold a plot of land to Thomas Cooper in 1830. He then built a house, which he opened as a single-room beerhouse called the **Forester's Arms** in 1852. He appointed George Hill to run the pub, who brewed a typical Black Country malty mild – a dark, sweet and strong ale. In 1914, it was leased to the Home Brewery (Quarry Bank), but Benjamin and Fredrick Hill continued home-brewing until 1935, advertising Fred Hill's Home Brew & Pure Ales. It later passed to Ansell's (Birmingham), before becoming a Holt, Plant & Deakin pub in the 1980s. Sometimes known as the Ridge Top, other long-serving licensees included Fred Raybould (1953-1975) and Frank (The Gas) and Mary Downes (1982-1991). In the 1960-1970s, Stan Webb performed here with his group, Chicken Shack, named after the tin shack behind the pub. Popular with ramblers, it often has music and other events and still serves a great pint of real ale with tasty hot pork rolls.

Just over the border in Stourton, the **Stewponey & Foley Arms** was another popular pub for Black Country folks. This stood at the junction of the main A449 and the road to Wollaston, opposite the tollhouse and Staffordshire and Worcestershire Canal. Originally Benjamin Hallen's house of 1744, it was rebuilt in the 1930s, with an outdoor swimming pool, which was very popular with local people and visitors arriving by the Kinver tram. Its name is said to derive from a local pronunciation of Estepona, where the founder of the tavern had been a soldier in Spain. Unfortunately, this local landmark was demolished in 2001 and replaced with private housing, but a Kinver tram pole remains on the road frontage!

WOLVERHAMPTON – PUBS RECALLING FAMOUS NAMES & LOCAL TRADES

From the late Middle Ages, pubs (or ale-houses, taverns and inns) needed to identify themselves in some way at a time when most people were illiterate. So simple signs evolved, ranging from a crooked piece of wood, holly bush, tradesman's sign, or a type of heraldic sign borrowed from religion or aristocratic coats of arms. There are probably upwards of 17,000 different signs for pubs, the most popular being the Red Lion, Crown and Royal Oak.

Wolverhampton was no different, with 13 pubs named the Crown or Old Crown, 11 Red Lions and nine Royal Oaks. But there were also 10 pubs named the Fox and eight named the Barley Mow, Beehive or New Inn.

Several Wolverhampton pubs are named after Kings, including the generic Kings Arms (7 pubs) and Kings Head (3 pubs). In Cromwell Road, the **King Charles** (1979-2016) recalled the 1642 Civil War when King Charles I visited Wolverhampton and local families, the Levesons and Giffards fought for the King, whilst the Wrottesleys and Lanes fought for Parliament. His son, Charles Stuart, visited Moseley Old Hall in 1649 before being restored to the throne as Charles II in 1660.

Several pubs are also named after Queens, including the generic Queen/Queens (3 pubs), Queens Arms/Old Queens Arms (8 pubs) and Queens Head/Old Queens Head (3 pubs). At the **Queen's Hotel** in North Street (1861), there was an underground passage leading to the theatre next door, which is believed to be haunted by long-dead actors. **Queen Victoria** was recalled in Ablow Street (1866-1920) and at the **Victoria** (1851-1983) in Pountney Street, **Victoria House** (1861-1998) in Monmore Green Road and **New Victoria** in Heath Town. In Chapel Ash, the **Alexandra Hotel** (1864) was originally named the Princess Alexandra, who became the wife of King Edward VII.

In Railway Street, the **Prince Albert** (1861-2015) recalled Queen Victoria's consort. The Royal Commercial Hotel was upstairs, where Room 13 was haunted by 1920s landlady Miss Williams (who wore trousers and smoked a pipe) and her lover, Anna. Seven pubs in Wolverhampton were named after the **Prince of Wales,** usually referring to the Princes who became King Edward VII and King George V.

Several pubs were named after Dukes, including the generic **Duke's Head** (1851-1983) in Walsall Street. In Albany Street, the **Duke of Albany** (1911) was probably named after Queen Victoria's fourth son, Prince Leopold. The **Duke of York** is recalled in pubs in Princess Street (1818) and Little Brickkiln Street (1818-1916), and usually refers to Prince Frederick who commanded the Flanders Campaign in 1793. But at that time, he was only 30 years old, and there were few hills in the region where he fought!

Famous military figures are not forgotten in Wolverhampton. In Salop Street, the **Lord Nelson** (1833-2004) was named after the famous admiral who fought at the Battle of Trafalgar on *HMS Victory* in 1805. But less is probably known about **Lord Raglan,** who fought with the Duke of Wellington at the Battle of Waterloo in 1815 and in the Crimean War in 1853. He's remembered at a pub in Great Brickkiln Street (1860-2006). **The Wellington** (1855-1964) in North Road, **Wellington Arms** in Wadhams Hill (1849-1939) and **Duke of Wellington** (1818-1924) in Horseley Fields recalled the famous Duke himself.

In Canal Street, the **Admiral Vernon** (1818-1890) recalled a distinguished Royal Navy officer who saw active service during the War of Spanish Succession (1701-1714) and later in the War of Jenkins' Ear (1739), when he attacked Spanish settlements in the Caribbean. But he's probably best remembered for watering down the daily ration of rum given to sailors, giving him the nickname of "Old Grog"!

In North Street, the **Colonel Vernon** (1871-1966) recalled an officer who landed at Dover in 1660 with Charles II. Landlord Ted Adey ran the pub for 44 years from 1912, and it's probably best remembered for the parrot hanging on a perch who would often say "Yow 'ere agin"!

The **Chindit**, in Merridale Road, was formerly one of William Butler's (Wolverhampton) off-licenses and didn't become a pub until 1958, when its licence was granted partly as a tribute to Black Country war heroes. It's probably unique in the country, being named after Major-General Orde Charles Wingate's Chindit Regiment who, with the pub's first landlord, Harold Elliston, fought in Burma during the Second World War. Charles Wingate was an exponent of unconventional military thinking and knew the importance of surprise tactics. He had a self-reliant and aggressive philosophy of war, with the resources to stage large-scale operations, including deep-penetration jungle missions in Japanese-held territories such as Burma. However, the high casualty rate suffered by soldiers in his Chindit regiment, especially from disease, remains controversial to this day. Wingate believed that resistance to infection could be improved by instilling a tough mental attitude, rather than usual medical practices.

Politicians are also remembered in Wolverhampton. The **Gladstone** (1868-1972) in North Road and **Gladstone Arms** (1871-1910) in Horseley Fields recalled the famous British statesman and Liberal politician who became Prime Minister between 1868-1892. In Dudley Road, the **Melbourne Arms** (1871-1979) recalled the British Prime Minister of 1834, who also gave his name to the capital city of Victoria, Australia.

Sir Robert Peel was the founder of the modern police force and British Prime Minister in 1834 and 1841, and was remembered at the **Peels Arms** (1855-1959) in Peel Street. In Dudley Street, the **Lord John Russell** (1833) recalled the reforming politician who helped to enfranchise growing industrial towns and became Prime Minister between 1846-1865.

Daniel O'Connell was a famous political leader of Ireland's Roman Catholic majority in the first half of the 19th century, who championed liberal and reform causes at Westminster's Parliament. His name was recalled at pubs in Montrose Street (1857-1960) and East Park (1960-2006).

Several pubs were named after the local landed gentry. In Dudley Street, the **Dudley Arms** (1874-1957) was named after the Earl of Dudley, who owned local collieries and iron and steelworks. The Giffard family, who were based nearby in Brewood at Chillington, is recalled at the **Giffard Arms** in Victoria Street. Originally dating from 1818, the pub was rebuilt in 1927 for Butler's Brewery to the designs of James Swann, as an accurate rendition of a period house in Tudor stonework. It's allegedly haunted by a former landlord, a local lady of the night called Anne Horton and a little girl.

The **Baggotts Arms** in Coleman Street (1871) and Moore Street (1860-1967) probably recall the Baggott family of Staffordshire, whose family home was at Blithefield Hall. Not all members of the Baggott family were particularly upstanding – Charles Baggott was convicted in Worcester in 1829 and transported aboard the *Claudine* ship to New South Wales. The Wrottesley family were local landowners in Tettenhall, whose name is remembered at the **Wrottesley Arms** (1990) in Perton.

At Chapel Ash, the **Combermere Arms** (1861) takes its name from the former monastery and country house near Nantwich, Cheshire, home to Viscount Combermere. It retains original features from its alterations of 1925 and is included in CAMRA's national inventory of heritage pubs, but it's probably best remembered for the old lime tree which grows in the gents' outside toilet!

The **Hatherton Arms** (1855) recalls Baron Hatherton (Edward Littleton), who was based at Hatherton Hall near Cannock, and who had substantial estates in Staffordshire, including around Penkridge and Great Wyrley. In Fordhouses, the **Harrowby Arms** (1957) is named after the Earl of Harrowby's Ryder family, whose ancestral home is at Sandon Hall, Staffordshire.

In Lichfield Street, the **Sir Tatton Sykes** (1851-2008) was named after the squire of Sledmere, a baronet horse jockey and breeder with a stud of 200 horses. He witnessed the St Leger Stakes over 70 times and won the race on his own horse in 1846.

The **Bradford Arms** in Commercial Road (1853-1983) recalled the Earl of Bradford, who supported King Charles I in the Civil War and was also a local landowner with a family home at Weston Park in Staffordshire.

Famous local people are not forgotten at Wolverhampton's pubs. In North Street, the **Molineux Hotel** was originally built in 1740 as the residence of local ironmaster, Benjamin Molineux, and became a hotel in 1871. The hotel closed in 1979, is Grade II listed and was restored as the City Archives in 2009.

In Tettenhall Wood, the **Mount Hotel** was originally the home of Sir Charles Mander, local industrialist, benefactor and former Mayor of Wolverhampton. In Penn, the **Bruford Arms** may recall William and Mary Bruford who lived at Compton Hill Lodge, Compton. William was involved in quarrying sand locally and also helped to establish the Steam Brewery in Market Place in 1864.

In Upper Villiers Street, the **Villiers Arms** (1871-1990) recalled Charles Pelham Villiers, a long-serving MP for Wolverhampton (1835-1885). In Chapel Ash, the **Clarendon Hotel** (1849) recalls the Villiers family who also took the title of Earl of Clarendon. The **George Wallis** in Victoria Street (1998) recalls the famous Wolverhampton industrial design artist who worked for local japanners, Ryton and Walton, painting the centres of tea trays, and went on to help oversee the Great Exhibition of 1851.

In Princess Street, the **Greyhound** originally dated from 1818 and was allegedly haunted by a policeman and a local robber, "Jack the Hat". After being renamed several times, it now recalls **Billy Wright**, one of the greatest Wolves captains, who won over 100 caps for England and led Wolves to victory in the FA Cup in 1949 and League Championship in 1958/1959.

As in most towns, Wolverhampton paid homage to writer William Shakespeare, at the **Shakespeare** in Horseley Fields (1833-1981), along with shorter-lived pubs in Garrick Street (1850-1865) and Little Brickkiln Street (1850-1907). Also in Little Brickkiln Street, the **Sir John Falstaff** (1833-1912) recalled a Shakesparian character in his *Henry IV*, *Henry V* and *Merry Wives of Windsor* plays.

Wolverhampton came of age during the Victorian period, with heavy industry based on coal, limestone, clay, brickworks and iron and steel foundries. Other trades, including safe, lock and key-making, hollow-ware manufacture, paints, enamelling and japanning, electrical machinery, railway works, and bicycle, motorcycle, car and tyre manufacturing also flourished. In fact, between 1879-1896, there were over 190 independent cycle makers in the town. So, it's not surprising that hundreds of pubs grew up to slake the workers' thirsts, some of which were named after those trades.

Coal mining developed around Wolverhampton in the 18th-19th centuries. This industry is recalled in five pubs named the **Jolly Collier,** along with the **New Jolly Collier** in Old Heath Road, **Miners Arms** (1833) in Green Lane and **Old Miners Arms** (1861-1906), a home-brew pub in Duke Street.

Iron and steelmaking were remembered at the **Steelhouse Tavern** in Steelhouse Lane (1871-1964), **Forge Hammer** in Bilston Street (1851-1914) and **Rolling Mill** in Lower Horseley Fields (1868-1917). Particular trades were recalled at the **Fitters Arms** in Whitmore Reans (1871-1965), **Moulders Arms** in St James' Street (1864-1910) and Steelhouse Lane (1880-1937), **Smiths Arms** in Bilston Road (1864-1911) and **Shinglers Arms** in Shrubbery Street (1866). Gunmaking is recalled at the **Gunmakers Arms** in Graisley Road (1861-1956) and Trysull Road (1874), where landlord Thomas Rigby also made gun locks.

Woodworking was reflected at the **Joiners Arms** in Darlington Street (1866-1926), whilst the **Painters Arms** in Bilston Street (1858-1921) and Horseley Fields (1871-1877) recalled another local trade. Japanning was a specialised craft, recalled at the **Japanners Arms** in Pool Street (1881-1926).

There were four pubs named the **Bricklayers** or **Brickmakers Arms,** but all were gone by 1910. In 1858, William Perry (Tipton Slasher) was accused of assaulting customers at the **Old Bricklayers Arms** in Walsall Street (1818-1907), whilst the **Builders Arms** in Derry Street (1851) once had a fine Butler's Brewery mural on the side wall. In Broad Gauge Way, the modern **Blue Brick** (2007) recalls the particular type of hard blue bricks made in Staffordshire.

The town once depended on farming, which is recollected by eight pubs named the **Barley Mow,** the oldest examples being at Penn Common (1630) and Pipers Row (1792-1983). Four pubs were named the **Wheatsheaf,** including those in Market Street (1855), Great Brickkiln Street (1871-1938) and Horseley Fields (1861-1931). The **Plough** is recalled at pubs in Bilston Road (1861) and John Street (1818-1907), along with four pubs called the **Plough Harrow,** including those in Bromley Street (1871-1958), Pipers Row (1857-1923) and Worcester Street (1855).

Beekeeping was another local interest, which is reflected at eight pubs named the **Beehive,** including those in Dudley Street (1850-1884), Newhampton Road West (1871-1931), Oxford Street (1864-1934), Salop Street (1871-1907) and Coventry Street, built for local stonemason, Benjamin Woolaston in 1861.

Farm animals are not forgotten either. Seven pubs were named the **Bull's Head,** including in Bilston Street (1855-1981), where we'd also find the **Red Cow** (1850-1981), along with its namesake in Dudley Street (1818-1929). There was also a **Lamb** in Wulfruna Street (1845-1931) and three **Hen & Chickens,** including those at Eagle Street (1864) and Snow Hill (1818-1940). Forestry was recalled at the **Foresters Arms** at Birmingham New Road (1868-2008) and North Road (1871-1919), along with the **Woodman** in Little Chapel Street (1851-1938).

Six pubs were named the **Boat,** recalling the importance of canals in the development of the town. Most were short-lived, but the pub in Compton Road (1834) lasted until 1928, whilst its namesake in Southampton Street (1828-1920) was a home-brew pub alongside the Birmingham Canal at the 4th lock house. The importance of canals was also recalled at the **Navigation** in Bilston Road (1818-1936) and **Old Navigation** in Commercial Road (1850-1936).

Many pubs brewed their own beer and there were also several breweries in the town. This trade was recalled at the **Brewers Arms** in Brickkiln Street (1864-1907) and Berry Street (1858-1873), along with the **Jolly Brewer** in Commercial Road (1913). The **Malt Shovel** in Walsall Street (1833-1914) and Willenhall Road (1868) also reflected this trade, as did the **Hop Pole** in Market Place (1792-1858) and Oxley (1938-2015).

Pubs named the **Coach & Horses** recalled the time when stagecoaches stopped at pubs on their journeys to places as far away as Liverpool and London. Two were first licensed in 1818, in

Bilston Road and Snow Hill, which lasted until the 1960s, with their namesake in Cannock Road (1864) closing in 1996. Some might have preferred more basic travel in the **Waggon & Horses,** recalled in Bilston Road (1818-1985), Cannock Road (1866-2008) and Great Brickkiln Street (1866-1935).

In Stafford Street, the **Locomotive** (1866-1976) recalled the nearby Great Western Railway's steam locomotive works. This railway company was also remembered at the **Great Western Hotel** in Stafford Street (1871-1976), along with the **Great Western** in Southampton Street (1861-1927) and Sun Street (1864), a noted real ale tavern serving Holden's beers. In Berry Street, the **London & North-Western Railway Hotel** (1873-1967) recalled the other main railway company in the town, along with the **London & North Western Inn** at Bushbury (1881-1931) and **LNWR Refreshment Rooms** (1871-1881) at the railway station itself. Railways were also remembered at the **Railway** in Lower Horseley Fields (1841-1872) and Berry Street (1845-1861), along with the **Railway Guard** in Pearson Street (1866) and Pipers Row (1857).

The cycle and car making industry was once prosperous in Wolverhampton, and is recalled at the **Sunbeam** in Railway Drive (2016) and Penn Road (1976-1995) (see below). The motorcycling industry was also remembered at the **Villiers Arms** in Upper Villiers Street (1861-1990). Neither industry could operate without the **Wheel,** recalled at Corn Hill (1841-1983), Faulkland Street (1861-1906), Whitmore Reans (1856-1965) and Wolverhampton Road (1860-2001).

Horse racing is still popular in Wolverhampton. It's recalled at the **Winning Post** in Glentworth Gardens (1982), **Starting Gate** at Penn Fields (2018), **Tipster** in Dunstall Road (1977-2004) and **Grandstand** in Horseley Fields (1833-1860), along with the **Horse & Jockey** in Bilston Street (1818-1975) and Salop Street (1833-1872).

Other historic sports, such as cockfighting, were recalled at the **Fighting Cocks** in Dudley Road (1833-1993), whilst fox hunting was reflected at 11 pubs named the **Fox,** including those in All Saints' Road (1871-1924), School Street (1858-2011) and Zoar Street (1864-1957). The **Hare & Hounds** is another sport, recalled at Bilston Road (179?) and Church Lane (1818-1960), along with the **New Hare & Hounds** in Bishop Street (1871-1960).

Football is not forgotten, with several landlords being ex-football players. In Molineux Street, the **Wanderer** (1822-2013) was popular with Wolverhampton Wanderers FC. Originally the Fox, it was rebuilt in 1914 but demolished a century later. In Waterloo Road, the **Goalpost** (1982) was previously known as Kettering Villa and became Red Roofs Hotel, but was later renamed the Leaping Wolf and last known as Lounge 107. In Exchange Street, the **Wanderers Return** was formerly the Corn Exchange, which became Exchange Vaults in 1866, but was renamed in 2019. It's allegedly haunted by Capn. Roger Tart, a First World War soldier, and Andrew Beswick, a Second World War sailor.

Wolverhampton had many pubs named after a fascinating range of famous people and recalling local trades and industries. Few survive today, but they retain many memories.

A Sunbeam in Wolverhampton

There are two pubs called the **Sunbeam** in Wolverhampton, in Railway Drive and Penn Road. The Sunbeam was "the Supreme Car", developed by Ludlow-born John Marston. He started making Sunbeam bicycles at Sunbeamland in Paul Street from the 1870s, with the name being suggested by his wife, Ellen. In the late 1890s, his right-hand man, Thomas Cureton, persuaded him to build a motor car, and they drew up a specification for an experimental prototype in 1899. The vehicle was built by Henry Dinsdale and Harry Wood in a disused coachhouse in Upper Villiers Street. The first road test took place on the hilly route from Wolverhampton to Bridgnorth at a speed of 14mph.

A second prototype was exhibited at the Crystal Palace National Show in 1901. There he met Maxwell Maberley-Smith, who offered John Marston the rights to build a most unusual four-wheeled motorised vehicle, with one wheel at the front and back and two wheels on the sides. It was marketed as the Sunbeam-Mabley car and sold for £140.

He extended the factory in Upper Villiers Street and began to build more conventional motor cars, and by 1903, his Sunbeam car was "the Sensation of the National Show".

By 1904, he was selling his Silent Sunbeam for 430 guineas and in March 1905 the company was formally registered as the Sunbeam Motor Car Company Ltd. His cars regularly won reliability trials and even included a two-way non-stop run between Lands End and John O'Groats! In 1909, he joined forces with French trained engineer, Herve Coatalen, and the company went from strength-to-strength, designing and building many new models. By 1912, his six-cylinder Sunbeam Double Landaulette was selling for £740 and his cars were running in the French Grand Prix and the Isle of Man Tourist Trophy. However, car production was reduced during the First World War and by 1919, the Wolverhampton factory was only producing aircraft and aircraft engines.

After the war, car production returned, but due to financial problems, the company amalgamated with Talbot in 1920 to form Sunbeam-Talbot. By this time, the Moorfield Works had expanded greatly and car production increased. On the race track, there was both success with winning, but tragedy with drivers killed. In 1922, Kenelm Guinness broke the last World Land Speed record at Brooklands in a 350hp Sunbeam, reaching over 133mph. By 1923, the company had become involved with Malcolm Campbell and Henry Segrave's speed records both in Denmark and at Saltburn and Pendine Sands, achieving a speed of over 150mph. Back at the works, new car models were built, including the first 1,000hp twin-engined Sunbeam car, which was raced in Daytona, USA at over 200mph.

However, the company later began its decline, and was purchased by Rootes in 1935. They kept the Sunbeam name for some of their models, but closed the car-building plant in Wolverhampton. A sad end for a fine company, but a good tale to tell over a pint or two of Banks's Sunbeam at the Sunbeam pub!

WOLVERHAMPTON – OLDEST PUBS

Wolverhampton can be traced back to the Middle Ages (*Wulfruna and Heantun*), when its wealth was based on the woollen trade, but it came of age in the 19th century with the discovery of coal and ironstone in the district. By 1750, its population was barely 7,500, but as heavy industry and other trades flourished, by 1801 it had grown to 12,000. A century later it had grown to over 94,000 and by 1951 was over 162,000.

All this heavy industry was thirsty work, so it's not surprising that hundreds of pubs and several breweries grew up to slake workers' thirsts. Over the years, licensing records list over 800 pubs and beerhouses in the wider Wolverhampton area, of which fewer than 100 remain. They range from historic town centre pubs and hotels, once the hub of the town's social and commercial life, to street-corner and terraced locals, more imposing suburban roadhouses and modern theme based pubs.

In the old days, your choice of pub was usually restricted to how far you could walk, where your friends were, or whether you preferred a pint of Banks's mild or Butler's Spring. Before then, many pubs brewed their own beer, but they were later taken over by larger commercial breweries. At that time, the main attractions of pubs were probably limited to darts, dominoes or cribbage, or whether the pub had a football or cricket team, or bowling or angling club. Unusual events were not a post-war phenomenon – topless women boxers used to fight regularly at the **White Hart** in Worcester Street, and the pub is reputedly haunted by one of them!

There is some dispute about the oldest licensed premises in Wolverhampton. This chapter covers some of the oldest pubs in the town – those licensed before 1800 or in premises older than that.

Just south of the town centre in Goldthorn Hill, the **Blue Bell** was originally a tavern in the 16th century. Known as Hill Cottage after it closed, it's one of the few surviving timber-framed buildings in the town.

In Victoria Street, the **Old Barrel** was thought to date back to 1600, but the first licence wasn't recorded until 1822. Originally a home-brew pub, it was rebuilt in 1896 before being converted into a shop in 1962. Nearby, the **Hand** had a plaque dating the half-timbered building to 1300, but it is said to have been a pub in 1609. It later became a bakery and is fondly remembered as Lindy Lou, the name of a children's clothing shop in the 1960-1970s. Further along Victoria Street was the **Hand & Bottle,** dating from before 1802, but closed in 1927 and later demolished.

Dating from 1630, the **Barley Mow** at Penn Common was first licensed in 1851, whilst the **Star & Garter** (1635) in Victoria Street was one of the town's commercial hotels with stagecoaches running to Birmingham, Dudley, Bridgnorth, Shrewsbury and Worcester. It was rebuilt in 1836 and was home to several local clubs, including Wolverhampton Cricket Club, Gun Club and Florist Society, Literary, Quaver and Pickwick Clubs, but was demolished in 1964 as part of the Mander Centre redevelopment.

In Stafford Street, the **George Hotel** originally dated from 1735 and was first licensed in 1833. It was rebuilt a century later, renamed the Varsity in 1993 and taken over by the University of Wolverhampton in 2012.

The **Molineux Hotel** was originally built as a residence for local ironmaster, Benjamin Molineux, around 1740 and became a hotel in 1871. In 1860, its extensive pleasure gardens, popular for cycle racing and now forming part of the Wolves ground, were opened to the public. Landlords John Jack Addenbrooke played for the team and became manager in 1885, whilst Albert Harry Paulton was manager/director of the football club after the First World War. It was also home to the local bowling team, cycling club and canine society. In 1897, it was acquired by

Butler's Springfield Brewery, but closed in 1979. The building is Grade II listed and was restored and reopened as the City Archives in 2009.

Queen Square and Lichfield Street were the old heart of the city, at the centre of a spider's-web of roads and passageways that lead in all directions. Queen Square was the site of the town's original market, dating from 1285, but later, old timber-framed buildings were replaced by much grander Georgian and Victorian buildings. It was also home to several ancient hostelries.

The **Swan** was first licensed in 1770 and was one of the town's main commercial hotels, excise office and coaching inn, but was replaced by a bank in 1877. The **Woolpack** dated from 1780, whilst parts of the **Lych Gate Tavern** date back to 1726. It was previously a wine vaults and offices, but became a Black Country Ales' pub in 2012. In Lichfield Street, the **Noahs Ark** was established as a popular home-brew pub by 1792, but was rebuilt in 1883 and later acquired by Frank Myatt's (Wolverhampton) Brewery.

King Street was also home to several venerable hostelries. The **Old Still,** dating from 1750, is Grade II listed and probably the oldest pub surviving in the town centre. Originally Richard Henshaw's private house, by 1818, he had converted it into the Old Saracen's Head, with its own brewery. In 1894, it was renamed the Old Still and entertained performers from the Grand Theatre, ranging from opera soprano Dame Maggie Teyte to Les Dawson! Landlord Dicky Rhodes played for Wolves between 1926-1935, but in the 1900s, a licensee hung himself and still haunts the pub, as do the ghosts of Martha and a small crying child.

In 1760, Mary Clarke had established **Madame Clarke's Ale & Porter Stores** in King Street. It's a fine Georgian house converted into a pub and is now Grade II listed. When kept by Madame Clarke, it was known as a house of ill repute, where the ladies of the night chalked their prices on the soles of their shoes! It became the City Bar in 2001 and is now known as the Grain Store, but be careful, since Madame Clarke still haunts the pub as the Grey Lady! Nearby, the **Talbot Hotel** was first licensed in 1780 and was another commercial hotel, rebuilt to the designs of J.V. Boswell for Butler's Brewery in 1933, before becoming a betting shop in 2010. It was reputedly haunted by two ghosts, Scratching Fanny who used to scratch the door to be let in, and George, a jovial character who appears once a year.

Other early pubs include the **Castle** (1770) in Dudley Street, a coaching inn whose first licensee was Widow Foster. In North Street, the **Lion** was another commercial hotel dating from 1780 as the Red Lion. The Town Commissioners held their first meeting here in the 1770s, but it was closed after 1850. First licensed in 1792 were the **Dog & Partridge** in Canal Street, **Hop Pole** in Market Place, **Hare & Hounds** in Bilston Road, **Fountain** in New Street, **Golden Cup** in Victoria Street, **Old Anchor** in St John's Street and **Old Crown** in Horse Fair, but all were gone by the end of that century. Wolves player, Billy Harthill, kept the **Barley Mow** in Pipers Row, but it was demolished in 1983.

Of these early pubs, few remain today. Several have been converted into other uses and many have been demolished, some as a result of town centre redevelopment. Only the **Old Still** survives as a "proper" pub – long may it prosper!

WORDSLEY

Wordsley lies on the western fringe of the Black Country and was once a rural community, which started to develop along the main Saltway road from Stourbridge to Kingswinford from the late 17th century. It had a flourishing nailmaking industry and soon began to establish several glassworks and brickworks. It was also home to Webbs, the Royal seedsmen, famous for their "Wordsley Wonder" pea and "Wordsley Queen" potato. Much of the historic fabric of the village has been lost through demolition and redevelopment, but several old inns and taverns survive. Over the years, almost 40 pubs served the area, of which around a dozen remain today.

The oldest pub in Wordsley is undoubtedly the **Old Cat** on the corner of High Street and Lawnswood Road. Originally two cottages dating from the late 1700s, it was first licensed in 1812 and is now a Grade II listed building. In the early days, it was kept by butchers, John and Sarah Cooper, and frequented by hearty rustic types from nearby farms. In the 1850s, it was called the Cat & Cushion, and from 1957, it was kept by Thomas and Martha Matthews for nearly 20 years. It's also allegedly haunted by the ghost of a Cavalier, a vestige of the fateful journey made by Charles II through Wordsley after the Battle of Worcester.

Further up High Street is the **New Inn,** dating from 1822 and unusually facing south. It's been a Batham's (Brierley Hill) pub since 2008. A few doors away was the **Wheatsheaf,** dating from 1818. From 1878-1891, it was owned and kept by Edward Geary from Pittsburgh, USA, but became a shop in 1968. The **Queen's Head** (1854) is well-placed on the corner of Queen Street, and is reputedly haunted by a ghost who knocks pennies off the bar counter and likes to listen to music. It became a Holt, Plant & Deakin pub in 1988, and is now a popular Black Country Ales' real ale pub.

Several old inns were grouped around Wordsley Green, including the **Old Red Lion** (1845). John and Jane Dalrymple brewed their own beer here from 1908-1919, but it was rebuilt and became a supermarket in 2012. Along The Green itself was the aptly-named **Inn on the Green,** built in 1862 as the Green Tavern, but renamed the Raven in 1899. Originally a home-brew pub, it had a bowling green and pigeon club, but it was replaced by new houses in 2002. Almost next door was the **George & Dragon,** another home-brew pub, originally built in 1864 as the Woodman, rebuilt in 1957, but demolished in 2007. Just around the corner was the **Exchange** (1872-1909), a Wordsley Brewery pub.

In 1860, John Northwood established his glassmaking "factory in the country" on the corner of Barnett Street, which is recalled by the **Glasscutters Arms** (1870). Until 1926, it was kept by William Newman and his family, followed by Frederick Loach until 1940, and has a thriving bowls club. Around the corner in Barnett Lane was the **Cherry Tree** (1854-1906), whilst along Lawnswood Road was the unusually named **Thull Ghaut** (1870-1922), a Hanson's pub which recalled the steep road and rail route through the mountains in India near Mumbai. In the surrounding countryside is Lawnswood House, built in 1816 in Regency style for the Foley family, and later owned by geologist Colonel Thomas Fletcher, Jack Bean (who manufactured Bean cars) and Alfred Marsh of Marsh and Baxter's meat business. From 2019, it became the **Roe Deer,** a popular Brunning & Price restaurant/pub.

Returning to the High Street, several pubs were grouped near Holy Trinity Church, opened in 1831. The oldest is the **Rose & Crown,** first licensed in 1795 and a home-brew pub until 1926. It was later acquired by Showell's Crosswells Brewery (Langley) and Davenport's (Birmingham). Opposite was an old house where Charles II paused to enjoy some "small beer, bread and cheese" on his journey in 1651. Next to the School of Art was the **Cottage of Content** (1822-1851), with the **Harmonic Tavern** (1849-1925) next to the war memorial.

On the corner of Brewery Street (now Brierley Hill Road) was the **Old White Hart,** dating from 1818, with its pot-bellied stove in the bar, but it closed in 1979. A few doors away was the **Old Bear** (1870-1922). The aptly-named Brewery Street was not only home to Edward Oakes' **Wordsley Brewery** (1858-1906), but also its taphouse, the **Lion** (1850-1909). New housing in Crownoakes Drive (recalling Edward Oakes) now occupies the site (see below).

Further along Brierley Hill Road was the **Old Boat Inn** (1822), kept by Daniel and Emma Gill for nearly 50 years until 1932, which closed in 1938. Not far away was the **Swan** (1835-2008), remembered for the 23 local miners who emigrated to Hudson Bay in 1854 in search of gold. The **Black Horse** (1851) was replaced by new housing in 1916.

The **Samson & Lion** dates from the opening of the Stourbridge Canal in 1779 and remains a traditional canalside hostelry. In the early days, it was a home-brew pub, serving beer to the bargees and stabling their horses. Early landlord James Smith operated canal boats, whilst later landlord, Samuel Hill, was also a furniture dealer. Just beyond the canal bridge, we mustn't forget the **Bottle & Glass**, built in 1834. It was another Wordsley Brewery pub, backing on to the canal, but was moved brick-by-brick to the Black Country Living Museum in 1982, where it's still lit by gas lights.

Returning to High Street and crossing the canal bridge, we soon spot the Red House Glass Cone, built in 1790, opposite the new **Glassworks** pub. On the corner of Vine Street, the **Vine** dated from 1822, but became a fish and chip shop in 2012. Initially named the Old Jacob's Well, it was renamed the Duke of Wellington in 1822, the Spotted Leopard in 1832, was rebuilt and became Mad O'Rourke's Pie & Grill Factory in 2010. One of the early landlords was Richard Mills, who not only founded the Albert Glassworks opposite the pub, but was also the grandfather of Gerald Mills, founder of publishers Mills & Boon! In 1869, Elijah Harris had a grocery shop in Bridge Street which he converted into a beerhouse called the **Bird in Hand.** Its name recalls the sport of hawking and it's now a popular CAMRA award-winning real ale pub.

There were several pubs along High Street, Audnam, all of which have been demolished. They included the **Gladstone Inn** (1870-2006), part of a terrace of houses rebuilt in 1956, which became a Holt, Plant & Deakin pub and was then briefly known as Roosters. Nearby was the **Marquis of Granby** (1829-1912), named after John Manners, Commander-in-Chief of the Forces, who helped retiring soldiers to set up pubs. A few doors away were the **Rose & Crown** (1818-1930), another Wordsley Brewery pub, and the **Turk's Head** (1818-1956).

From brewery to cinema

Edward Oakes had established the Lion Brewery behind the **Lion** pub in Brewery Street by 1858, after opening this beerhouse in 1850. By 1875, his brewery was producing 600 bushels of malt per week. He was also a hop merchant, farmer and mineral water manufacturer, but overreached himself and became bankrupt in 1895. He sold the brewery with 13 tied houses to Collis & Co. (Stourbridge) and emigrated to the USA. They continued brewing as the Wordsley Brewery, but by 1906, they were also bankrupt and sold the brewery, its three maltings and 29 pubs to the Hereford & Tredegar Brewery. They had no intention of brewing here, so sold the buildings to Anthony Bayley, who converted the brewery into the Olympia Cinema in 1912. The last film was shown in 1959 and the buildings were demolished in 1969 and later replaced by housing (Crownoakes Drive).

BREWERIES

Heath Robinson's Perfect Brewery

BROWNHILLS BREWERIES – WILLIAM ROBERTS' STATION BREWERY

I recently called into the Shoulder of Mutton pub in Brownhills. Whilst enjoying my pint, I couldn't help noticing an etched glass window in the rear door of the bar, with the words *"Roberts' Noted Ales"*. I needed to know more about this local brewery. My initial research revealed little, but thanks to Brownhills-Bob and his friends, I was able to piece together the story of this local entrepreneur and philanthropist who was one of the true fathers of modern Brownhills.

William Roberts was born in December 1828 in Shenstone, close to the Bulls Head public house, but the family soon moved to Coppice Side in Brownhills. In his youth, he worked on his father's farm and in the local coal mines. When his mother died, he obtained work on the South Staffordshire Railway, starting as a plate-layer, but rising quickly to the position of ganger or foreman. In later years, the railway locomotive emblem would feature on his advertisements, bottles and crockery. In 1847, he moved away to work on the railways in Durham and Huddersfield (including the notorious Standedge Tunnel), and later for Hartlepool Council. While working in Yarm, he met Ann Bradley, who he married in 1852.

When his father died in 1860, William made his first venture into the licensed trade at the Tower Inn, Potter's Hill, Aston. But after nine months, he moved back to Brownhills and took over the Station Hotel, also setting up the brewery behind the pub. This was to be his home for over 45 years and was the centre of the local community, frequented by the elite of the town. An advert of 1884 advertised *"William Roberts' Brownhills Celebrated Station Ales ... brewed from choice Malt and Hops, and the purest water in existence that have so won their way into popular favour that Brownhills Brewery has become a household word"*. He sometimes engaged a theatrical party to entertain his clients at the hotel. They arrived by train at Brownhills station, and everyone went to meet the entertainers and see them off the next day.

In 1887, he sold the pub and brewery to Showell's Brewery (Langley), but almost immediately bought it back, paying £2,000 more than he'd sold it for! He then transformed the pub into a three-bar hotel, complete with music hall and brewery. This was now the kingdom of William Roberts, where he carried out and developed his business. At its height, he owned 26 pubs and two off-licenses, mainly in Brownhills, Pelsall, Bloxwich and Walsall, all within a 6-mile radius of the brewery. He not only gave the town employment in his brewery and entertainment in his public houses, but also helped to give the town its own fire brigade.

William Roberts also had interests in a distillery in Belfast and in the Lichfield Brewery Company. He owned several properties in the Brownhills area, including three large farming estates, and took a great interest in agriculture and breeding prize cattle and pigs. As well as being a successful businessman, he also played an active part in local government. He was first elected to the Brownhills Local Health Board in April 1877, becoming its chairman from 1892-1894. In 1897, he was elected to a seat on Brownhills Urban District Council and in 1904 became chairman until his death. In council matters, as in his own business, he was a rigid economist, but often brought forward schemes to benefit the rate-payers, such as the local sewage farm. He took a prominent part in the erection of the Public Buildings at Brownhills in 1887 and also presented the council with a new Merryweather Gem steam fire engine in 1898.

He was a charitable man who was always willing to support a fair cause, such as supplying food to starving miners and their families during the miners' strike of 1893. At times like the King's Coronation, he entertained the town's old people and others. He was a member of the local Lodges, including the Oddfellows and Foresters, and also made regular financial donations to local hospitals. In 1865, he donated part of the land on which the new Mount Zion Chapel was built, and in May 1899, gave every resident of Brownhills over 80 the sum of 5s to commemorate the 80th anniversary of Queen Victoria.

As a Justice of the Peace he would often pay the fines of miscreants brought before him if he thought the charge was unfair. He had very strong Christian beliefs, and at one time held the position of Warden at St James' Church. However, the church tried to discredit him because of his brewery business, and he never forgave them for trying to blacken his character. When the church wanted to arrange a concert in aid of the church bells fund, William offered to pay for the bells himself if only the church would give him a fair hearing. But when they did meet to discuss the matter, the Vicar, Revd Arrowsmith, refused to talk to him.

William Roberts died in February 1906, aged 77, leaving an estate valued at an incredible £126,868 (equivalent to £16.4m in today's money). Such was his devotion to council duties that he even apologised in advance for his impending death and the trouble it would cause. His funeral was the largest seen in Brownhills to that day, with 20 carriages taking the mourners from the Station Hotel to St James' Church. Flags flew at half-mast and the route was lined by thousands of spectators. Having no children of his own, William left most of his estate to his wife Ann and his nephew George. In his will, he asked them to try and make a go of the brewery business, but George died in January 1910, aged 44, and William's wife Ann followed in July 1910, aged 77. William, Ann and George are buried together in St James' Churchyard and their memory is perpetuated by an annual charity that still doles out money from their bequests at Christmas.

After Ann's death, the estate was divided up and sold off. Most of the Roberts' family fortune was inherited by Clara Cresswell, who had been a helper at the Station Hotel and a close companion to Ann. In 1925, the brewery was acquired by Eley's Brewery (Stafford) and closed in 1928 when it passed to William Butler & Co. (Wolverhampton). The Station Hotel survived through several hands, but finally closed in November 1983 and was demolished in 1990 to be replaced by a supermarket.

It's a real pity that, apart from his tombstone in the church graveyard, there's no public memorial in Brownhills to William Roberts, as one of the town's greatest benefactors and public servants. Many of the brewery's pubs have long gone, but occasionally you may see an etched glass or mirror, a ceramic mug or an old bottle to bring back some memories of a true father of modern Brownhills.

DUDLEY BREWERIES

Dudley is well known as the home-brew capital of the Midlands, with around 150 pubs once brewing their own beer on the premises, but there were also several commercial breweries in and around the town centre.

Probably the most well-known local brewery was **Hanson's.** Originally established as a wine and spirits business in 1847 by Thomas Hanson, when he died in 1870, his widow, Julia, took over the company and expanded the business. When she died in 1894, her sons, Thomas & William, started to buy up local pubs, including the Peacock Hotel and brewery in 1895. In 1897, they built a new brewery next door and by 1919, had over 100 tied houses. They later took over Frederick Tandy's Brewery (Kidderminster) and by 1934 had taken over Smith & William's Town Brewery (Round Oak) with its 60 tied houses in the biggest sale of licensed property in the area at the time.

As part of this £120,000 deal, they also bought the Stewponey & Foley Arms Hotel at Stourton and the White Hart Hotel in Kinver, and in 1942, they took over the Red Lion Brewery in Lower Gornal. However, over the years, Wolverhampton & Dudley Breweries had been buying shares in the company, and by 1943 had gained a controlling interest. The production of Hanson's Bitter then shifted to Wolverhampton, but Hanson's distinctive dark Mild continued to be brewed at Dudley until 1991 when the brewery closed, however it did continue at Wolverhampton until 2007. Wolverhampton & Dudley Breweries eventually amalgamated with Marston's (Burton-on-Trent).

Most of the other breweries had a much shorter life. In Kates Hill, Henry Cox established the **Dudley New Brewery** in 1820, and rebuilt it as a 10-quarter brewery in 1830, adding two malthouses. By 1835, it had been renamed as Henry Cox & Co. to avoid confusion with the Dudley Old Brewery at Burnt Tree. However, in 1840, the brewery, with two copper furnaces, mash tuns and vats, was put up for auction and sold in May 1841. Along with the adjoining Malt Shovel pub, it became **Kates Hill Brewery,** ran by Samuel Salt from 1862. From 1895-1910, it was managed by his son-in-law, John Foley, when it was acquired by Thomas Plant (Netherton) and brewing ceased.

Joseph Plant established the **Diamond Brewery** in Cromwell Street, Kates Hill, in 1899, but he was bankrupt by 1901 and sold it to Hutchings & Jackson. By 1916, John Frederick Cecil Jackson bought out his partner and registered the company as J.F.C. Jackson, retaining the old brewery. The brewery, along with the Black Horse, Loving Lamb and other tied houses, were eventually acquired by Darby's Brewery (West Bromwich) in 1937.

In Hall Street, George England established the **Dudley Brewery** in 1823. By 1851, it was being run by his son, George Joseph, employing 35 men, including one who stole five bags of malt and sold them to a Netherton publican. By 1867, George was bankrupt and the brewery was bought by William Smith (Netherton), but a year later, George England and Rous John Cooper bought it back for £7,000. In 1871, Rous Cooper bought out George England, but in 1874, a tall chimney stack fell in a gale and caused £200 of damage to the brewery. By 1881, the company was almost bankrupt and was taken over by George Thompson & Son who, by then, also owned the Victoria Brewery. In 1890, the new company, Dudley & Victoria Breweries, merged with Banks & Co. and Fox Brewery (Wolverhampton) to become Wolverhampton Dudley Breweries.

In 1873, John Dawes established the **Victoria Brewery** at the Victoria Vaults in Hall Street, brewing Dawes' Sovereign Pale Ale – "the best Dinner Ale extant". However he became bankrupt in 1880, when the business was bought by George Thompson & Son, and became part of Wolverhampton & Dudley Breweries in 1890.

Henry & Benjamin Woodhouse began brewing at the **Alma Brewery** behind the Alma Inn in Hall Street in 1901. In 1914, they moved across the road to take over the then-vacant Victoria Brewery, renaming it the Alma Brewery. They later moved to the Queen's Cross Brewery in 1917.

In 1873, Matthew Smith, a local councillor and alderman, established the **Queen's Cross Brewery** adjoining the Lamp at Queen's Cross. This was a three-storey 10-quarter brewery producing 500 barrels of beer a week. It was also known as the Dudley Hop Ale Brewery, since it also brewed a non-alcoholic sweet bottled beer of that name. After Matthew Smith's death in 1914, the brewery was bought by Henry & Benjamin Woodhouse, but brewing ceased in 1934. In 1950, the pub and brewery were taken over by Daniel Batham (Brierley Hill). The pub has won local CAMRA awards and the former brewery was converted into overnight accommodation.

The **Black Horse Brewery** was behind the Black Horse pub in Greystone Street. Jack Downing, formerly of the Leopard, bought it from the Diamond Brewery in 1901. He was a well-known local character, who became a successful brewer and businessman. In today's money, he was a multi-millionaire, owning a brewery, 11 taverns and a motor car! He was also very successful in pigeon racing, and kept canaries and a world-champion racing dog. He sold the business to W. Butler (Wolverhampton) in 1923.

The **Cricketer's Arms Brewery** was at the Horse & Jockey in King Street, dating from 1822. The pub was renamed in the 1870s when Dudley Cricket Club made it their home. By 1913, Henry Jones had built a 10-quarter brewery here, brewing 400 barrels of beer a week, and later installing a bottling plant. The brewery closed in 1910 when it was taken over by the Diamond Brewery and the pub closed in 1922.

At Burnt Tree, local businessmen, James Bourne, Joseph Royle, Thomas Wainwright & Thomas Hawkes established the **Dudley Porter & Ale Brewery** in 1805. It was a three-storey 10-quarter brewery producing 300 barrels of beer a week. In 1828, after a series of buyouts, it changed its name to the Dudley Old Brewery to distinguish it from Henry Cox's Brewery at Kates Hill, but the company collapsed in 1835 and was taken over by Joshua Scholefield. In 1846, it was briefly renamed the Royal Brewery and then bought by Samuel Allsop & Sons (Burton-on-Trent) in 1861. It later passed to Tetley Walker and eventually to Allied Breweries.

The British Oak in Salop Street was originally a home-brew house established by Benjamin Cole in 1871, but it ceased brewing in 1898 and the pub was temporarily closed in the mid 1980s. However, Ian Skitt resumed brewing at the **British Oak Brewery** in 1988 and brewed a range of popular beers, including Castle Ruin, Eve 'ill Bitter and Colonel Pickering's Porter. Brewing ceased in 1996 and the pub closed in 2003.

Many will remember the **Gipsies Tent** in Steppingstone Street. Dating from 1841 as the Jolly Collier, it was bought by Thomas Millard in 1867 and remained in the family's ownership for over a century. In 1886, he built the Little Model Brewery and when he died in 1899, his widow, Harriet took over, followed by her son, Harry. It was modernised in 1914 and passed to brothers Bert & Don Millard (who were both tee-totallers) in 1951. They continued brewing until 1961, but the pub finally closed in 1980.

It's a pity that the town has lost all its indigenous breweries, but at least we can still have a decent pint in many of the remaining pubs.

DUDLEY BREWERIES – BATHAM'S

We all like a good pint of Batham's, whether it's the straw-coloured bitter with a sweet aftertaste or the classic mild, drunk by thousands of Black Country workers. Batham's were a family born to brew beer, with the sixth generation now involved in creating and serving legendary Black Country beers. Most folks know that it's brewed at the Delph Brewery in Brierley Hill, next to the Bull & Bladder. But what else don't you know about Batham's?

The first **Daniel Batham** was born in Quarry Bank in 1806 and became a nailmaker. In 1825, he married Eliza Cartwright and moved to a house in New Street near the corner of Queen Street, with its own nailmaking shop at the rear. They had nine children, including Daniel Jnr (Daniel II), who was born in 1840 and was later to establish the brewery. In fact, Batham's first links to brewing go back to the 1850s, when Bromley shopkeeper, William Batham, gained a beer licence as a result of the Duke of Wellington's Beerhouse Act of 1830.

Like many Black Country lads, **Daniel II**'s first job was in the local coal mines. In April 1865, he married 21-year-old Charlotte Billingham at St Thomas' Church, Dudley, and moved to High Street, Cradley Heath in the 1870s. Charlotte was the daughter of local chainmaker, Joseph Billingham and his wife Susannah, part of an extended family who were involved in metal and chainmaking, farming, brewing and meat processing. Whilst Charlotte was at home, taking in lodgers and rearing five children (including Daniel III), she found she had a talent for brewing beer in the tiny brewhouse out the back. This may be because her uncle was Benjamin Benny Fiddler Billingham, who kept the Bell Inn near Five Ways, and was also a farmer and brewer. By 1867, she was brewing a sweet, dark mild ale, which was popular with her family and lodgers.

In Cradley Heath, they lived not far from the White Horse Inn, opposite the present-day Rose & Crown. It was then owned by John Attwood, and would become their future home. By 1881, times were hard after Daniel gave up working in the mines, so they would help out at this nearby pub. By 1882, Daniel had become its landlord, whilst he and Charlotte brewed the beer. The White Horse had originally been a butcher's shop with a beerhouse, and the slaughterhouse had been converted into a small brewery. With all the thirsty miners and factory workers drinking his beer, trade at the pub grew, and two of his sons, Daniel III (born in 1867) and Caleb, began to help him brew the beer. Daniel II also started to collect cut glass and displayed it behind the bar, providing another excuse for a pint or two!

Daniel II sold his beer not only at the White Horse, but also to other pubs and beerhouses in Dudley, Stourbridge and the local area. He kept the pub until 1922, when it was sold for £3,455 – a remarkable 40 years tenure, before it finally closed in 1971. In 1904, he expanded his empire by acquiring the King William, a home-brew beerhouse in Cole Street, Netherton, and in 1905 he bought the Vine in Brierley Hill.

Daniel II was nicknamed "Dan Crusty". No one is certain why, but it could be because he was bad-tempered or tight with money, or both! Nevertheless, from an unemployed coal miner, he had become a successful local brewer and licensee who laid the foundations for Batham's brewing heritage. He kept the King William for eight years, when it passed to his son, **Daniel III,** who had married Myra Detheridge, the daughter of a blacksmith, in July 1896. She was known locally as Lady Bountiful, and is remembered for her tea parties on the bowling green behind the pub. It was later kept by Daniel III's eldest son, Arthur Joseph, until it was sold to Julia Hanson (Dudley) in 1921. Sadly, his mother, Charlotte Batham, died in 1906, followed by his father, Daniel II, in 1922.

Meanwhile, by 1905, Daniel III had moved to the Vine, but because of serious subsidence, the pub had to be rebuilt in 1912, with the grander title of the Vine Hotel. At the same time, he constructed a purpose-built model tower brewery, which remains the cornerstone of the Batham's brewing enterprise. The pub is often referred to as the Bull & Bladder, recalling that in the 1820s, it was previously a butcher's shop with an adjoining slaughterhouse owned by Joseph Attwood. It's also memorable for the Shakespearian quotation (from *The Two Gentlemen of Verona*), *"Blessing of Your Heart: You Brew Good Ale"*. From its opening, it became a model of a good community pub, hosting many local organisations, such as the Vine Pipe Club, Royal Antediluvian Order of Buffaloes and the local pigeon club. Batham's other tag-line relates to the adjoining Delph Brewery – "The Birthplace of Genuine Beer". However, this wasn't the first Delph Brewery; that was further along Delph Road, behind the Duke William (which became the Dock & Iron), operated by George Elwell, but by 1912, it had collapsed due to mining subsidence.

When Daniel III's wife, Myra, died in 1920, he tended to stay at the family home at Blakedown, leaving his sons, Arthur Joseph, Daniel IV and Caleb William, to run the pub and brewery. In 1922, they sold the White Horse Inn at Cradley, along with other properties bought over the years, totalling £7,221 in all. Although this was a period of consolidation, some growth was necessary to utilise the capacity of the brewery, and so more pubs were added to the tied estate, including the Royal Oak (Lye) in 1923, and Bird in Hand (Oldswinford), Brickmakers Arms (Lye) and Spread Eagle (Brierley Hill) in 1926. In later years, these pubs would be sold, but by a remarkable quirk of fate, the Bird in Hand became a Batham's pub once again in 2019. In 1928, while other brewers were still using horses and carts, Batham's propelled themselves into the modern world by buying their first motorised dray lorry to deliver the beer, built by F.J. Fildes of Stourbridge on a Bean (Dudley) chassis.

By the 1930s, Batham's had around 10 pubs, but the business was shaken by a dispute between Daniel IV and his brother Caleb, who had run up serious debts while running the Brickmakers Arms. He continued to work for the family business, but Batham's had to sell several pubs to pay his debts. In 1936, the company was restructured as a partnership between Daniel III and his eldest son, Arthur Joseph. However, the family was dealt a further blow in June 1939, when Daniel III died whilst he was living at the Vine, aged 72. Over the years, he had been a local councillor on Brierley Hill Urban District Council and a key member of the Licensed Victuallers Association. Unfortunately, more pubs had to be sold to pay his death duties.

After Daniel's death, **Arthur Joseph Batham** effectively controlled the company, formally registering it as Daniel Batham & Sons Ltd in 1941. After recovering from injuries whilst serving in the East Yorkshire Regiment in the First World War, he became a professional brewer, trained by Ross McKenzie of Spreckley's Worcester Brewery, and married his second cousin, Doris Batham, in 1925. At this time, Caleb Batham was still involved with the brewery and lived next door. The company began to acquire or lease further pubs, including the Swan (Brierley Hill), Elephant & Castle (Quarry Bank), Hare & Hounds (Kidderminster), Royal Exchange (Stourbridge) and Lamp Tavern (Dudley).

By the 1950s, things were looking good. In 1950, Batham's supplied their Delph Strong Ale to the Oxford boat crew (a pint a day for each crew member) in the annual boat race with Cambridge. However, they'd either had too little or too much Delph Ale, since they lost by $3\frac{1}{2}$ lengths!

In 1951, Batham's leased the Swan Inn at Chaddesley Corbett from the Trustees of King Henry VIII and opened another important chapter in the company's history. Batham's Bitter, regarded by some as one of the finest beers around, would never have been brewed if it was not for the pernickety taste buds of the regulars in this quiet Worcestershire village and the brewing skills of Daniel Bertram Arthur Batham. The traditional mild ale, so popular in the Black Country, was not to the liking of these country folk, so Batham's created a pale ale, Batham's Bitter, which is now the company's flagship beer.

Daniel Bertram Arthur Batham (the son of Arthur Joseph and Doris Batham) had joined the company in 1951 after graduating from Birmingham University's School of Brewing. In 1953, talks about merging with Holden's, another local brewer at Woodsetton, to reduce production costs and stave off takeover threats from larger breweries, came to nothing. In the same year, Batham's bought the Plough & Harrow in Kinver. In 1954, Batham's won a diploma for Delph Strong Ale at the London Brewers' Exhibition, rising to first prize in 1968 and 1972. Despite the rise in keg beer, by 1971, cask beer was back on the agenda, supported by CAMRA and, in 1972, the *Daily Mirror* voted Batham's as having the cheapest beer in Britain!

Sadly, Arthur Joseph Batham died in January 1974, leaving his son, Daniel Bertram Arthur (better known as Arthur Batham) to run the company. He married Dorothy Jean Turner, who became company secretary and had two sons and a daughter. His eldest son, Timothy, was born in 1958 and became a professionally trained brewer, learning his trade under the direction of Philip Brown at Wolverhampton & Dudley Breweries. In 1981, he married Linda Cartwright, brewing beer the day after the wedding, just before they went on their honeymoon to Corfu! They have three daughters, Ruth, Claire and Alice, who carry on the family traditions. Claire managed the Plough & Harrow pub and helps to run the pubs, whilst Alice is a qualified brewer who won the Young Brewer of the Year competition in 2019. Arthur's younger son, Matthew, trained in hotel management and married Deborah Smith, with three children Lauren, Hannah and Joseph. Arthur's daughter, Jane Myra, is a teacher and married John Spicer, with two daughters, Katy and Emily. The family name will certainly live on!

After the takeover of the local Simpkiss Brewery in December 1985, Batham's expressed fears that they could be the next target. Tim Batham said "We are not looking to sell, but it is my father's view that if someone came up with an offer we couldn't refuse, it would be ridiculous not to take it". But he also said "I would like us to carry on as we are. We have had a good year – our pub and free trade is up, we are brewing to capacity, and I see no reason why we should not stay independent".

By the 1990s, Batham's had nine tied houses – the famous Batham's nine, which would form a popular pub crawl. In 1991, Batham's Best Bitter was voted a winner in the Best Bitter category at CAMRA's Great British Beer Festival in London. In 2005, Batham's extended its empire into another country by acquiring Y Giler Arms near Betws-y-Coed in North Wales, but sold the pub a few years later. When Daniel Arthur Batham died in January 2010, aged 76, Tim and Matthew took over the company. Tim now controls the brewery side of the company, while Matthew looks after the pubs. Martin Birch, born in Quarry Bank and previously a brewer at Watney's and Hanson's, became head brewer in 2009. When he took over as head brewer he said "I still have to pinch myself when I think how lucky I am to be brewing Batham's beer. It must be every local man's dream!"

Many folks may not know that, in 2009, Batham's began its association with motorcycle racing by sponsoring Michael Rutter on his privately-entered Suzuki in the Isle of Man TT (he came 7th). Batham's continued to support Michael Rutter, including the British Superbike Championship and Macau Grand Prix, and established Batham's Racing in 2018, a team managed by Michael. His father, Tony, was one of the greatest motorcycle racers of all time, who also used to like a pint of Batham's! By 2020, Batham's had proved itself as a competent and competitive team, gaining official status and technical support direct from BMW, and continues to race successfully.

In 2010, Batham's acquired a historic Bean dray lorry, one of only three remaining, similar to the original one bought in 1928, and restored it as a promotional vehicle. Matthew Batham said

"It has been fascinating recreating a part of Batham's long history, transforming the old Bean back to the beautiful vehicle it has become today". The Bean dray lorry had led an exciting life, making many television and show appearances, before Stourbridge restorers, S.W. Sheppard, brought it back to its former glory. But beer wasn't forgotten, since in 2016, Batham's Mild and XXX gained gold and silver awards in CAMRA's West Midlands Regional Champion Beers of Britain competition, and both the beers and The Vine regularly receive local CAMRA awards.

2017 marked the 140th anniversary of Batham's, which was founded in 1877. The company continues to thrive, producing around 8,000 barrels of beer a year, using the finest materials, including Flagon barley malt, Fuggles and Goldings hops and yeast originating from Hanson's (Dudley). The biggest seller is Batham's Best Bitter, accounting for over 97% of production, but the long-term survival of Batham's Mild (which has something of a cult following with real ale drinkers) depends on local Black Country folk continuing to drink it! At Christmas, many locals look forward to Batham's XXX, a stronger winter brew. Batham's Best Bitter is also available all-year-round in bottles.

Over the years, Batham's have owned or leased more than 25 pubs and now have a tied estate of 12 pubs, many of which are steeped in history, including the Britannia (Upper Gornal), Fox & Grapes (Pensnett), New Inn (Wordsley), Plough (Shenstone) and Unicorn (Wollaston). Their beers are also available in more than 20 selected pubs and 30 off-licences in the free trade. And the name of Arthur Joseph Batham lives on at Batham's latest acquisition, the King Arthur at Hagley. Long may they prosper!

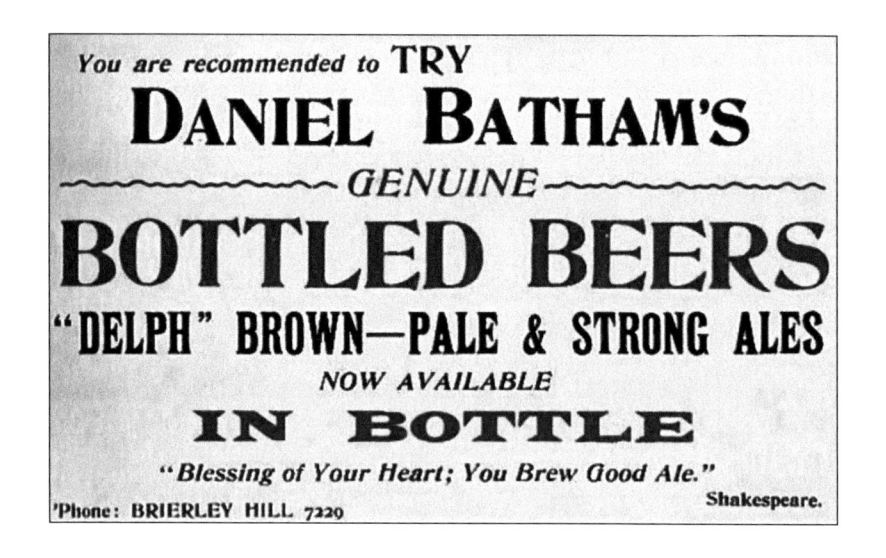

DUDLEY BREWERIES – HOLDEN'S

The story of brewing by the Holden family begins in 1875 with **Edwin Alfred Holden.** He was the youngest of seven boys, who first became an apprentice boot maker, working with his father and brother. Later, he found himself in lodgings behind the Old Swan in Netherton, which like so many local pubs at the time was a home-brew house. There were also several local breweries, including John Rolinson's Five Ways Brewery and Thomas Round's Steam Brewery.

Edwin spent much of his time in the **Trust in Providence** pub, where he met brewer and landlord, Benjamin Round's daughter, Lucy Blanche. They were married in October 1898 at St Andrew's Church in Netherton, and then took over the **Britannia Inn** in Northfield Road. In 1904, they moved to the **Struggling Man** at Shavers End, Dudley, where Edwin gave considerable support to Dudley Town Football Club who met in the pub. In 1907, they moved to the **Horse & Jockey** in Lower Gornal, and later moved on to the **Bloomfield Inn** at Tipton.

In 1910, they took over the tenancy of the **Summerhouse** in Woodsetton. During their time here, Edwin used his pony and trap to visit other nearby pubs with his beloved dog, whose claim to fame was that he had bitten most of his customers! They stayed at the Summerhouse until 1920, and bought the freehold of the **Park Inn** in George Street for £750 in August 1915. This was also a home-brew pub, where Harry Ossie Round brewed a strong, dark mild ale, with a special strong ale at Christmas. The pub was also known for its roaring log fire, free sandwiches on Friday nights, clay pipe smoking contests and a fine bowling green.

In 1920, they established Holden's Brewery at the Park Inn, but later that year, Edwin died aged just 45, and the business was taken over by his wife, Lucy. In 1938, the licence and company passed to her son, Edwin Teddy Holden, who had previously studied brewing at Birmingham University. Meanwhile, Lucy worked hard for local charities and expanded the tied estate, buying the **Painter's Arms** in Coseley from Butler's (Wolverhampton) Brewery for £2,375 as a present for Teddy. He kept this pub from 1929-1932, but also helped Harry Field with the brewing business at the Park Inn. He later became a local councillor, before marrying his wife, Clara, who he'd met at the Painters Arms, in 1938. Unfortunately, his mother, Lucy, died a few weeks before the wedding, aged just 60.

In 1939, Teddy acquired Atkinson's old malthouse behind the Park Inn and installed a new brewing plant here as the Hopden Brewery, with Harry Field as head brewer. In 1940, his daughter, Maureen Blanche, was born. From 1940-1944, both Teddy and Harry Field were brewing beer for the local RAF stations war effort. In 1944, Teddy added the **New Inn** at Coseley to his estate, slightly "bomb damaged", for £2,000. By 1945, a new bottling plant had been added at the brewery by brothers, Sam and Wilfred Hammond, Clara's brothers.

In September 1945, Teddy's son, also Edwin, was born. Further pubs were acquired, including the **Green Dragon** in Bradley, **Old Mill** in Upper Gornal, **Blue Gates** in Dudley, **Miner's Arms** (Chapel House) in Lower Gornal and **Rose & Crown** in Brierley Hill. In 1953, talks about merging with Batham's, another local brewer in Brierley Hill, to reduce production costs and stave off takeover threats from larger breweries, came to nothing.

In 1961, the Hopden Brewery was rebuilt and enlarged, with a new boiler house and second-hand copper and hopback, enabling 80-90 barrels of beer (25,000 pints) to be produced each week. The company was registered as Holden's Brewery Ltd in 1964.

In 1965, Teddy's only son, young Edwin, joined the company, after serving an apprenticeship at McMullen's Brewery in Hertford. He was engaged to Therese (Tess) Baker and they married in 1968. More pubs were acquired, including the **Cottage Spring** in Wednesbury, **Royal Exchange** in Bilston (later renamed the Trumpet) and the **Wheatsheaf** in Carters Green. Around this time Holden's Golden was launched and became a popular local bitter.

The 1970s saw the introduction of the "Black Country beer drinker logo" and the move to draught cask-conditioned beer. At that time, the brewery was producing around 200 barrels of beer a week (57,500 pints), including its very dark traditional mild, brewed by head brewer, Cliff Garner. In November 1971, Edwin and Therese's son, Jonathan Edwin Holden was born, followed by Lucie Victoria in 1973 and Abagail Blanche in 1980.

By the 1980s, Holden's had seen some difficult years of trading, but the expanding brewery had a growing reputation. However, in January 1981, Chairman Teddy Holden died suddenly, aged 74, just a few days after his fellow brewer, Dennis Simpkiss.

The brewery settled down under the third Edwin Holden until 2002, and more pubs were acquired, including the **Swan Inn** (Jasper's) in Cradley Heath, **Prince of Wales** in Wednesbury, **Elephant & Castle** in Bromley and **Old Bulls Head** in Sedgley, along with the iconic, award-winning **Great Western** in Wolverhampton.

In 1991, Jonathan Edwin joined the company after serving an apprenticeship with Morrell's Brewery in Oxford. Jonathan was instrumental in creating and launching Holden's new flagship beer, Golden Glow. The **Bell** at Trysull, **Shrubbery Cottage** at Oldswinford and the **Lamp** at Bloxwich were also added to the portfolio of pubs. By 1998, Holden's had refurbished the former **Codsall** railway station, bringing together two of Edwin's passions, beer and trains. Lucy and Abagail joined their brother at the company in the late 1990s.

In December 2002, Edwin sadly died, aged 57, but left the company in great stead. Over the next 10 years, three more pubs were acquired, including the **Waterfall** in Old Hill. By this time, the brewery had a tied estate of around 20 pubs with a further 90 free-trade outlets. In 2012, Holden's embarked on major expansion plans, extending the brewery and increasing production from 50,000-75,000 pints a week.

The brewery is still run by the fourth generation of the Holden family, who are just as committed to their proud history and heritage and to the generations to come. The Holden family are justly proud to have been brewing traditional Black Country real ales at the Hopden Brewery for over 100 years, producing what some might say are some of the finest ales in the area.

The Hopden Brewery is a traditional brewery, with a gravity mill, open fermentation vessels and proper coppers, with a brewing capacity of 36 barrels (10,368 pints for each brew). Over the years, Holden's has brewed many beers, including its core range of Black Country Mild (3.7%), Black Country Bitter (3.9%), Golden Glow (4.4%) and Special (5.1%). Seasonal and limited-edition beers have included Old Ale and XL Old Ale (8.5%) and a stout (3.7%), along with a Royal Wedding bottled beer (1986) and Tremor, commemorating the Great Dudley Earthquake of 2002! Holden's also bottle beer for themselves and other local breweries.

Cheers, and long may they prosper!

DUDLEY BREWERIES – SIMPKISS

The story of brewing by the Simpkiss family began in 1854, when **William Simkiss** bought the Potters Arms home-brew pub in Potter Street, in the Rocks area of the Delph, Brierley Hill. He was a potter by trade, but by 1859, had added a "p" to his surname and changed his occupation to a licensed victualler. He died in 1871.

By 1861, his son, **William Henry Simpkiss,** had taken over the pub and was carrying on a successful ginger beer and mineral water business there. In 1869, he borrowed £700 and, with additional contributions from the Lidstone family, bought the Royal Oak at Round Oak in Brierley Hill from Edward Smithyman. This site had a history of brewing beer, going back to 1797, and was on the main road to Dudley and close to the railway and canal. There was also a fast-growing population working in the local iron and steelworks, glassworks and brickworks. A few years later, Henry built a brewery on land behind the pub, but since he had little experience of brewing beer, immediately engaged 21-year-old Hercules Hazlehurst as head brewer. By 1890, Henry had bought three more pubs and the brewery was producing 250-350 barrels of beer a week.

By 1896, the business was such a successful and developing company, with around 30 pubs, that North Worcestershire Breweries (Stourbridge) made Henry an offer he couldn't refuse. He sold the brewery and most of the pubs for £20,000 and then retired until he died in 1905, aged 63. In 1897, the brewery passed to Elwell & Williams, who renamed it the Town Brewery. In 1934, Dudley based Julia Hanson & Sons bought the brewery and over 50 pubs (including the Stewponey & Foley Arms at Stourton) in one of the biggest sales of licensed premises at the time, at a cost of more than £120,000. However, Hanson's were more interested in the pubs and closed the brewery soon afterwards. By 1967, it had been replaced by a new fire station.

In 1903, Henry's 29-year-old son, **Joseph Paskin Simpkiss,** bought the Swan Brewery in Evers Street, Quarry Bank with money financed by his father, and renamed it the Home Brewery. Over the next few years, the company acquired 23 pubs, and by the outbreak of the First World War was producing over 300 barrels of beer a week. Despite swingeing increases in beer duty and taxes and tighter licensing restrictions, Simpkiss' maintained the price of their beer and provided a cheaper 2% light beer to works canteens. However, in 1916, J.P. Simpkiss lost the brewery in a curious court case which revealed that, for some reason, he had signed over the business to his office manager, William Clewes, who promptly ousted him and formed a partnership with head brewer, William Proctor. The brewery closed in 1921 and was demolished in 1959.

Joseph Paskin Simpkiss then became a travelling representative for Elwell & Williams of the Town Brewery until 1919. By then, he had raised enough money to buy the Foley Arms in Brettell Lane, Brierley Hill for £3,000 from Henry Bolton, who was brewing beer there. This was an established inn, originally known as the Wellington Arms, dating back to at least 1822. It was also on the main road to Dudley and next to the railway station and canal. Now 45-years-old, Joseph Paskin had to establish his new business again, brewing in a room that later became the pub lounge and, by 1925, he was producing 145 barrels of beer/week. In 1926, his 19-year-old son, Dennis, who had been an assistant brewer at the Ashton Gate Brewery in Bristol, joined his father in the family business. At this time, the range of beers included IPA, XXX, old ale and mild ale, and the company had acquired five other pubs.

In 1934, Joseph Paskin built a new brewery behind the pub on the site of an old iron foundry and cottages, designed by Dennis Simpkiss and named the Dennis Brewery after him. In 1936, a bottling plant was installed and by this time, the five-quarter brewery could produce up to 250 barrels of beer/week. In 1938, the company was registered as J.P. Simpkiss & Son, but shortly afterwards, Joseph died. Dennis took over the company, buying further pubs and two farms. Horace Perks, who had worked at the brewery for 30 years, became manager, with Teddy Guise as head brewer. They were later joined by Ken Hamilton as office manager from Darby's Brewery (West Bromwich).

In 1955, Simpkiss began an association with Johnson & Phipps Ltd, who operated the Anglo Malt Brewery in Wolverhampton. The companies soon merged and established the new company as JPS Breweries Ltd. Production of beer increased by installing brewing equipment from Darby's Brewery, and the partnership lasted 14 years until Alan Phipps retired.

In 1960, Dennis' son, **Jonathan Patrick Simpkiss,** joined the company. By 1965, the bottling business had been transferred to Holden's of Woodsetton and, in 1973, Ansell's installed a kegging line at the brewery. National notoriety was achieved in 1977 with the production of Jubilation beer, brewed for the Royal Silver Jubilee and bottled by Horace Perks. By this time, the company had reverted to J.P. Simpkiss & Son Ltd. In 1979, a 60th anniversary brew was launched to commemorate brewing at the Foley Arms, with each bottle signed by the head brewer, Trevor Pratt.

In 1981, Dennis Simpkiss died and Jonathan Simpkiss became managing director of the business. In 1984, Greenall-Whitley made a takeover bid for the company, but this offer was initially rejected. However, in July 1985 the company agreed to sell the brewery and its 15 tied houses for £1.9m to Greenall's. I can well remember joining local CAMRA members parading a coffin up Brierley Hill High Street to signal the loss of the company. Soon afterwards, Greenall's closed the brewery with the loss of 20 jobs, and it was demolished three years later. Greenall's went on to acquire Davenport's (Birmingham) and for some time their beers were served in the former Simpkiss pubs. It's also believed that Jonathan Simpkiss is now living as a tax-exile in the Isle of Man!

J.P. Simpkiss brewed a range of beers, the most regular being Simpkiss Bitter and Simpkiss Old Ale. Until 1981, a mild ale was brewed and Supreme and AK were introduced in 1984. Bottled beers included Nut Brown Ale, Black Country Bitter, Extra Special Bitter, Special Home-Brewed Ale and No.1 Old Ale. Over the years, more than 40 tied houses sold Simpkiss beers.

Although the Simpkiss Brewery has gone, the name lingers on, since the Enville Brewery has acquired the recipe for Simpkiss Bitter. They've relaunched it as Simpkiss Ale (4%), recalling a taste you'll remember and never forget!

LANGLEY BREWERIES – CROSSWELLS

Walter Showell was born in Birmingham in 1832, where he spent his formative years with his aunt at Ashted Row. He started his career as a trainee chemist and moved to Oldbury, where he joined Charles Tonge as an apprentice at his chemist's shop in Birmingham Street. In 1854, he met and married Sarah Harthill, the daughter of a master miller, which led to a career change. With his background as a chemist, he began collaborating with his father-in-law, Joseph Harthill, in his malting business. With his financial backing, he soon established the small Victoria Brewery in Simpson Street, Oldbury, not far from the Dog & Pheasant. Walter's beer recipes were popular with local drinkers and the business expanded.

During this period, he bought a large piece of land next to the Great Western Railway line in Crosswells Street, Langley Green, including Crosswells Springs, which early monks had called "The Wells of the Cross". In 1874, he constructed his new Crosswells Brewery here, which was such a success that in 1881 he built a new maltings at Langley, next to the Titford Canal and railway. A second 90-quarter brewery was added in 1884 with further extensions a year later. The brewery had its own company band, fire brigade and fire engine. In 1884, the company was formally registered and in 1887, Walter handed over control to his son, Charles.

The beers from Crosswells Brewery were advertised as *"ales brewed from the choicest malt and hops, and the purest water in existence, have so won their way into popular favour that the Crosswells has become a household word"*. There was a good range of *"palatable, wholesome and invigorating beers"*, including fine and superior dinner ales, table beer, mild, bitter and pale ales, brown stout and porter, best and strong old ale. The nearest tied house to the brewery was the **Crosswells Inn** in Station Road, Langley, previously kept by local agent, William Smith, and acquired in 1890.

The company expanded their outlets to supply beer to the Black Country and Birmingham, and in 1889 acquired Taylor's Hockley Brewery, adding another 40 tied houses in Birmingham. A year later, they acquired Sarah Marsland's Brookfield Brewery in Stockport, but this exposed the company to some risk in supplying beers to more remote locations.

In 1894, Showell's acquired the Brewers Investment Corporation, which doubled the number of pubs owned in Birmingham, and moved their head offices to Great Charles Street in Birmingham. The canal between Langley and Birmingham provided an efficient transport link between the brewery and a new distribution warehouse based at Crescent Wharf, off Broad Street, where 6,000 casks of ale could be stored. By 1896, they also had a brewery at Ely in Cardiff, but had to sell the Stockport Brewery for £250,000 due to a financial crisis. Further acquisitions in London and the South-West proved to be rather ambitious, which along with the downturn in the country's economy, led to the decline of the company. In 1898, their London pubs were bought by Reffell's Bexley Brewery, with a series of financial difficulties and prosecution.

By 1900, Showell's were widening their markets, supplying beer and stout to the Egyptian army of the Khedive, delivering 15,000 barrels of beer a year. At the shareholders' AGM in the same year, it was reported that the company was in good health, paying 15% dividends over the last four years and with annual net profits of over £92,000 (equivalent to over £12.1m in today's money). Around this time, Harry Twyford was one of the main directors of the company. By the end of the Victorian Age, Showell's had developed into a large regional brewery with a tied estate of almost 200 pubs.

In 1901, Walter Showell passed away at Stourton Hall, the family home near Kinver, aged 68, leaving a wife and daughter. At that time, he was a household name in Oldbury, as one who did so much for the people among whom he lived and worked. He had taken a prominent part in public life, becoming chairman of the Local Public Health Board and Board of Guardians. He had built a small church in Rounds Green, and contributed to the cost of the new parish church at Langley and the repair of the chancel at Kinver Church. He also helped to establish the Hospital Saturday Movement in Oldbury. He'd travelled widely, and was one of the first to ascend Mount Blanc. In 1885, he had stood unsuccessfully as a candidate for parliament and, at the time of his death, was an Alderman on Worcestershire County Council.

By 1912, the company was feeling the pinch, with declining profits of barely £9,500, mostly associated with the high cost of brewing materials. In 1914, his sons sold the company to Samuel Allsopp & Sons (Burton-on-Trent), along with its 194 pubs and 30 off-licences. At the final shareholders' meeting the accounts showed an apparent turn-round in profits, recorded as £65,224. The brewing plant was put up for sale in 1918, and Crosswells Brewery closed shortly afterwards. Samuel Allsopp leased all the pubs to Ind Coope & Allsopp, who used the brewery as a depot, and by 1961, had become part of Allied Breweries and later part of Carlsberg-Tetley.

Although most of the brewery buildings were demolished, some remain as part of a distillers company making Langley gin! In 1944, Langley Maltings was sold to Wolverhampton & Dudley Breweries and until 2006 was one of the few remaining traditional floor maltings. Listed as a historic building (Grade II), it remains a prominent canalside feature, but was seriously damaged by fire in 2009 and is on the top of the Victorian Society's list of endangered buildings.

So, although Showell's Crosswells Brewery has long gone, many of the company's pubs remain, often with some original features of the brewery, and still serving an excellent pint of beer.

LANGLEY BREWERIES – HOLT, PLANT & DEAKIN

Holt, Plant & Deakin was set up in 1984 by Allied Breweries as part of a marketing plan to enliven some struggling former Ansell's pubs in the Black Country. They came up with the idea of forming a chain of branded pubs supplied by a new micro-brewery at Langley. The enterprise used the names of three former breweries in the Allied portfolio, Holt's (Birmingham), Thomas Plant's Steam Brewery (Netherton) and James Deakin's Manchester Brewery. The brewery cost £100,000 to establish and produced up to 5,000 gallons a week of their stronger Holt's Entire beer.

Under the stewardship of general manager, Andrew Thompson, and company secretary, Andrew Holt, the selected pubs were refitted and given a Victorian appearance, at a cost of over £350,000. They had carved wood, open fires in black fire grates and furnishings that made it look like you'd stepped back in a time machine. Whilst some thought this was a questionable project, the beer was excellent, and Holt's Entire became a favourite tipple for many real ale fans.

The brewery was located at the former New Inn at Langley, run by Dave Rawsthorne. He had 11 years brewing experience, with an MSc brewing degree from the Brewing School at Birmingham University. The brewery was launched in September 1984, with the New Inn reopened as the Brewery Tap. In this "spit-and-sawdust" pub, you could look through a window to see the workings of the brewery. Although all the Entire was brewed at Langley, the regular mild and bitter came from Allied's Brewery at Warrington, to a recipe formulated to meet Black Country tastes. The Langley Brewery not only brewed the stronger Entire ale (4.4%), but also Deakin's Downfall (5.9%) and Plant's Progress (5.9%), as well as an occasional Christmas ale.

After the Brewery Tap, the first pub to be opened as part of the Holt, Plant & Deakin chain was the Fountain Inn at Tipton. They initially supplied six tied houses, including the Crosswells in Langley (former taphouse of Showell's Brewery), Crown & Cushion (Ocker Hill), Mount Pleasant (Sedgley), Dudley Port (Dudley Port) and Posada (Wolverhampton). Although many of the selected pubs were old Victorian locals, they were less successful in converting more modern pubs such as the Gladstone Arms at Wordsley. At its height, Holt, Plant & Deakin had a tied estate of around 50 pubs, mainly in and around the Black Country.

To keep pace with demand, they opened a second micro-brewery in 1989 at the Ship & Rainbow (renamed the Holt's Brewery Tap) in Wolverhampton, capable of producing 120 barrels of beer a week. But this led to the brand losing its focus and confusion, and the beer didn't always taste the same. After most of the brewing was switched to Wolverhampton, the project started to fail and was wound up in 1996. But most of the pubs survived and several still feature remnants of the old brand, including etched windows and signs, such as at the Plough & Harrow in Stourbridge. After the brewery closed, the pubs were sold to the Firkin group, who resumed brewing at Wolverhampton (renamed the Fermenter & Firkin at a cost of £330,000) for a short time to supply their local chain of tied houses. But brewing finally ceased in 1999 after the locals thought their beer was not as distinctive as the previous Entire.

Dave Rawsthorne, the man responsible for launching Holt's Entire, then went to the Old Swan, Netherton, to recreate the ale under the Pardoe's/Old Swan name. Later, he spent time at the Titanic Brewery in Stoke-on-Trent and Enville in South Staffordshire. He also helped to create Beckbury Bitter for the Hop & Stagger Brewery in Shropshire, before retiring.

I can well remember sampling glasses of Holt's Entire at several of their pubs, and their doorstop butties were unbeatable. A sad loss, but at least Entire beer survives under the Old Swan name, and Holt, Plant & Deakin's brewery memorabilia is very collectable.

BREWED ENTIRELY FOR THE BLACK COUNTRY

Holts Entire is a new strong bitter brewed in Oldbury for the Black Country taste.

You won't get it anywhere but the Holts pubs round here.

And once you've tried it you may find there's nowhere else you'll be entirely satisfied. Holts Entire. It's what's been missing round here.

HOLTS

IT'S WHAT'S BEEN MISSING IN THE BLACK COUNTRY.

TRADITIONAL HOLTS ENTIRE ALES

HOLT PLANT & DEAKIN · OLDBURY

MICRO-BREWERIES

The Black Country was home to many home-brew pubs and breweries. Indeed, Dudley was said to be the home-brew capital of the Midlands. But over the years, nearly all of the home-brew pubs have gone, and many of the smaller-scale independent breweries have been lost or taken over. However, the area is now home to almost 20 new micro-breweries, most established within the last decade or so, that complement some of the older independent breweries such as Batham's & Holden's.

A micro-brewery is typically a brewery that produces limited amounts of beer, certainly less than the large breweries, and is usually independently owned and uses traditional methods of producing beer. Such breweries are often perceived as having an emphasis on enthusiasm, new flavours and innovative beers.

In terms of micro-breweries, Dudley retains its title of "micro-brewery capital of the Black Country", with almost a dozen producing a variety of beers. In and around Stourbridge, they include the **Green Duck Brewery** in Rufford Road. This was set up by three friends in 2012, with its 10-barrel brewery producing hop-forward beers that are approachable and easy to drink. The Taproom (Badelynge Bar – meaning a row of ducks) is usually open on Fridays and Saturdays. **Craddock's Brewery,** based at the Duke William in Coventry Street, was established by Dave Craddock in 2011, and now has five pubs, including the Plough & Harrow in Stourbridge.

At Lye, John and Christopher Sadler converted a former printworks into the Windsor Castle Pub and Brewery in 2004, which became the home of Sadler's Peaky Blinder ales. They later moved to a new brewery in the railway station yard, but this was acquired and closed by a multi-national company. Meanwhile, Emily Sadler and her partner, Gareth, recommenced brewing at the Windsor Castle at the **Printworks Brewery,** with many of the beers named after printers' typefaces. Unfortunately, it closed in December 2023. In 2018, **Beat Brewery** moved to the Old Forge Trading Estate from North Curry (Somerset). Its beers reflected the owners' musical inspirations, with names like Raver, New Wave and Metal Head. Its large taproom became a popular music and events venue but it closed in November 2022.

At Quarry Bank, James and Tom Fownes set up **Fownes Brewery** at the Two Woods Lane Industrial Estate in 2019, after previously establishing a three-barrel brewery at the Jolly Crispin in Upper Gornal in 2012. Their beers are based on their "Dwarfen" fantasy world of King Korvak and his brewmaster, Broddy Firebeard, with beers such as King Korvak's Saga and Firebird's Old Favourite. One of their most memorable moments was when their beer was served in the Stranger's Bar at the House of Commons in 2013. In 2023, the brewery was sold to Dean Cartwright (of the Britannia, Rowley) and moved to Kidderminster.

Since 1992, **Black Country Ales** has established an estate of around 50 real ale pubs throughout the Black Country and beyond. It's based on the micro-brewery behind the Old Bull's Head, Lower Gornal, which was previously home to Bradley's Brewery, originally established by Edward Guest in 1834. It was resurrected in 2004 and now brews popular beers such as Bradley's Finest Golden, Fireside and Pig on the Wall, along with seasonal beers, such as Plum Pig and Chain Ale.

At Sedgley, the Beacon Hotel is a home-brew pub dating from 1852, which was acquired by **Sarah Hughes** in 1921. Brewing ceased in 1958, but in 1984, John Hughes (Sarah's grandson) restarted brewing at the traditional Victorian tower brewery, including the famous Sarah Hughes Dark Ruby Mild. Netherton is, of course, well known for the **Old Swan Brewery**, home to Pardoe's ales. Also in Netherton, beer sommelier, Roberto Ross, opened his Cult of Oak micro-brewery in 2019.

At Halesowen, cycling and brewing enthusiasts, Scott Povey and Sharon Bryant, set up their eight-barrel **Fixed Wheel Brewery** in 2014 at Long Lane, near Blackheath. Their core beers, many of which are based on cycling themes, include the award-winning Blackheath Stout. The taproom is usually open on Fridays and Saturdays, and the brewery also supplies their micro-pub, the **Wheelie Thirsty** at Old Hill. In Rowley Village, Dean Cartwright moved his **Pig Iron Brewery,** originally established at Brierley Hill in 2015, to the Britannia pub, and now brews popular beers such as Workin' Mon's Mild.

Walsall is also home to several micro-breweries. In 2015, Andy Dukes and his wife, Charlotte, established **AJ's Ales,** and later moved their four-barrel brewery to Ashmore Industrial Estate. The taproom often opens on the last Saturday of the month. At Bloxwich, home-brewer, Karol Kawecki set up his **New Invention Brewery** at Pinfold Industrial Estate in 2019. He uses his 30Hl micro-brewery to brew a range of modern beers, some of which are very fruity! The taproom is usually open on Fridays and Saturdays.

Brownhills is home to two micro-breweries. Brewing began at the **Backyard Brewery** at Gatehouse Trading Estate in 2008 and expanded in 2012. This 12-barrel plant brews up to 50 barrels a week and supplies several local pubs, including Wetherspoon's. Phil Bennett began brewing at **Beowulf Brewery** in Yardley, Birmingham in 1997, before moving to the artisan and manufacturing craft units at Chasewater Country Park. Beowulf brews a core range of popular beers, along with seasonal specials, which are widely available in pubs throughout the Black Country.

West Bromwich is not completely devoid of micro-breweries within the wider Sandwell area. At Tipton, the **Toll End Brewery** is based at the Waggon & Horses in Toll End Road. Its four-barrel micro-brewery opened in 2004, with one of its signature beers named after the brewer's daughter, Phoebe. **Davenport's** was an old brewery established in Birmingham in 1829, with the well remembered Beer-at-Home tag-line. The name was later acquired by another company and the current brewery occupies an industrial unit in Smethwick. Its 7.5 barrel plant produces a range of beers, some based on recipes from the old Davenport's and Highgate Breweries.

At Bilston, the **Newbridge Brewery** was set up in 2015 at Tudor House, with a five-barrel plant. Its name recalls a brewery of the same name in Tettenhall Road, Wolverhampton, operated by John Pearson and Arthur Thompson in the 1870s.

Just outside the Black Country in South Staffordshire, two breweries supply beer to many of our local pubs. **Enville Brewery** is sited at Cox Green in a picturesque Victorian farm complex, using traditional steam brewing and natural well water. First established in 1993, its signature beer, Enville Ale, is based on an old 19th century recipe for beekeeper's ale. In 2004, Dave and Carol Kelly established the **Kinver Brewery,** which moved to its current farmyard setting in 2012 with a new 10-barrel plant.

So, brewing is far from dead in the Black Country! The traditional, older established breweries such as Batham's & Holden's are complemented by a range of newer micro-breweries and craft breweries, widening and enlivening the variety of traditional and modern beers available in our pubs and clubs. Long may they prosper!

NETHERTON – BREWERIES & HOME-BREW PUBS

Netherton is probably best known for its long-established home-brew pub, the **Old Swan**. But in the 1900s, more than 100 pubs and alehouses served the town and its wider area, including over 40 home-brew houses and a surprising number of breweries. Most of these pubs and breweries have long gone, and today there are barely a handful of pubs remaining in and around the town. But it is fascinating to find the many family links and connections between the pubs and breweries.

OLD SWAN
The **Old Swan** in Halesowen Road is affectionately known as Ma Pardoe's, after long-serving landlady, Doris Pardoe. There was a pub here in 1835 when Joseph Turner was the earliest recorded landlord. The present pub and brewery date from 1863, when John Young was the owner, and later, Thomas Hartshorne and his family owned the pub and brewery for over 90 years from 1872-1964. In 1932, he offered the tenancy of the pub to Frederick and Doris Pardoe, who were then running the British Oak in Sweet Turf. When they moved in, Ben Cole was the brewer who was succeeded by Solomon Cooksey and then by his son George Cooksey, who stayed until 1988. But in December 1936, Fred Pardoe was found guilty of adding sugar to the beer to increase its strength, defrauding the Inland Revenue, and was fined £25. When he died in 1952, aged 59, his widow Doris (a tee-totaller) took over and bought the freehold of the pub in 1964. By the 1970s, the pub was a legend in beer-drinking circles, and was one of only four home-brew pubs remaining at the time of CAMRA's first Good Beer Guide in 1974. The brewery has a capacity of 28 barrels a week, with fermenting vessels of unlined timber.

Doris Pardoe died in April 1984 and the pub was kept by her daughter and her husband, Brenda and Sidney Allport, but within a year it was up for sale. A few troubled years followed, when the pub was owned by various companies (including CAMRA), and it was eventually bought by Punch Taverns. In 1985-1987 and from 2000 it has been kept by Tim Newey, who pulled his first pint here (13p) when he was 18 years old. He is also part-time organist at St Andrew's Parish Church and tirelessly maintains the traditional character of this Grade II listed Victorian gem, with its iconic interior which is included in CAMRA's National Inventory. Tim previously kept the Elephant & Castle in Dudley Wood when it was a Holt, Plant & Deakin pub, the short-lived local brewery set up at Langley by Ansell's in 1984. When this brewery folded in 1996, David Rawsthorne, former head brewer, moved to the Old Swan, where he recreated the Entire beer brewed by HP&D. Brewing still continues to this day and, as the sign proclaims, *"The Ales brewed at this establishment are the purest in the Borough"*.

JOHN ROLINSON AND THE FIVE WAYS BREWERY
John Rolinson was part of a brewing tradition in Netherton. In 1852, he bought the **Bricklayers Arms** in Church Street, but by 1864 had moved to the **Five Ways Inn** in St Andrew's Street, a home-brew house run by Thomas Penbury. In 1881, he built a 15-quarter brewery on land behind the pub, which could produce 850 barrels of beer a week to supply six tied houses. He also had a malting house in Northfield Road, behind the Loving Lamb Inn. Unfortunately, due to excise problems and financial difficulties, by 1896 the company was close to bankruptcy, but his son, Daniel Rolinson, was able to buy back the brewery and its pubs. However, more financial problems occurred, so to raise money, the company went public. Despite his financial problems, Daniel became a town councillor in 1896, and lived nearby at Hill House (*"the finest in the whole of Netherton"*). In 1905, the Public Analyst confirmed that he was brewing *"wholesome beer of very*

good quality". Daniel then became something of a country gentleman, buying farms and hotels, and also built a brickworks off Cinder Bank and founded the Baptist End Colliery. But things didn't go well and by 1910 he was declared bankrupt. The company had many pubs in Netherton, but the brewery and its 58 tied houses were eventually bought by Wolverhampton & Dudley Breweries in 1912.

THE STEAM BREWERY

William Round, an illiterate butty collier, was also a key player in Netherton breweries. In 1830, two doors away from the Castle Inn, he opened the **Cottage Spring Inn**, converted from two terraced houses, and built a small brewery at the back of the pub in 1837. When he died in 1854, his son Samuel Round took over and in 1861 built a new eight-quarter tower brewery using the Union (Burton-on-Trent) fermentation system. It had a steam boiler, thus giving the brewery its name, and produced 280 barrels of beer a week. It was second only to John Rolinson's brewery, with whom there was friendly rivalry. Samuel died in December 1874, leaving his young son, Jabez Round, to run the pubs and brewery. But a year later, he sold the brewery to Thomas Plant, who established Thomas Plant's Steam Brewery, brewing 16 draught beers. In 1892, he bought the adjoining Castle Inn from Thomas and William Hotchkiss, and this became the taproom for the Steam Brewery.

Thomas Plant died in 1896 and, with no son to succeed him, the company passed to his executors. Plant's was registered as a company in 1901, with John Shaw as brewery manager. In 1912, the brewery was bought by the Hereford & Tredegar Brewery and closed in 1914. It reopened a year later, but was never financially viable, and was taken over by Ansell's in 1936, along with 63 tied houses. The brewery was closed again in 1946, and the site was redeveloped for housing. In 1967, the Castle Inn and Cottage Spring were both demolished, and replaced with the modern **Mash Tun** pub (well located as one of the Holt, Plant & Deakin pubs), but this was replaced with modern apartments in 1999.

PRIMROSE HILL BREWERY

In 1896, Elijah Bywater bought the Primrose Hill Brewery at the rear of the **Bird in Hand** in Chapel Street from William Onslow, who had brewed beer here from 1840. Elijah had also run the football team when he kept the Britannia in Northfield Road (who lost 9-0 against Rowley White Star in 1890!) He also owned the **Colliers Arms** (Chapel Street) and the **Star** (Cradley Road), both home-brew houses. In 1896, Elijah sold the Bird in Hand to North Worcestershire Breweries, but kept the brewery and continued to brew with his son, Thomas Bywater, until 1926 and later with Wilfred Simms until 1936. The pub was rebuilt in 1909 by Wolverhampton & Dudley Breweries, but it closed in 1970 and became offices.

WHEELWRIGHT'S ARMS BREWERY

On the corner of Castle Street and Griffin Street, the **Wheelwright's Arms** dated back to 1832. Samuel Kendrick Houghton, a wheelwright from Droitwich, established a brewery here in 1873. In 1885, he leased the premises to Joseph Davies, who purchased the freehold in 1888 and bought several local beerhouses. His son, Joseph, married Sarah Cooksey, the sister of Solomon Cooksey, brewer at the Old Swan. After Joseph Snr died, his grandson, Joseph, took over, but sold the pub, brewery and its 11 tied houses to M&B in June 1942.

THE BATHAM'S CONNECTION
Netherton has a connection with Batham's, now brewing at The Delph in Brierley Hill. After 22 years of home brewing and running the White Horse in Cradley, Daniel Batham moved into the **King William** in Cole Street, and held a housewarming party to celebrate the opening of his new brewery in August 1901. His son, Daniel Batham Jnr, ran the pub from 1912-1915, when his wife, Myra Batham (also known as the Lady Bountiful), held tea parties on the bowling green. His eldest son, Arthur Joseph Batham, then aged only 18, kept the pub from 1921-1926.

TOMMY BOOTH
Tommy Booth was another legendary Black Country brewer who took over the **King William** in Cole Street in 1915 from Daniel Batham. In 1920, he bought the **Blue Pig** in St Andrew's Street from Joseph Homer for £2,300. Tommy rebuilt the disused brewery, assisted by Solomon Cooksey as brewer. He then bought some other Black Country pubs, including the Red Lion in Gornal Wood, where he built another brewery in 1935. By 1939, he had opened a new brewery in Corbyns Hall, near Pensnett, which lasted until he died in 1952. Tommy's career owed much to the Batham family; indeed, Daniel Batham gave him a gold sovereign from his first week's takings, which he kept mounted on his gold watch chain.

THE HOLDEN'S CONNECTION
Netherton also has a connection with another Black Country brewery, Holden's, founded by former shoemaker Edwin Holden. He married Lucy Blanche Round, daughter of Benjamin Round, who brewed beer at the **Trust in Providence** pub in Washington Street. In 1898, he persuaded Edwin to take the tenancy of the **Britannia Inn** in Northfield Road, and they eventually moved to the **Park Inn,** Woodsetton, establishing Holden's Hopden Brewery, with Harry Ossie Round as brewer.

NETHERTON NEW BREWERY
This was situated behind the **Old Pack Horse** in Hill Street, a home-brew house run by Daniel Hampton. In 1872, Richard Rolinson took over the pub and, with William Onslow, opened the Netherton New Brewery in 1875. However, he overreached himself and was bankrupt by 1885. He suffered further mishap in March 1895 when the brewery was almost destroyed by fire, but luckily he had paid the insurance premium two days earlier. In 1900, the brewery was amalgamated with the Five Ways Brewery, run by his son, John Rolinson.

NETHERTON OLD BREWERY
Sited in High Street behind the **Castle Inn,** this brewery was developed from 1835 by former miner Thomas Hotchkiss. When he died in 1874, his sons, Thomas and William, carried on the business as "The Old Brewery, Ale & Porter Brewers, Sweet Turf, Netherton". Brewing ceased in 1892, when the pub and brewery were sold to Thomas Plant.

NETHERTON BREWERY
The Netherton Brewery was founded by William Woodward Smith in 1852 on the corner of Cinder Bank. He also kept the nearby **Hope Tavern,** where Samuel Clempson had brewed in the 1880s, and he briefly operated the Dudley Brewery in Hall Street, Dudley.

HOME-BREW PUBS

Netherton abounded in home-brew pubs, a tradition which dated back to the early 1800s. Home-brewer Charles Cartwright was running the **British Oak** in Sweet Turf before 1861, and later leased it to Michael Hodgkins in the late 19th century. The last brewer was Edward Prince in 1930, just before the pub was kept by Frederick and Doris Pardoe, who moved to the Old Swan in 1932. In High Street, the **New Inn** dated back to 1870, when Samuel Taylor was licensee, and was a home-brew house in the 1890s. In 1901, it was advertised for sale, including a *"16-bushel mash tun, 200 gallon steam boiler and five fermenting vessels"*. The pub was bought by North Worcestershire Breweries and the brewery closed.

In Simms Lane, Joseph Smart brewed at the **Golden Lion,** where in 1888, he was fined £10 for defrauding the Inland Revenue by adding sugar to his brew to increase the strength of the beer. In St John's Street, the **Queen's Head** was established in 1875 by the Billingham family, led by Francis Billingham, who owned the pub for nearly 50 years and used the small brewery at the rear until 1935. In Harrison's Fold, the **Bull's Head** was first recorded as a home-brew house in 1828, where Sarah Crew and Thomas Round brewed. It was briefly home to the short-lived Dudley & District Brewery (1896-1897), and in 1926 became the base for the Netherton Bottling Company before it was eventually taken over by Wolverhampton & Dudley Breweries.

In St Thomas' Street, William Burchill established the **White Horse** in 1870, but brewing ceased in 1938 when it was taken over by Ansell's and closed a year later. In Hill Street, the **Old Cottage Inn** was a pre-1870 home-brew house kept until 1910 by John and Abagail Hampton. Here, Abagail would get a candle and go down the cellar stairs to serve beer direct from the cask.

In Cradley Road, William Tibbetts brewed beer at the **Reindeer** from 1896, but brewing ceased in 1936 when the pub was leased to Butler's and closed in 1938. Sarah Rolinson, matriarch of the Rolinson brewing dynasty, was landlady of the **Blue Bell** from 1781 when it was a home-brew pub. Brewing continued here until 1930 under Thomas Harris, but the pub closed in 1939. At the **Star,** brewer George Chatham was fined £20 in August 1887 for defrauding the Inland Revenue by adding sugar to his brew to increase the strength of the beer. George Bywater later brewed here, whilst in 1917, John Dunn was fined £80 for serving after hours.

At Primrose Hill, on the corner of Washington Street, the **Loyal Washington** was named after William Washington, a one-time canal carrier and loyalist. He built a pub here around 1850 and was also Netherton's first councillor in 1865. It was a home-brew house, rebuilt in 1901, when it was bought by Plant's. At Darby End, Ann and Louisa Bird brewed fine beer at the **Rose & Crown** in Withymoor Road, before selling it to William Dunn in 1897, who passed it to his son, John Dunn, in 1920.

At Windmill End in St Peter's Road, Thomas Cooksey brewed at the **Fox & Goose** in the 1830s, whilst William Hotchkiss brewed at the **Boat** in the 1880s. The **Bull's Head** also had its own brewery. In Baptist End, on the corner of Swan Street, the **White Swan** dates back to 1830, where the Roe family, led by Mary Ann and James Roe, brewed here from 1880-1939. It is now known as **Turner's,** after long-serving landlord, Tommy Turner (1954-1980).

It seems that nearly every pub in Netherton was once a home-brew pub or home to a small brewery, with the Old Swan remaining as one of the few traditional, iconic pubs still with its own brewery. Long may it prosper!

SMETHWICK BREWERIES – CHESHIRE'S WINDMILL BREWERY

I recently travelled on the Severn Valley Railway and found myself in the Railwayman's Arms pub on Bridgnorth station platform. Here, I spotted a huge etched mirror over the fireplace advertising Cheshire's beers from the Windmill Brewery, Smethwick. I needed to know more.

Well, firstly, there was a windmill in Smethwick, hence Windmill Lane, Windmill Shopping Centre and Windmill Precinct. In fact, the windmill was sited off Windmill Lane, and was built around 1803 by William Croxhall, a miller who was also a local churchwarden, but it was largely out of use by 1860. His name is commemorated in Croxhall Way, which runs alongside the site of the windmill.

Edward Cheshire was born in Titford, Oldbury in 1842 and educated at Chance Brothers School. He started work at Chance's Chemical Works in Oldbury and married his wife, Ann. Around 1870, he began his career in the licensed trade as the licensee and brewer at the Clock pub in Rolfe Street. He later acquired and brewed at the New Church Inn in Windmill Lane. In 1886, he bought two fields surrounding the old windmill at Capes Farm and established the brewery on the corner of Windmill Lane and Ballot Street. He integrated the historic windmill into the building complex and used it as a grain store.

He registered the company's name in 1896, with a registered capital of £200,000, and two years later, took over six tied houses of Threfall's (Liverpool/Salford) Brewery, which included the Bull's Head in Smallbrook Street, Birmingham. By 1900, he had acquired several pubs, including the Old Talbot in Smethwick High Street, the Queen's Head in Londonderry Road and the Seven Stars in Cape Hill. At the height of its business, Cheshire's had a tied estate of over 45 pubs throughout Smethwick, Oldbury, West Bromwich, Wednesbury, Wolverhampton and Walsall. However, Cheshire's were themselves taken over by Mitchells & Butlers in 1913. The 40-quarter brewery closed the following year and was put up for sale in March 1915. For some time afterwards it was used as Scribbans bakery. The old windmill was demolished in 1949 and some of its working parts were moved to the Science Museum in London for display.

Edward Cheshire was a well-known and respected member of the local community. He served on the local Board of Health and later on the District Council. He was elected an alderman in 1899 and became Mayor of Smethwick in November 1902. He was also president of the Birmingham Children's Hospital, Cripples Union, Smethwick Aid Society and Smethwick Musical Society, and founded the Edward Cheshire Nursing Home in 1903. He was also a churchwarden at Smethwick Old Church and, in the early 1900s, donated land to extend its churchyard. He lived at Sunny Bank in Augustus Road, Edgbaston, but died in July 1919, aged 78, and was buried at the Old Church. His nephew, William Cheshire, was also a director of Cheshire's Brewery and joined the Holt Brewery (Birmingham) in 1910, becoming director in 1912. He was taken ill on a tramcar in December 1922 and died shortly afterwards, leaving an estate valued at £9,415 (equivalent to over £374,000 today). The family's name is commemorated in the name of nearby Cheshire Road.

The brewery was a profitable venture, reporting healthy profits and dividends during its 27-year life. In the early days, the brewery was very generous to its staff and local community, holding a capital dinner at the New Church Inn for their employees in 1897, catered for in excellent style. There was a hearty toast to the *"Success of Cheshire's Brewery Ltd"*, especially after increased trade meant increased wages! The beers brewed at Cheshire's were renowned for their *"high character, purity and brilliance, brewed from the choicest malt and hops"*. The range of beers included a mild ale, Guinea bitter, Grand Pale Ale and Family Ale, along with bottled stout. Some of the advertisements for their beers showed an idyllic element of romanticism, like the lady carrying bottled beers from the farmhouse past the old windmill.

The Windmill Brewery is long gone, and the site is now occupied by St Matthew's Church of England Primary School and new housing. Most of its pubs have disappeared too, but occasionally you may spot an old etched glass window or mirror advertising its beers. For example, at the Seven Stars (Cape Hill), there was a windmill motif high on the corner of the wall, and one of the oldest pubs in Smethwick, the Old Chapel (The Uplands), dating from 1732, was once owned by Cheshire's Brewery.

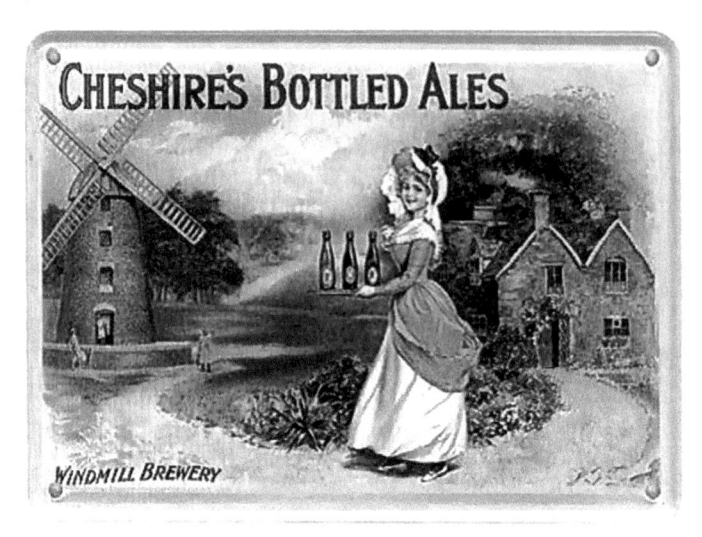

Windmill motif at the Seven Stars, Smethwick

STOURBRIDGE BREWERIES

Stourbridge is renowned for its high-quality glassmaking industry, but is much less remembered for its breweries, probably because there weren't that many! In the early days, most of Stourbridge's pubs were home-brew houses, where landlords brewed beer on the premises to their own individual recipes. From the late 1800s, commercial breweries, particularly from Lye, Netherton, Dudley, Wolverhampton and Birmingham, began to supply the town's pubs, along with around 100 independent home-brewers. Over the years, there were barely a handful of breweries in and around Stourbridge, but even now, several small-scale breweries still serve the town.

Probably the largest brewery in the town was the **Stourbridge Brewery** in Duke Street. This was originally established by John Wall in the 1850s, after expanding from his home-brew pub, but there was a damaging fire in 1867, and after he died it was run by his executors. In 1896, **North Worcestershire Breweries** was formed to acquire and amalgamate the Stourbridge Brewery, Rowley Brewery (Blackheath), White Swan Brewery (Oldbury) and Royal Oak Brewery (Round Oak), with a combined total of 135 tied houses, including the Talbot Hotel in Stourbridge town centre, and with a share capital of over £250,000. Brewing was then concentrated at Stourbridge where, after another fire, the brewery was reconstructed and enlarged as a new 80-quarter brewery, with its own well, 280ft deep. The foundation stone was laid with a silver trowel and oak mallet by Chairman Herbert Praed in August 1897, who was later knighted in 1906.

In 1907, the company bought most of the pubs in Wolverhampton owned by Deakin's Manchester Brewery. But by 1908, the enterprise was losing money and, along with its 152 pubs, was acquired by Wolverhampton & Dudley Breweries in 1909. The brewery had extensive cellars dating from 1856, 35ft deep and on three levels. In 1940, they served as a communal air-raid shelter, holding up to 1,000 people, including pupils and staff from King Edward VI Grammar School. The town's ring road now crosses the site of the brewery. The brewery's taphouse was the **Duke William** in Coventry Street, purpose-built in 1903 with terracotta and glazed brickwork and retaining many original features today, including a curved bar, bar-back and etched windows.

Another notable brewery was Edward Rutland's **Queen's Head Brewery** in Enville Street, behind the pub of the same name. The premises were acquired from Albert Hipkiss in 1898 by Rutland & Lett, who expanded the brewery and installed a bottling plant in 1900. Rutland's were prolific advertisers, and promoted their Harvest Beer in splendid condition in 1905. In 1924, the firm was registered as Edward Rutland & Son, with offices and a wine and spirits merchants at Bordeaux House on the corner of High Street and Foster Street. The company also had a handful of tied houses in Stourbridge, Kinver, Dudley, Amblecote and Halesowen. The brewery was taken over by Albert Hipkins in 1929, but was then acquired by Frederick Smith (Aston), along with its pubs, and closed in 1931. The brewery was later demolished, but its taphouse, the **Queen's Head,** remains as a local CAMRA award-winning Black Country Ales' pub.

Other smaller-scale breweries in the town included Rowland Hill's **Angel Brewery,** behind the Angel Inn in Coventry Street. It was registered under the name of H&F Kelley (1870-1910) and had at least four tied houses, but it was offered for sale at auction in 1911 and closed in 1923. Around 30 home-brew pubs are recorded, including the Bird in Hand (Oldswinford), Forester's Arms, Gate Hangs Well and Unicorn (Wollaston), Royal Exchange and Golden Lion (now Katie Fitzgerald's) (Enville Street), Mitre (Lower High Street) and Plough & Harrow (Worcester Street).

Two small-scale breweries in Lye also supplied the town's pubs, including the Penn family's **Cross Walks Brewery** (1914-1926) and **Herbert Newnam & Son,** established in 1885 behind the Seven Stars pub in Pedmore Road. During the 1930s, this brewery produced a very strong pale ale (10.5% Premier Cuvee) with the tag-line "Treat it with Respect", but the company was acquired and closed by Wolverhampton & Dudley Breweries in 1960.

More recently, Mill Race Lane was home to **Premier Midland Ales,** which was founded in 1988 by Eddie and Graeme Perks. However, it was short-lived and merged to form Pitfield Premier Brewing Co. in 1990. This company went into voluntary liquidation and was acquired by Wiltshire Brewery (Tisbury) in 1991, when brewing ceased. In 1994, the brewery and its seven tied houses were taken over by United Breweries of India, but that operation also crashed and the brewery closed. I can well remember drinking a glass of Maiden's Ruin – a 7.4% dark, fruity strong ale in the Moorings Tavern, just across the ring road beyond the end of Lower High Street.

Nowadays, the only brewery in Stourbridge town is **Craddock's,** established by Dave Craddock in 2011. In an interesting twist of fate, this brewery started life behind the Duke William in Coventry Street, once the taphouse of North Worcestershire Breweries. In the early days, Dottie the dray horse delivered the beer to Craddock's other local pub, the Plough & Harrow, near Mary Stevens Park in Worcester Street. The company now has five pubs, including the King Charles in Worcester, Talbot in Droitwich and Good Intent in Birmingham, which is a charity-led pub. Craddock's popular beers include Troll, Saxon Gold, Honey Ewe and Crazy Sheep.

Other smaller-scale local breweries also supply the town's pubs. In 2012, three friends established the **Green Duck** brewery and moved to Rufford Road in 2013, with its Badelynge Bar (badelynge is the name for a group of ducks!). Nearby, in Lye, **Beat Brewery** moved from North Curry in Somerset to the Old Forge Trading Estate in 2018. Its beers reflected the owners' musical inspirations, with names like Raver, New Wave and Metal Head. It's large taproom became a popular music and events venue but it closed in November 2022.

In the 1860s, the Sadler family owned the **Windsor Castle** in Dingle Street, Rounds Green, Oldbury, including John Sadler (the Grand Old Man of Oldbury). Nathaniel Sadler soon established his Windsor Castle Brewery here, and at its height, Thomas Sadler was supplying another 10 pubs. But brewing ceased in 1927 and the pub closed in 1956. Later, in 2004, John Christopher Sadler recalled their family's brewing heritage in Oldbury by converting a former printworks in Lye into the Windsor Castle Pub and Brewery. This became home to Sadler's Peaky Blinder ales, before moving to a site next to the railway station, which was later acquired and closed by a multi-national company. In 2019, Emily Sadler and her partner, Gareth, recommenced brewing at the Windsor Castle as the **Printworks Brewery,** with beers named after printer's typefaces (Verdana, Geneva and Helvetica), reflecting the family's printing heritage. In another quirk of fate, Printworks recently held a tap-takeover at the Queen's Head in Enville Street, the former home of Edward Rutland's brewery. However, the brewery and pub are currently closed.

And we mustn't forget **Kinver** and **Enville** breweries over the border in South Staffordshire, complementing the long-standing **Batham's** (Brierley Hill), **Holden's** (Dudley), **Beacon Hotel** (Sedgley) and **Old Swan** (Netherton) breweries.

So, although Stourbridge's old breweries are long gone, there are still a handful of small-scale local breweries in and around the town, brewing some excellent beers to sample in the many real ale pubs in and around the town centre.

WALSALL – OLD BREWERIES

Over the years, **Walsall** has been home to several breweries supplying the local pubs used by thirsty workers. Most are long gone, but they've now been joined by a new generation of micro-breweries, brewing high-quality craft beers for the local population to enjoy in their taprooms and local pubs.

The most memorable brewery in Walsall is probably the **Highgate Brewery.** It was built between 1895-1898 for James A. Fletcher, who ran a long-established wine and spirits merchants in Ablewell Street, to supply his 10 pubs. He chose the site in Sandymount Road due to its supply of pure brewing water from a local borehole. The building is a typical Victorian five-storey tower brewery which still survives; indeed it's listed as a historic building (Grade II). Fred Broadstock was the first brewer, and Agnes Mountfield became the country's first female brewer in 1914. During the early 1900s, Highgate began to acquire a few home-brew pubs and breweries, including Yardley & Ingram's Brewery at Bloxwich. In 1920, a bottling plant was installed, which also bottled Guinness, and a malt crushing mill came from Dresden in 1922.

In 1924, James Fletcher (Highgate Brewery), Bolton-born brewer John Lord (Town Brewery) and James Pritchard (Darlaston Brewery) joined forces to form Walsall Breweries Proprietory Ltd and promptly took over Arthur Beebee's Malt Shovel Brewery. In 1939, Mitchells & Butlers (M&B) took over this expanded company, along with over 50 tied houses and the brewery, which by then produced 1,000 barrels of beer a week. During the Second World War, M&B continued brewing at Highgate so that they could make full use of the limited rations of malt and hops. When it passed to the Bass group in 1961, it was the company's smallest brewery and was always under threat of closure, even though it produced 2,000 barrels of mild ale a week.

Following a management buy-out in 1995, Highgate became famous for its Highgate Mild and seasonal Highgate Old Ale. In 2000, it merged with Aston Manor Brewery and in 2007 passed to Global Star, which became the new incarnation of Davenport's, based in Smethwick. Brewing no longer takes place at Sandymount Road, although some original brewing equipment remains. The brewery has been put up for auction several times, and the Friends of Highgate Brewery continue to campaign for its future preservation.

Over the years there were several other breweries in and around Walsall. In 1871, James and Emma Bird established the **Butts Brewery** behind the Butts Inn but, along with its three tied houses, was acquired in 1920 by Butts Brewery Ltd. However, this enterprise was short-lived and by 1929 was in voluntary liquidation. In 1890, Sarah Allsop established the **Pleck Brewery** at the Royal Oak in Oxford Street. This brewery and its four pubs were later acquired by Messrs Leary and Son and then by Ansell's, when the brewery was demolished and the pub was rebuilt. In 1898, John Lord rebuilt the **Town Brewery** in Short Acre Street, next to the Black Horse Inn, and eventually had 16 tied houses. It became part of the Highgate consortium in 1924, and the brewery closed when it was taken over by M&B in 1939.

In 1904, Arthur Beebee established the **Malt Shovel Brewery** in Sandwell Street, close to the White Lion pub, but the 40-barrel brewery and its 12 pubs were taken over by the Highgate consortium in 1924. In Bath Street, Samuel Holmes ran the **Windmill Brewery** behind the Windmill pub from 1921-1937. In 1933, George Shelley Twist established **Twist's White Horse Brewery** in Wolverhampton Street, where his beer included *"Malt for Strength and Energy, Hops for the Appetite and Yeast for the Blood"*. In 1950, it was acquired by Atkinson's (Aston), along with its tied estate of 20 pubs, which then passed to M&B in 1959 who closed the brewery.

In **Bloxwich,** J.W. Brookes established the **Bloxwich Brewery** in Elmore Green Road, but this was taken over by Butler's (Wolverhampton) in 1923. At that time, it had 42 pubs, mainly in

151

Bloxwich, Walsall, Darlaston and Willenhall, including a small brewery behind the Royal Exchange (Bloxwich), now listed. The brewery closed in 1931. In Leamore Lane, Samuel Birch founded the **Crown Brewery** behind the Crown Inn in 1864. It was acquired by the Bird family in 1920 as a result of inter-family marriage and, at its height, had nine tied houses. Brewing ceased in 1965, but bottling continued until it was taken over by Ansell's (Aston) in 1967. In High Street, **Yardley & Ingrams** operated the **Victoria Brewery** in 1891, associated with wine and spirits merchants, J & J Yardley, until it was taken over by Highgate Brewery in the early 1900s.

In **Darlaston,** James Pritchard & Son founded the **Darlaston Brewery** behind the Bell in Church Street in 1849, but by 1924, it had become part of the Highgate consortium. The brewery closed when it was taken over by M&B in 1939 and the pub was demolished in 1956. In **Willenhall,** Jesse and Emily Lashford established **Lashford's Brewery** in the 1920s to supply the Springvale Tavern on the corner of St Anne's Road. They acquired a few more pubs and supplied the free trade, before diversifying into the leisure industry, converting an old football ground into a greyhound track. In 1930, the pubs, brewery and dog track were sold to Truman, Hanbury & Buxton for £34,500. Also in Willenhall, the **West Midlands Working Men's Club Brewery** was set up in 1920 to acquire Henry Mills' Old Oak Brewery in Walsall Road, along with its nine pubs, but this was bought by W. Butler & Co. (Wolverhampton) in 1922 and closed by 1932.

In **Rushall,** Frederick Harrison established the **Rushall Brewery** in Daw End in 1880, which was associated with **Laburnums Brewery** in Pelsall Lane, also in the Harrison family. In 1905, Thomas Shercliff and Henry Waters started brewing at the **Old Rushall Brewery** until 1920, when the premises were taken over by the Walsall & District Clubs Brewery, before being sold to Charrington's in 1960 and subsequently closed.

In **Brownhills, William Roberts' Brewery** was established behind the Station Hotel in 1860, but this was acquired in 1925 by Eley's Brewery (Stafford) and closed in 1928. The pub subsequently passed to William Butler & Co. (Wolverhampton). An etched window with the Roberts' logo survives in the Shoulder of Mutton in Brownhills.

Apart from commercial breweries, the Trade Directory of 1839 records a few common brewers in Walsall, including John Beckett's Dudley Brewery in Ablewell House, and Meakin & Son in George Street. Several pub landlords also brewed their own beer, including the Victoria (Lower Rushall Street), Littleton Arms (Littleton Street) and Royal Exchange (Bloxwich). Most of these pub breweries were closed in the 1920s, but the Watering Trough (Ablewell Street) continued under Norman Dawson as Walsall's last home-brew pub until the 1950s. However, new micro-breweries have opened more recently in and around Walsall, including **AJ's** (Long Acre), **New Invention** (Bloxwich), and **Backyard** and **Beowulf** (Brownhills).

So, even though most of Walsall's old breweries are long gone, you may spot an old bottle or glass, or an etched window at one of their former pubs. And we can still enjoy a drink of fine beer from the newer local micro-breweries in their taprooms and local pubs.

WEST BROMWICH – OLD BREWERIES

West Bromwich came of age in the 19th century, when the town experienced industrial and commercial growth in Victorian times, increasing its population from 5,687 in 1801 to over 65,000 a century later. At that time, more than 100 pubs served thirsty workers, many of them brewing their own home-made ales. But, as the century progressed, several commercial breweries were established, which were later subject to takeover and closure.

In 1777, the first recorded common brewer in West Bromwich was **Joseph Bullevent**. His wholesale brewery was "of service to the lower sort of people which they can sell to the working people at about Four or Sixpence per gallon".

Another early brewer was Abraham Fisher, first recorded in 1828 after establishing the **Greets Green Brewery**. Unfortunately, he died in 1833, but brewing continued with his wife, Sarah, and Louisa until 1846, when the brewery was sold.

From 1839-1842, Sarah's brother-in-law, Jesse Fisher, operated the **Stoney Lane Brewery** in Sandwell Road. In 1848, it was bought by James O'Connor and Robert Bennett, who promptly changed its name to the Burton Brewery. But their partnership was dissolved in 1853, and by 1859, Carey Heelas and Henry Bishop were running the brewery. Their involvement was short-lived and, by the 1860s, it had passed to John Morgan and Benjamin Wikeley. Brewing ceased by the late 1870s and the buildings were later taken over by safe manufacturer, Thomas Withers & Son.

One of the shortest-lived breweries was the **West Bromwich Brewery** in Churchfields, operated by John Chapman from the late 1840s until he became bankrupt in 1868.

In 1850, Daniel Williams was brewing beer at the small brewery behind the **Union Cross Inn** on the corner of Greets Green Road and Oldbury Road. By 1883, it had passed to William Bowen, whose brother John was one of seven subscribers who converted West Bromwich Albion into a limited company in 1891. Interestingly, William's sister married George Darby, whose son, Charles, founded Darby's Dunkirk Brewery. By 1890, it was a "modern brewing plant with well-seasoned casks, varying from 18-750 gallons". His son, William, took over in 1927 and, during this period, the **Union Cross Brewery** grew substantially, gaining eight tied houses. In 1945, it was taken over by William Butler & Co. (Wolverhampton), who promptly closed and sold the brewery.

In 1864, Charles Darby was running the **Dog & Duck** in Braybrook Street, and by 1871, his son, George, was licensee of the **Bush Inn** on the corner of Wood Lane and Claypit Lane. In 1895, his son, Charles, bought the pub and five years later bought Dunkirk Hall, Greets Green, one of the oldest buildings in the town. In 1902, he built the **Dunkirk Brewery** behind the pub, which he ran with his son, George. It became the largest in West Bromwich, but after Charles died in 1949, the brewery and over 100 tied houses had to be sold to pay death duties. In 1951, Mitchells & Butlers acquired the company, closed the brewery, and the premises were later demolished and replaced by housing.

In 1874, Samuel Woodhall founded his **High Street Brewery** and by 1885 had established the **Borough Brewery** behind the Fox & Dogs pub, recalling the time when West Bromwich became a County Borough. By 1914, he was brewing Old English mild, bitter, pale, old and family ales, along with porter and stout *"from the finest materials procurable borne out by the brilliancy, nourishing and appetising properties"*. After Samuel died in 1919, his son, Frank, ran the company until it was taken over in 1939 by Julia Hanson & Sons (Dudley), along with its 25 pubs.

In 1871, 24-year-old Arthur James Price was licensee of the **Lewisham Arms** in High Street. In 1887, he built a new brewery behind the pub, which 20 years later was supplying around 30 other tied houses. He had also carved his initials (AJP) into a lion on the front pediment of the pub. Unfortunately, he died in 1906 (aged 46); his funeral was described as one of the most imposing ever seen in the borough, with a cortege of over 30 vehicles. The brewery and 17 tied pubs were sold to Holder's (Birmingham) in 1908.

In 1888, rope manufacturer Thomas Oliver was running the **Farriers Arms** in Queen Street brewing his own beer. By 1897, he had built the **Sandwell Brewery** next to the rope works. He was another brewer who died young (at 48) in 1909, but the brewery continued under John Watkins, who registered the Throstle trademark in 1912. Although it continued to trade throughout the two World Wars, it was taken over by William Butler & Co. in 1945, along with its three tied houses.

From the 1880s, William, Thomas and Henry Brennand were well-known personalities in the licensed trade, holding the licences of several pubs in the town. By 1903, Thomas had built his **Malthouse Brewery** in Bratt Street, designed by noted London architects, Inskipp & Mackenzie, with its 350ft deep borehole, bottle-washing plant and stabling. He was later joined by his son, Henry, but Thomas died in 1928. The brewery closed two years later, becoming a salt and sweets factory and later a milk depot.

In 1887, George Arnold was licensee of the **New Inn** in New Street and by 1891, his son, Edward was running the pub. They were both brewers, and by 1903, George had built the **Dartmouth Brewery** behind the pub. Charles Perry, a well-known local figure and former player with West Bromwich Albion, later became director of the brewing company. By 1914, it was a modern, well-equipped brewery brewing "pure palatable and nourishing beverages", whilst Edward was a past Mayor, JP and Alderman of the town. By 1924, the company had merged with the **Sponwell Brewery** in Spon Lane, founded by Thomas Henry Bates in 1915, and renamed **Arnold & Bates Ltd.** But by 1928, it had been taken over by Darby's Dunkirk Brewery, with its nine tied houses, and closed shortly afterwards.

Thomas Spencer was the son of John Spencer, who ran the Phoenix ironworks in Greets Green for many years. In 1863, Thomas set up his first wine and spirits merchants (Dowdeswell & Spencer) with his brother-in-law, John Dowdeswell. In 1896, he set up an umbrella company (Birmingham Breweries Ltd) to acquire breweries and over 150 pubs, but it had a shaky financial start and by 1899 was in voluntary liquidation. But Thomas was undaunted and launched a new company (Spencer's Ltd) to run his in-house **Phoenix Brewery** in High Street, brewing Spencer's Celebrated Pure Family Home-Brewed Ales until he died in 1914. It was then run by his son, John, until 1928.

James Stanton was another former West Bromwich Albion player who, by 1906, was licensee of the **Dog & Duck** in Braybrook Street. By 1911, his son, Joseph, was helping him brew his own beer at the small brewery behind the pub, but this was acquired by Darby's Brewery in 1926.

West Bromwich has a long and eventful history of breweries, but all have been taken over or closed. However, the town still has a legacy of several pubs, once owned by these breweries, where memories of the past remain. Long may they prosper!

If you wish to know more about the history of breweries in West Bromwich, *The History of Brewing in West Bromwich and the most successful brewer Darby's* by Carol Harthill and Mark Bennett comes highly recommended.

WEST BROMWICH BREWERIES – DARBY'S DUNKIRK BREWERY

The Darby family's association with beer and brewing goes back to 1864, when Charles Darby was landlord of the **Dog & Duck** in Braybrook Street, West Bromwich. He kept the pub until 1881, but in 1870, the *Dudley Herald* reported that he'd been fined 20s for serving intoxicating liquor during prohibited hours.

After working at Chance's Glassworks, Charles' son, George, married Elizabeth Brown in 1860, whose family owned Bowen's Brewery in Greets Green. George was keen to enter the licensed trade and took his first pub, the **George** in Spon Lane, near the glassworks and a few doors away from the **Champion of England,** kept by William Perry (the Tipton Slasher).

By 1871, he'd moved on to the **Bush,** on the corner of Wood Lane at Greets Green, in an industrial area with four large ironworks, coal mines and brickworks. By 1891, George and his wife had raised four sons, George, Charles, Harry and Samuel, and five daughters, Alice, Mary, Elizabeth, Eleanor and Elsie. George started brewing his own beer at the pub and by 1894 had established Darby's Brewery here. The pub became one of the best inns in the town and George became a well-known local personality and a popular host, before being elected to the Town Council. He retired and died in 1910, aged 76.

In 1895, George's son, Charles and his wife, Ada, took over the Bush, and in 1900, purchased nearby **Dunkirk Hall** from the late Alderman Reuben Farley (recalled at the clock in Carter's Green). This building had a somewhat chequered history, being one of the oldest halls in West Bromwich, dating back to Tudor times. Its name may recall the time when Cromwell captured the French port of Dunkirk from the Spanish in 1658. Charles made some changes to the building and used most of it as a pub, named the **Dunkirk Inn.**

In 1902, Charles began to build a brewery behind the Dunkirk Inn, off Claypit Lane (now Whitgreave Street), which he named the **Dunkirk Brewery.** At the same time, his family moved out of the Bush to a house in Roebuck Lane and later to Handsworth Wood. The strong smell of beer brewing at the brewery was particularly remembered by children attending Greets Green School next door!

Charles later bought his second pub, the **Shakespeare Inn** at Toll End, Tipton. In 1915, Charles' son, George, joined the company, starting at the brewery at 4.00am each morning, and two years later, his son, also Charles, joined the brewery. George was called up to serve in the Great War, and his son learnt the brewing trade from the foreman, along with many women who had come to work in the brewery.

At the end of the First World War, George returned to the brewery and, by this time, Darby's had an estate of around 30 pubs. George looked after the brewery, with Charles doing the book-keeping. By 1923, Darby's had become a limited company and changed its name to Darby's Brewery Ltd in 1927. A year later, they acquired the Sponwell Brewery in Spon Lane from Arnold & Bates Ltd, adding another 17 pubs.

In the 1920s, Darby's continued to expand their estate of pubs, including the **Golden Cup** in Cross Street, **Stone Cross** (Stone Cross) and **Victoria** in Lyng Lane, and by 1939, they had around 100 pubs. Darby's adopted a rather innovative approach to their licensed trade, employing managers for their pubs, rather than tenants. They were paid 10% of the weekly takings and were trusted to do their own stock-taking, encouraging them to generate more trade. This approach resulted in Darby's pubs increasing their trade from two barrels to 7-10 barrels of beer a week.

Charles introduced lounge bars into the pubs, with ladies toilets, to attract a wider clientele. He would regularly visit the pubs in his pony and trap, after which the horse would find its own way back to the brewery with Charles asleep in the trap! The brewery workers were also well looked after, with a subsidised canteen. There was also a busy bottling plant, where they not only bottled their own beers, but also bottled Guinness.

In the 1930s, Charles decided to rebuild some of his most popular pubs, employing a local Walsall architect with a passion for art-deco designs and green tiled roofs. In 1932, the tax on beer was doubled, and Charles thought seriously about giving up brewing. Darby's only sold their own beers (with the exception of Guinness) and he'd always charged a penny less than Mitchells & Butlers for his beers. Nevertheless, he carried on brewing and, in 1937, Darby's acquired John Jackson's Diamond Brewery (Dudley), expanding the business further.

The original **Bush Inn** had been added to the Darby's estate in 1929, and was rebuilt as a flagship pub in 1937, with its trademark green tiled roof. Coming back full circle, former West Bromwich Albion player, James Stanton, who'd brewed Stanton's Ales, sold the **Dog & Duck** to Darby's Brewery in 1932, but it closed in 1959.

By 1947, Charles had even bought a Rolls Royce for the brewery, but he died in November 1949 at the age of 78. He was buried at All Saints' Churchyard, West Bromwich with his wife, Ada, but a huge sum of money had to be paid in death duties. In 1951, after much soul-searching, sons George and Charles had no alternative but to sell the company, along with over 100 pubs, to Mitchells & Butlers, who had some family links with the Darby family and the brewery. Although they hoped that Dunkirk Brewery would continue brewing, M&B closed it within a year. However, M&B continued to brew one of Darby's most popular beers, Darby's Pale Ale, for a few years at their Cape Hill brewery, but locals said it didn't taste the same as the original beer. Later, Charles Darby CBE, the great-grandson of George Darby, became Chairman and Chief Executive of Bass M&B.

After the sale, some of the brewing equipment from the Dunkirk Brewery went to the Simpkiss Brewery in Brierley Hill. They were also joined by former Darby's office manager, Ken Hamilton. Most of Darby's pubs continued to trade, including the Dunkirk Inn, but sadly this was closed and demolished in 1977. The brewery was also later demolished and replaced by flats and houses.

The **Bush** prospered as a popular community pub until the 1980s, when it was renamed Darby's. But it closed in 2000 and was converted into a community centre with flats in 2002. In August 2018, the Friends of Dartmouth Park erected a blue plaque on the site of the original Bush Inn, outlining the history and significance of George and Charles Darby and the Dunkirk Brewery. They also saved and restored a sign advertising Darby's Ales painted on the brickwork of a former Darby's pub in Lombard Street, West Bromwich, which is now on the perimeter wall of Dartmouth Park.

Darby's were the largest, most successful and last brewers in West Bromwich, and memorabilia, such as jugs, bottles and beer mats, have become very collectable. Many of their pubs survive and still contain memories of this popular brewery. Long may they prosper!

If you wish to know more about the history of Darby's Brewery, The History of Brewing in West Bromwich and the most successful brewer Darby's by Carol Harthill and Mark Bennett comes highly recommended.

WOLVERHAMPTON – BREWERIES

Wolverhampton came of age in the 19th century with the discovery of coal and ironstone in the district. Heavy industry developed, which was thirsty work, so it's not surprising that hundreds of pubs grew up to slake the workers' thirsts. In the early days, most pubs brewed their own beer, but towards the end of the 19th century, several commercial breweries were established. Probably the most well known are Wolverhampton & Dudley Breweries (Banks's Park Brewery) and William Butler's Springfield Brewery, but there were many other smaller breweries, most of which were taken over or closed.

Probably the oldest recorded brewery in Wolverhampton was **Jones & Co.** of Snow Hill, originally registered by James, Taylor & Co. in 1792, but passed to William Jones in 1802.

In 1840, **William Butler** was brewing beer at the Old Shoppe in John Street, Priestfield, and later set up the **Priestfield Brewery.** In 1873, he bought land at Springfield and built the new **Springfield Brewery** a year later, which was capable of producing 400 barrels a week. In 1881, a new 60-quarter tower brewery, now Grade II listed, was built, designed by London architects, R.C. Sinclair, making a total capacity of 120-quarters, producing 1,500 barrels a week, with further expansion in 1885. Butler's sons, William and Edwin, joined shortly afterwards and, by 1891, the company had a registered capital of £3 million.

After William Butler Snr died in 1893, control passed to his eldest son, William. He embarked on further expansion, acquiring Downing's Black Horse Brewery (Dudley), Cahill's Swan Brewery, Great Western Street Brewery (Wolverhampton), Bloxwich Brewery, Cannock Brewery and Eley's Brewery (Stafford). By the time the company was taken over by Mitchells & Butler's (Smethwick) in 1960, it had over 800 pubs, and brewing ceased at Springfield in 1991. Much of the site was cleared and some old buildings were damaged by fire, but others are to be restored and put to good use by the University of Wolverhampton (see below).

Wolverhampton & Dudley Breweries (W&D) was formed in 1890 to amalgamate Henry Banks's Park Brewery, Charles Smith's Fox Brewery and George Thompson's Dudley & Victoria Breweries, along with their 193 pubs. In 1894, Edwin Thompson became managing director and his family played a key role in the company for over a century. In 1898, a new 60-quarter brewery was built, designed by London architect, Arthur Kinder, and W&D then began its expansion plans. From 1909, W&D acquired several local breweries, including North Worcestershire Breweries (Stourbridge), John Rolinson (Netherton), Kidderminster Brewery and City Brewery (Lichfield). In 1943, they acquired Julia Hanson & Sons (Dudley), and continued brewing there until 1991.

Further expansion took place in the 1960s and, by 1990, W&D had over 800 pubs. Edwin Thompson celebrated their centenary by burying a time capsule of cask ale at the brewery. In the 1990s, managing director, David Thompson, embarked on even more expansion, acquiring Cameron's (Hartlepool) and half the pubs of Hoskin's (Leicester). By 1997, W&D had become Britain's largest independent brewery and, in 1999, acquired Mansfield Brewery and joined forces with Marston's (Burton-on-Trent). This brought its estate to almost 1,800 pubs and now, as Marstons plc, it has pubs (and breweries) in nearly all parts of the country.

Frank Myatt was brewing at the Cross Keys pub in 1900 and later moved to the nearby Albany Brewery, but sold the business to Eley's (Stafford) in 1909. He then established another brewery at the West End Inn and later acquired 26 pubs from Allsopp & Sons (Burton-on-Trent), along with the West Midland's pubs of Deakin's Manchester Brewery. He became Mayor of Wolverhampton in 1917 and, in 1919, he took over Old Wolverhampton Breweries, along with its 124 pubs. In 1927, Wolverhampton City Council acquired his premises by compulsory purchase and his remaining 94 pubs were sold to Holt's (Birmingham).

Market Street was a popular location for smaller breweries. Price, Yearsely, Mottram & Co. originally established the **Wolverhampton Brewery** in 1849, but they'd gone by 1855. In 1864, Booth, Bruford & Co. founded their **Steam Brewery,** but it was acquired by Charles Chater in 1890.

Hipkins, Meek & Co. were established in 1854 and later evolved into the **South Staffordshire Brewery.** In 1891, a new tower brewery was built to the designs of Arthur Kinder, which was later operated by Charles Chater and J & J Yardley (Bloxwich & Darlaston). **Old Wolverhampton Breweries** was founded in 1871 by Reuben Turner, who acquired South Staffordshire Brewery in 1910, but it was bought by Frank Myatt in 1919 and passed to Holt's in 1927.

William Tress & Turner's **Smithfield Brewery** was acquired by James Twyman in 1841, but had passed to Reuben Turner by 1854. In 1896, it was acquired by **Staffordshire United Breweries,** but they were dissolved by 1903, and the premises were later bought by Ansell's (Birmingham). Brewing continued until 1920 and the buildings were later replaced by a Marks & Spencer store.

There were many short-lived breweries in and around the town. At Penn Common, the **Penn Brewery** was originally part of the Earl of Dudley's estate. It was established by John Millard in 1860, but taken over by Burton Brewery in 1897 who sold it to **Wolverhampton District Brewery** in 1899 with its 11 pubs. Their **Victoria Brewery** in Wesley Street, Bradley was founded a year earlier, but went into liquidation in 1902 and was later acquired by Ansell's.

John Pearson and Arthur Thompson ran the **Newbridge Brewery** in Tettenhall Road between 1875-1884. Evans & Co.'s **Cannock Road Brewery** was in liquidation and sold by 1875. William Russell founded the **Great Western Street Brewery** in 1877 and brewed Russell's Family Ale until 1912, but it passed to William Butler in 1932. In 1893, Patrick Connolly registered the **Fountain Brewery** in Little Brickkiln Street, but it was wound up three years later. Jacob Cartwright built the **Tettenhall Wood New Brewery** in 1896, and brewed there with Catherine until 1920.

Stratton & Co. originally founded the **Anglo-Malt Brewery** in Lichfield Street around 1904, but after passing to Johnson & Phipps, it merged with J.P. Simpkiss & Co. (Brierley Hill) in 1955. James Cahill established his **Swan Brewery** at Heath Town in 1907, which was taken over by William Butler in 1919. In Bilston Road, Edwin Lawrence originally established Harmer & Co.'s **Midland Brewery** before 1909, but it was taken over by Ansell's in 1945. **George Hill** established his brewery in Park Street in 1915, but it was acquired by Atkinson's (Birmingham) in 1919. In 1920, Rogers & Calcutt registered their **Eagle Street Brewery,** which Atkinson's also acquired in 1925.

Several small breweries began life at pubs. **Shelton Brewery** was behind the Queens Arms in Graisley Row and was brewing by 1869, but this ceased in 1959 when it was bought by Bird's Crown Brewery (Bloxwich). Louis Connolly operated the **Grapes Brewery** in Chapel Ash from 1896-1922. In Bilston Road, Griffiths & Cattell brewed at the **Coach & Horses Brewery** until it was taken over by South Staffordshire Brewery in 1895. Over the years, around 125 pubs have been listed as home-brew pubs.

Finally, we mustn't forget **Holt, Plant & Deakin's** micro-brewery at the Ship & Rainbow in Dudley Road, set up by Ansell's in 1984 shortly after its first micro-brewery opened in Langley. It produced 5,000 gallons a week of Entire beer and eventually supplied 47 pubs. Brewing ceased in 1996, when it was taken over by the Firkin chain of pubs. Some may also remember the shorter-lived **Goldthorn Brewery,** where Paul Bradburn brewed his Heart Throb beer between 2001-2004.

Wolverhampton has a long and eventful history of breweries, but all but one has been taken over or closed. However, the town still has a legacy of several pubs, once owned by these breweries, where memories of the past remain. Long may they prosper!

The future of Springfield Brewery

Springfield Brewery dates back to 1873, when William Butler built his new brewery. In 1881, he added a new 60-quarter tower brewery, designed by London architects, R.C. Sinclair, capable of producing 1,500 barrels of beer per week. After further expansion and acquisition of other smaller local breweries, William Butler's extraordinary vision and business acumen paved the way for a Black Country success story that would eventually grow to employ up to 900 workers. In fact, he changed the course of Black Country brewing history, and the Springfield Brewery became a landmark and part of Wolverhampton's fame and folklore. Unfortunately, William died in 1893, after establishing Wolverhampton's largest brewery and a crucial element in the town's manufacturing base.

Meanwhile, another William Butler was brewing up plans in Birmingham, setting up the Crown Brewery in 1875 and later joining forces with Henry Mitchell and establishing Mitchells & Butlers Cape Hill Brewery in Smethwick in 1886. It is perhaps somewhat ironic that Springfield Brewery was taken over by Mitchells & Butlers in 1960, along with its tied estate of over 800 pubs; brewing ceased in 1991.

There's a fascinating tale about "rolling out the barrel" when apprentice coopers completed their five years of training at Springfield Brewery. The apprentice would be trussed up in a cask that he'd made, covered with wood shavings, sawdust and cinders, doused with water and rolled around the cooper's yard. He was then tipped out of the cask in a dazed and wet condition, whilst his colleagues toasted him with a glass of ale! The site of the Springfield Brewery included many iconic features, including the gatehouse and 1922 clock tower, and much of the brewery is Grade II listed. It was neglected and abandoned for 20 years and subject to a ferocious blaze in 2004, destroying many of the brewery's characteristic features.

However, in 2014, the site was taken over by the University of Wolverhampton, who revealed plans for a key strategic £120 million project, helping to regenerate this part of Wolverhampton. They aimed to turn the brewery site into a new super-campus for the School of Architecture & Built Environment, with over 1,200 students, specialist teaching and social learning spaces, including laboratories, multi-disciplinary workshops, lecture theatre, offices and meeting rooms. The site is also home to the new £17.5m National Brownfield Institute.

The new Springfield Campus is now Europe's largest university centre of construction excellence and focuses on innovations linked to sustainable housing and the circular economy, delivering new skills, training and job opportunities in the construction industry. It's also hoped to provide houses and apartments, and even an on-site micro-brewery!

Although the loss of the brewery is regrettable, I think William Butler would be pleased to know that his former brewery site is being put to good use by the University of Wolverhampton. A positive note on which to end our story.

ACKNOWLEDGEMENTS

Primary research sources:
Hitchmough's Black Country Pubs – Tony Hitchmough (www.longpull.co.uk)
The History of Batham's Black Country Brewers – John Richards (1993)
A History of Holden's Black Country Brewery – John Richards (1986)
A History of Simpkiss Breweries – John Richards (1984)
Black Country Breweries – Joseph McKenna (2010)
Birmingham Breweries – Joseph McKenna (2005)
Black Country Bugle (various articles)
The Blackcountryman (various articles)
Ales & Tales – Dudley & South Staffs/Stourbridge & Halesowen CAMRA (various articles)
   CAMRA (Campaign for Real Ale)
Black Country Society
Brewery History Society
Pub History Society
Alan Godfrey Maps (Old Ordnance Survey Maps)
Web/social media sites of pubs and breweries
Local press, including Dudley News, Stourbridge News, Halesowen News, Walsall Chronicle, Birmingham Post & Mail and Express & Star

Other research sources:
20th Century Pub – Jessica Boak & Ray Barley (2017)
A Brief History in Time: Halesowen pubs – topbeercrew (2016)
A Century of Wolverhampton – Ned Williams (1999)
A Cradley Album – Peter Barnsley (1994)
A History of Halesowen – Julian Hunt (2004)
A History of Stourbridge – Nigel Perry (2001)
A History of Wollaston – History of Wollaston (HOW) Group (2004)
A Memorable Medley of Great Black Country Characters – Aristotle Tump (1986)
A Photographic History of Lye & Wollescote during the Redevelopment of the 1950s-1970s Pat Dunn, Colin Wooldridge & Harry Cartwright (2013)
Beer & Spirits – David Taylor & Andrew Homer (2010)
Bilston, Tettenhall & Wednesfield – Mary Mills & Tracey Williams (1998)
Black Country Pubs in Old Photographs – Robin Pearson & Jean Wade (1991)
Black Country Ghosts & Hauntings – Andrew Homer (2017)
Dictionary of Pub Names – Leslie Dunkling & Gordon Wright (1987)
Dudley Through Time – Peter Glews (2010)
Haunted Black Country – Philip Solomon (2009)
Highgate Brewery – Keith J. Lloyd (1980)
History Around Us: Halesowen – John Billingham (1991/1996)
Halesowen Sketches – Bill Hazlehurst (2020-2022)
Lye Waste – A Very Horrible History – T. Jones (2015)
Memories of the Black Country – Alton Douglas (1985)
Memories of West Bromwich – Alton Douglas (1990)
Memories of Wolverhampton – Alton Douglas (1988)
Real Heritage Pubs of the Midlands – CAMRA (2015)

Rowley Regis: A History – Edward Chitham (2006)
Stourbridge in Times Past – H. Jack Haden (1980)
The Black Country – Andrew Homer (2019)
The Family Brewers of Britain – Roger Protz (CAMRA) (2020)
The History of Brewing in West Bromwich and the most successful brewer Darby's – Carol Harthill, Mark Barrett & the Friends of Dartmouth Park (2021)
The Historic Inns of Walsall – Walsall Chronicle/Walsall Library & Museum Services (1981)
The History of the Black Country – J. Wilson-Jones
This is Wednesfield Our Wednesfield – Ray Fellows (2010)
Tipton Through Time – Keith Hodgkins (2011)
Walsall as it was – John Benson & Trevor Raybould (1978)
Wednesfield Our Heritage – Ray Fellows (2011)
Wednesbury Through Time – Ian M. Bott (2011)
West Smethwick – Lilian M. Jewkes & Ewart J. Johnson (2017)
What's Happened to Quarry Bank? – Ned Williams & the Mount Pleasant History Group (1999)
What's Happened to Wolverhampton? – Ned Williams (1997)
Wolverhampton – Mary Mills & Tracey Williams (1996)
Wolverhampton Memories – True North (2001)
Wolverhampton Pubs – Alec Brew (2004)
Wolverhampton Photographic Memories – David Clarke (2005)

Britain in Old Photographs series (published by Sutton Publishing/History Press):
Bilston, Bradley & Ladymoor – Ron Davies & Roy Hawthorne (2000)
Bilston, Bradley & Ladymoor: A Second Selection – by Ron Davies (2002)
Bilston, Bradley & Ladymoor: A Third Selection – by Ron Davies (2003)
Bilston, Bradley & Ladymoor: A Sixth Selection – by Ron and Joan Davies (2009)
Bilston, Bradley & Ladymoor: A Seventh Selection – by Ron Davies (2011)
Blackheath – Anthony H. Page (2000)
Blackheath, A Second Selection – Anthony H. Page (2002)
Blackheath, A Third Selection – Anthony H. Page (2007)
Brierley Hill – Stan Hill (1995)
Brierley Hill, Brockmoor, Bromley & Pensett – Ned Williams & Mount Pleasant Local History Group (2010)
Brierley Hill, Round Oak, Harts Hill, Level Street, Merry Hill, Quarry Bank, Mill Street,
The Delph, Silver End Hawbush – Ned Williams & Mount Pleasant Local History Group (2011)
Cradley Heath, Old Hill and District – Ron Moss & Bob Clarke (1998)
Cradley Heath, Old Hill and District: A Second Selection – Ron Moss (2004)
Darlaston, Moxley & Bentley – Ian M. Bott (2000)
Dudley – H. Atkins, D. Matthews & S. Robins (1998)
Dudley & Netherton Remembered – Ned Williams (2010)
Great Bridge & District – Terry Price (2000)
Great Bridge Memories – Terry Price (2004)
Great Bridge Revisited – Terry Price (2002)
Halesowen – David L. Eades (1998)
Halesowen: A Second Selection – David L. Eades (2000)

Lye & Wollescote – Denys Brooks & Pat Dunn (1997)
Lye & Wollescote: A Second Selection – Pat Dunn (2003)
Lye & Wollescote: A Third Selection – Pat Dunn (2003)
Lye & Wollescote: A Fourth Selection – Pat Dunn & Colin Wooldridge (2013)
Netherton – Ned Williams (2006)
Netherton: People & Places – Ned Williams (2009)
Oldbury, Langley & Warley – Terry Daniels (2002)
Quarry Bank – Ned Williams & Mount Pleasant Local History Group (1998)
Quarry Bank: Past & Present – Ned Williams & Mount Pleasant Local History Group (2003)
Quarry Bank and the Delph – Ned Williams & Mount Pleasant Local History Group (2009)
Rowley – Anthony H. Page (2001)
Rowley Revisited – Anthony H. Page (2014)
Sedgley & District – Trevor Genge (1995)
Sedgley & District: A Second Selection – Trevor Genge (1997)
Sedgley & District: A Third Selection – Trevor Genge (1999)
Sedgley & District: A Fifth Selection – Trevor Genge (2004)
Sedgley, Coseley & The Gornals – Trevor Genge (2001)
Smethwick in Old Photographs – John Maddison (1993)
Stourbridge, Wollaston & Amblecote – Bob Clarke & Michael Reuter (1997)
Stourbridge, Wollaston & Amblecote: A Second Selection – Bob Clarke & Michael Reuter (2000)
Tipton – John Brimble & Keith Hodgkins (1995)
Tipton: A Second Selection – John Brimble & Keith Hodgkins (1997)
Tipton: A Third Selection – Keith Hodgkins & John Brimble (2001)
Walsall Past and Present – David F. Vodden (1999)
Walsall Revisited – David F. Vodden (1997)
Wednesbury in Old Photographs – Robin Pearson (1989)
Wednesbury in Old Photographs – Ian M. Bott (1994)
Wednesbury Memories – Ian M. Bott (2004)
Wednesbury Revisited – Ian M. Bott (1998)
Wednesfield and Heath Town – Elizabeth A. Rees & Mary Mills (1992)
West Bromwich Revisited – David F. Vodden (1999)
West Bromwich Memories – Terry Price (2006)
West Bromwich Yesterdays – Terry Price (2010)
Wordsley Past & Present – Stan Hill (2010)

Organisations & individuals:
Amblecote History Society
Black Country Muse
Bloxwich Tallygraph
Cradley Links
Angus Dunphy
Dr Malcolm Dixon
Bill Hazlehurst
Friends of Highgate Brewery

Tony Garrington
Langley Local History Society
Andrew Maxam
John Midwood
Pelsall History Society
Sedgley Local History Society
Mark Taylor
Tipton Archives
Tipton Civic Society
Walsall Library & Museum Services
Wednesbury Local History Society
Wordsley History Society

Web-sites and social media:
brownhillsbob.com
camra.org.uk
historywebsite.co.uk
lowergornal.co.uk
midlandspubs.co.uk
topbeercrew.com

NOTES ON PUB INFORMATION

Most of the information on pubs is taken from Hitchmough's Black Country Pubs database (www.longpull.co.uk). Modern licensing records don't go back much earlier than the early 1800s, so the opening date of a pub is usually the date of the first recorded licence. However, if it is known that the pub or building is older than this, that date is usually given.

The date of closure is usually the last recorded licence or the last known date of the pub actually closing. The dates that licensees held the pub licence are based on the licensing records. However, in some cases, the licensee was absent and the pub was managed by someone else. The licensing records are backed-up by information in the Census records. Many of the stories told about the pub, its licensees, customers and events are based on contemporary articles in the local press or from other recognised sources. All information is provided in good faith, from reliable research sources, errors and omissions excepted.

What's in a name?
- A **beer retailer** was a person allowed to sell beer and cider.
- A **licensed victualler** was licensed to sell beer, cider, wines and spirits.
- An **alehouse** or **beerhouse** was a house licensed to sell ale or beer, often simply in someone's house, with a Beerhouse licence, allowing them to only sell beer, with their number growing after the 1830 Beerhouse Act. A full licence allowed them to sell beer, cider, wines and spirits.
- A **tavern** tended to be larger and also sold wine, tending to attract a better class of customer. During the 17th century, a tavern was the meeting place for a "gentleman".
- **Vaults** were similar establishments that concentrated on selling wine.
- An **inn** was typically a house selling beer, cider, wines and spirits that accommodated travellers, particularly along the coaching network and turnpike roads. Some were "coaching houses" or "posting houses", served by horse-drawn coaches and omnibuses for travellers and post.
- A **public house** embraced all these licensed premises, first recorded in 1669, but becoming more regulated by 1880.
- The **modern pub** sells beer, cider, wines and spirits, and many have now diversified to provide meals, some are more akin to restaurants.
- A **hotel** is an establishment providing accommodation, meals and other services for travellers and tourists, akin to a modern version of the "inn", but often larger.
- A **tied house** is a public house which can only serve beer supplied by a particular brewery or pub company.
- A **free house** is a public house which is not tied to a particular brewery or company to supply its beer.
- A **micro-pub** is a more recent phenomenon, described as a small licensed establishment, usually consisting of just one small room, which "listens to its customers and promotes conversation, mainly serves cask ales, dabbles in traditional pub snacks, but shuns all forms of electronic entertainment".
- A **taproom** is a room in which alcoholic drinks, especially beer, are available on tap, such as in a bar in a pub or hotel, but also refers to the bar at, or nearest to, a particular brewery.